# Italian Neofascism

To David

# Italian Neofascism

## The Strategy of Tension and the Politics of Nonreconciliation

Anna Cento Bull

*Berghahn Books*
New York • Oxford

First published in 2007 by
**Berghahn Books**
www.berghahnbooks.com

©2007 Anna Cento Bull

**Library of Congress Cataloging-in-Publication Data**

Cento Bull, Anna, 1951-
  Italian neofascism : the strategy of tension and the politics of
  nonreconciliation / Anna Cento Bull.
     p. cm.
  Includes bibliographical references and index.
  ISBN 978-1-84545-335-0 (hardback : alk. paper)
  1. Fascism--Italy. 2. Terrorism--Italy. 3. Italy--Politics and government--
  1976-1994. I. Title.

JC481.C39 2007
324.245'038--dc22
                              2007044679

**British Library Cataloguing in Publication Data**

A catalogue record for this book is available from the British Library

Printed in the United States on acid-free paper

ISBN: 978-1-84545-335-0 (hardback)

# Contents

# List of Abbreviations

| | |
|---|---|
| AN | Avanguardia Nazionale |
| BR | Brigate Rosse |
| DC | Democrazia Cristiana |
| DS | Democratici di Sinistra |
| GAP | Gruppi di Azione Partigiana |
| MAR | Movimento di Azione Rivoluzionaria |
| MS-FT | Movimento Sociale-Fiamma Tricolore |
| MSI | Movimento Sociale Italiano |
| NAR | Nuclei Armati Rivoluzionari |
| NDS | Nuclei Territoriali di Difesa dello Stato |
| ON | Ordine Nuovo |
| PCI | Partito Comunista Italiano |
| PDS | Partito Democratico della Sinistra |
| PSI | Partito Socialista Italiano |
| TP | Terza Posizione |

# Preface

This has been without doubt the most difficult book I have written to date. It is also a different book from the one I had planned to write.

I lived in Italy in the late 1960s and early 1970s, and again between 1978 and 1985, and was deeply affected by the events of those years, starting with the bombing attack of 12 December 1969, at Piazza Fontana, Milan. Since then, I have repeatedly tried to make sense of the many massacres of innocent civilians (*stragismo*) carried out in Italy during the period of the Cold War. Following the most recent investigations and trials, I believed that it was now possible to achieve a balanced, evidence-based reconstruction of *stragismo* and the Strategy of Tension. The latter used the massacres as means, aimed at creating an atmosphere of terror in the country, whereas the goal was some form of authoritarian or presidential political system.

To complement existing judicial material, I decided to interview some ex-protagonists of the radical neofascist movement, as well as representatives and intellectuals of the right, initially with a view to treating them as possible oral *sources*, particularly in view of the demise of the old neofascist party, the Movimento Sociale Italiano (MSI), and its transformation into a democratic party, Alleanza Nazionale, which has distanced itself from both fascism and neofascism. However, it soon became clear that the stories they were prepared to tell did not constitute sources for reconstructing the past, but a plurality of *voices* through which a shared representation of a 'community of belonging' was being affirmed and deeply felt grievances were being expressed. While I found it very difficult to relate to the reconstructions put forward by the right, given that I come from the opposite side of the political spectrum and was unprepared to be faced with such uncompromising attitudes, I also wanted as much as possible to understand their positions.

The result has been this book, which is by necessity a book of two halves, rather than a comprehensive reconstruction of *stragismo*. In Part I, I have assembled the main evidence concerning the massacres as unearthed by successive judicial investigations and trials. I have also explored the reconstructions of *stragismo* and the Strategy of Tension put forward by a number of well-established and reputable, mainly left-of-centre, professional and scholarly people, as well as a leading witness for the prosecution, himself a neofascist. Despite significant differences of interpretation, the trial findings and these people's reconstructions have one thing in common: that the massacres were carried out by radical neofascist groups.

In Part II, I examine the reconstructions put forward by the neo- and post-fascist right, which reverse the previous interpretations. I consider their narratives primarily as 'narratives of victimhood', whereby the neofascists are constructed as victims, as opposed to perpetrators, of *stragismo* and the Strategy of Tension. To an extent they are also codified narratives which leave little room for a critical reappraisal of the past. One example is that of Stefano Delle Chiaie, who in 1997, during a hearing of a Parliamentary Commission of Inquiry, stated, with reference to his 'wronged' image, that 'Fantasy, plus more fantasy, plus archival news create the monster'. When I met him outside the block of flats where I would interview him, in October 2005, he greeted me with the same words, thereby clearly indicating that his story was not going to change in any significant way from his previous renditions.

Finally, I explore the reasons for this clear-cut division of opinions and narratives, and I consider its wider political significance.

In many ways, therefore, this is not the book I intended to write. It is, however, the only one that I could write given the current state of the judicial process and of political relations in Italy. I hope that one day it will become possible to write the original book I had in mind.

# Acknowledgements

I wish to thank the Arts and Humanities Research Council for awarding me funded leave in 2006 under its Research Scheme Leave, and for sponsoring a research trip to Italy in October 2005. Thanks to its generous support, I was able to carry out a number of extremely valuable interviews and bring to completion my research, as well as this book.

All the people who agreed to be interviewed and who helped to make the interviews possible are owed special thanks. I did not receive any refusal for an interview, with the exception of Roberto Fiore, former leader of the extreme-right group Terza Posizione and current leader of Forza Nuova. I would like to thank Giano Accame, Adalberto Baldoni, Paolo Bolognesi, Saverio Ferrari, Aldo Giannuli, Manlio Milani, Pier Paolo Pelizzaro, Ferdinando Pincioni, Sandro Provvisionato and Guido Salvini, for giving up some of their time to talk to me and in most cases also for giving me access to judicial and/or parliamentary material. My thanks also go to Gabriele Adinolfi, Marcello De Angelis, Stefano Delle Chiaie, Giuseppe Dimitri and Giuseppe Valerio Fioravanti, all of whom agreed to be interviewed on sensitive and even personal matters. Shortly after I interviewed him, on 30 March 2006, Giuseppe Dimitri died in a road accident. To his family, especially to Giano Accame, I offer my sincere condolences. I would also like to thank Roberto Bartali, Annamaria Brunner, Giorgio Cazzaniga, Roberto Chiarini, Sabrina Fantauzzi and Maria Ocello whose assistance proved invaluable in order to contact some of the persons I wished to interview.

For the photo appearing on the front cover, I would like to thank Lucia Clerici and Alessandra Fadini. They took various pictures in December 2006, on the 37th anniversary of the bomb attack carried out in Piazza Fontana, Milan. My thanks also go to Elisabetta Nadalutti for helping to transcribe the interviews, and to Verina Jones for obtaining copies of two articles from the *Observer*, published in December 1969.

I am indebted to Roger Eatwell, Mark Gilbert, and Berghahn's official reader of the manuscript, Michel Huysseune, for their very helpful comments and advice. The book is of much better quality thanks to their exacting and constructive criticisms. I am, of course, responsible for any remaining weaknesses.

Finally, I wish to thank my husband, David, to whom this book is dedicated, for his constant support and for reading through the manuscript and making linguistic and stylistic corrections.

# CHAPTER 1
## Introduction

This book compares and contrasts the narratives put forward by the Italian radical and postfascist right, through its political representatives, intellectuals and protagonists, with the judicial findings on – and the mainstream interpretations of – the political violence perpetrated in the 1960s and 1970s, with specific reference to terrorist bombing massacres collectively known as *stragismo*. The book examines the evidence concerning the role of Italian neofascism in *stragismo*, as established by successive judicial investigations and trials, and then analyses the reconstructions of these same events made by the right. As this work will show, the contrast between the two could not be greater.

The analysis takes into consideration issues of postconflict national reconciliation, which are generally applied to countries that have experienced a transition from an authoritarian regime to a liberal democracy and/or have emerged from a bloody and prolonged civil war, rather than to democratic countries like Italy. Yet it can be argued that Italy went through a period of violent conflict in the late 1960s and 1970s which was directly related to the Cold War and to the 1943–45 civil war, and which has left a legacy of bitter divisions and recriminations, as well as preventing a truth recovery process about past crimes and the achievement of full justice. It has also been a longstanding topos among Italian academics, politicians, journalists and the general public that Italy after 1945 represented a case of an 'incomplete', 'blocked' or indeed 'anomalous' democracy, given the lack of alternation of parties or coalitions of parties in government, the existence of strong anti-system parties, and limited sovereignty (Ambrogetti 1999; Di Nolfo 1998; Pecchioli 1995; Ronchey 1982; Santino 1997; Tullio-Altan 1995).

By applying the literature on truth telling and reconciliation to the Italian case, the book addresses the question of how far the country has progressed on the road of becoming a fully fledged democracy and overcoming entrenched ideological divisions. The focus is on the extreme right, specifically the transformation of the old neofascist Movimento Sociale Italiano (MSI) into the postfascist Alleanza Nazionale and the extent to which the new party has established its democratic credentials through a critical reevaluation of its more recent past, distancing itself from the radical groups to its right and accepting the legitimacy of the judicial process as regards crimes related to *stragismo*. This does not exclude questioning the validity of individual trial verdicts, but it does necessitate refuting the view, typical of the radical right, that the entire judiciary is part of a leftist conspiracy or that Italian neofascism was systematically and unfairly criminalised and used as an innocent scapegoat by evil villains.

The book is divided into two parts. Part I analyses the most recent judicial findings and the main interpretations which take into account these findings and/or are in accordance with them. Part II examines the reconstructions put forward by representatives and sympathisers of the radical and postfascist right, both in the form of intellectuals, journalists and politicians, and in the form of ex-leaders of Italian neofascist groups operating in the 1960s and 1970s. Before we discuss the research questions which have informed this work, it is useful to give an overview of the political violence carried out in Italy during the period of the Cold War. It is also necessary to provide a definition for this violence and to examine its legacy upon, and implications for, Italian society and politics today. Finally, a brief outline of Italian neofascism after 1945 will help to place this study in context.

## Political violence in Italy during the Cold War

Italy was a deeply divided nation after the end of the Second World War, as a result of the 'civil war' between supporters of the Italian Social Republic (or Republic of Salò, from the name of its capital on Lake Garda), the regime set up by Mussolini and diehard fascists with the support of the Germans in November 1943, and the anti-fascist Resistance movement, which left deep scars and legacies. Internal divisions also grew worse in consequence of the onset of the Cold War, whose fault line split the country into two, albeit not in physical and territorial terms, as was the case for Germany. Rather, the divide was ideological, political, social and cultural. It was also military, at least in the sense that the means of violence were not a prerogative and a monopoly of the state, but were also in the possession of paramilitary organisations, each of which was ready to take up arms and engage in battle should the need arise. In the opinion of Timothy Smith (1991: 1), the role of Italy after the Second World War was that of a microcosm of the Cold War: 'Italy, one of the defeated nations of World War II, contained many of the major elements that produced the cold war and which led to one of the significant developments of that conflict: two armed camps capable of mutual destruction.'

As the former President of the Republic Francesco Cossiga stated, both the Catholics and the communists could rely on armed groups. Each group had as its main aims to defend themselves from any attack by their perceived enemies and to ensure the safety of political leaders and activists in case of a descent into civil war. This was confirmed by other prominent Christian Democratic politicians, including Paolo Emilio Taviani, according to whom the Catholics put their own weapons to rest after the 1948 elections, which marked the decisive victory of his party: 'As for the arms, I want to recall that our "volunteers for freedom" possessed them too. We were ready to use them, if necessary … It was only after the Christian Democratic victory that the weapons were handed over' (interview with Paolo Emilio Taviani, *Avvenire*, 1 April 1998: 22). As for the so-called 'Gladio Rossa', that, is, a paramilitary organisation within the Italian Communist party, its existence is now well documented (Pelizzaro 1997; Donno 2001; Turi 2004). It is believed that it remained operational until at least the mid-1950s. It has also been hypothesised that a third paramilitary group was operating in Italy at the time, made up of the remnants of ex-combatants of the Italian Social Republic who feared for their lives as a result of reprisals on the part of the communists, as indeed happened after the war in some parts of northern Italy, the so-called Triangle of Death, recently the subject of controversial books written by the journalist Giampaolo Pansa (2003; 2005). In short, a revival of the civil war which had taken place in 1943–45 represented a real possibility, but after the general elections of 1948, which saw the triumph of Christian Democracy over the Fronte Popolare, the coalition between socialists and communists, political relations were gradually normalised. For most of the 1950s the country was governed by stable coalitions made up of trusted parties of the centre and centre right, whose anti-communist credentials were well established.

By the late 1950s, however, this 'centrist' coalition experienced a loss of political support and votes, which required Christian Democracy to look for new partners. The only solution was to coopt some other party in the governing coalition, by turning either to the Movimento Sociale Italiano, or, alternatively, to the socialist or communist parties. The Christian Democrats tried the first solution in 1960, when the Tambroni government was formed with the support of the MSI, but this wrought widespread protest demonstrations in the country. They started negotiating with the PSI (Partito Socialista Italiano) in the early 1960s, thanks to the thawing of East-West relations and to an increasingly favourable attitude on the part of the USA under the Kennedy administration (Nuti 2002). The 'Opening to the Left' was finally sanctioned by the American President J.F. Kennedy during a trip to Italy in 1963, having already secured the approval of Pope John XXIII. However, in both Italy and the USA there was substantial opposition to this policy: 'the Kennedy administration undermined the position of Italian political leaders who counted on Washington to prevent, and not facilitate, an opening to the left' (Nuti 2002: 47). More importantly, the new centre-left coalition governments did not appear to have any significant impact upon reducing the strength and influence of the Communist Party. On the contrary, the PCI (Partito Comunista Italiano) increased its percentage of votes at successive elections, while the trade unions went on a wage offensive in the early 1960s and again in 1968–69, when a high level of militancy and a wave of protest and unrest by workers and students appeared to signal to many conservative forces that the country was on the brink of collapse or of a revolution.

From then onwards, the country witnessed an appalling series of acts of subversion and violence, which reached its peak in the 1970s – the so-called 'years of lead' – culminating first in the murder of Aldo Moro, President of the Christian Democratic Party, carried out in May 1978 by the Red Brigades, and then a bomb attack at Bologna railway station on 2 August 1980. Generally speaking, one can distinguish between three types of 'subversion': a first type, consisting of a sustained bombing campaign; a second type, consisting of planned or attempted coups d'état; and a third strand, related to an armed conflict carried out by paramilitary groups.

The first type of violence, known as *stragismo* from the term *strage* (massacre), started in 1969, with a series of bomb attacks at Milan's Fiera Campionaria and Central Station, on 25 April, resulting in twenty people wounded, as well as attacks on various trains, on 8–9 August of the same year, which injured ten people. Later in the same year, on 12 December 1969, bombs were planted in various public places in Milan and Rome, one of which exploded in a crowded bank in Piazza Fontana, Milan, resulting in seventeen people dead and eighty-four wounded. After various bloody attacks in 1972 and 1973, the following year witnessed an escalation of this type of violence. On 28 May 1974, a bomb exploded at a crowded anti-fascist demonstration in Piazza della Loggia, in Brescia, resulting in eight people dead and 103 wounded. A few months later, on 4 August 1974, in San Benedetto Val di Sambro, a bomb exploded on a crowded train, the *Italicus*; twelve passengers were killed and forty-four wounded. After six relatively quiet years on this front, the bombing campaign resumed on 2 August 1980 with an attack at Bologna railway station which resulted in eighty-five dead and 200 wounded. Four years later, on 23 December 1984, a bomb exploded on a train, the *Rapido 904*, resulting in fifteen people dead and more than 100 wounded. For almost a decade this seemed the last act of a campaign which no organisation claimed as its own, either in its entirety or in relation to single episodes. There were to be other attacks in 1993, however, at a time when the First Republic was collapsing under the weight of judicial investigations into political corruption and voters' mistrust of the political elites. In particular, a bomb exploded in Florence on 27 May 1993, killing five people, and another in Milan during the night between 27 and 28 July 1993, again resulting in five deaths.

The second type of subversive acts allegedly started in 1964, soon after the Socialist Party had started to collaborate with the Christian Democrats in centre-left coalition governments, the so-called 'Opening to the Left'. General Giovanni de Lorenzo, commander of the *Carabinieri* armed force and head of the Italian secret services, then named SIFAR, drew up a plan for a coup d'état, known as 'Plan Solo', with the connivance of President of the Republic Antonio Segni. As part of his activities, General de Lorenzo compiled roughly 150,000 dossiers on people considered dangerous, including politicians, priests and trade unionists. The Plan was made public by two journalists, Lino Jannuzzi and Eugenio Scalfari, in the weekly *L'Espresso*, in May 1967. Plan Solo was followed by the Borghese attempted coup of 7 December 1970, known as the 'Night of Tora Tora', from the conspirators' secret password, clearly inspired by the code used by the Japanese after Pearl Harbor to show that complete surprise was achieved. Led by the ex-supporter of the Italian Social Republic, Prince Junio Valerio Borghese, now at the head of a group known as Fronte Nazionale, the coup aimed at forcing the President of the Republic to dissolve Parliament and to form an emergency government of military and civilians (Monti 2006). Further plots took place between 1972 and 1974, planned under the leadership of ex-Ambassador Randolfo Pacciardi and ex-partisan Edgardo Sogno.

The last type of violence escalated in the 1970s and consisted of acts of 'guerrilla warfare', including shootings of individuals, robberies, kidnappings, beatings and threats, perpetrated both by extreme-left and extreme-right organisations. The former were predominant as regards the number of groups and of participants involved. The main organisations were the Brigate Rosse ('Red Brigades'), Prima Linea ('Front Line'), Potere Operaio ('Workers' Power') and Nuclei Armati Proletari ('Proletarian Armed Nuclei'). Other organisations, such as Lotta Continua ('The Struggle Continues'), while not embracing the armed struggle, often justified, and occasionally practised, the revolutionary use of political violence. The latter consisted mainly of Lotta di Popolo ('People's Struggle'), Terza Posizione ('Third Position'), Costruiamo l'Azione ('Let Us Build Action'), and above all the Nuclei Armati Rivoluzionari ('Revolutionary Armed Nuclei'). The extreme-left groups targeted individual politicians, judges, journalists, policemen, who were considered to be at the service of the 'imperialist state' which had to be destroyed to open the way for a proletarian revolution. They also systematically targeted their longstanding enemies, the neofascists, thus keeping up the fight initiated during the Resistance. The Resistance, in fact, provided in many cases 'the inspiration for justifying terrorist activity' (Cooke 2006: 182), much in the same way as the Italian Social Republic provided the inspiration for the terrorist activity on the right. In either case, the violence was also directed at the respective 'father parties': the Communist Party, which in the eyes of the extreme-left activists had betrayed the ideals of the Resistance and the revolutionary cause, and the Movimento Sociale Italiano, the neofascist party, which the young extreme-right activists equally blamed for its compromising attitude towards Italian democracy and the political establishment and also for abandoning them to the reprisals and attacks perpetrated by the extreme-left groups. The radical-right groups shared their targets with the extreme left: policemen, judges, journalists; in addition, they also targeted the extreme left. As Piero Ignazi commented: 'The only difference was their cultural-ideological premisses. Whereas the leftists' reference point continued to be the neo-Marxist critique of society, the right-wingers adopted Julius Evola's ideas of the political soldier and the rejection of the modern world. On both left and right, violence became a standard political resource' (2006: 24).

These three types of political violence had different goals, protagonists and outcomes, and have also left different legacies in Italy today. The third type of violence is the most straightforward to account for in terms of its origins, motivations, protagonists and outcomes, as well as in terms of its legacy upon the country today. It was ideologically inspired; it was directed against the 'system' and the 'falsely revolutionary' political parties; it consisted primarily of young extreme activists; and, in the first half of the 1980s, was effectively dealt with by the state. While at first slow to react and to face up to the terrorist threat, in fact, the state later was able to rise to the challenge and to bring this type of violence to a close, through a combination of tough police measures and significant incentives, in the shape of reduced sentences, for those terrorists who 'repented' and confessed to their crimes. However, this strategy has clearly left a divisive legacy in terms of its morality, since different perpetrators have ended up with widely different sentences, on the basis of whether they 'repented' and confessed or refused to 'collaborate' with the magistrates and/or turn witnesses for the prosecution. As a result, people responsible for serious crimes have ended up with more lenient sentences than those responsible for lesser crimes. In addition, many relatives of the victims of extreme-left and extreme-right violence feel that justice has not been achieved and political expediency has prevailed. There is also a long-standing controversy concerning the kidnapping and assassination of Aldo Moro, which many believe was masterminded by obscure forces in the context of the Cold War, similarly to *stragismo*. Finally, this type of violence has left a legacy in the form of widespread resentment and a collective sense of grievance among the political right today, whose representatives believe that the extreme right by and large was a victim of this kind of violence and was deliberately targeted by the extreme left, not defended by the police, and abandoned by the MSI. The extreme right, in their own view, took up the armed struggle only as a last resort in order to defend their members from being physically exterminated. This specific legacy of the armed struggle will be examined in Part II.

The second type of violence is still in part shrouded in mystery as regards its aims and protagonists. It was clearly inspired by what were perceived as pressing and 'legitimate' fears concerning an imminent left insurrection (which may in turn have been artificially exaggerated or possibly even made up). It was conceived and masterminded by different protagonists, including veteran combatants of the Italian Social Republic, neofascists and freemasons, whose common glue was visceral anti-communism. Finally, it involved at least sections of the intelligence services and the armed forces as well as sections of the Christian Democratic Party. In the case of the Borghese coup, there is judicial and testimonial evidence in support of the hypothesis that the coup attracted the consent of the CIA, which was worried about a growing Communist threat in Italy (Monti 2006), and that it secured the support of the Mafia (Arcuri 2004). This type of subversion was never implemented, hence it did not actually involve the use of violence, although there would without doubt have been recourse to violence had any of the intended coups been carried out.

In terms of its legacy, this type of subversion has arguably had the least impact on present-day Italian politics and society, not least because it has often been dismissed as consisting of naïve, picturesque and hopelessly amateurish episodes. Recent judicial investigations, however, belied this benign version of putschism and linked it to *stragismo*. Nevertheless, since Italian democracy proved resilient and was able to withstand these acts of subversion, there appears to be a prevailing consensus that there is no need to dwell on what could have happened during the Cold War but was ultimately thwarted. As far as the radical and postfascist right are concerned, this type of subversion is by and large acknowledged in their reconstructions, as will be discussed in Part II. However, the links with other forces, specifically Italian and American intelligence structures, not to mention the Mafia, tend to be strongly refuted, and the autonomy of Italian neofascism proudly asserted.

The first type of violence – *stragismo* – is the most mysterious, the most bloody, the most sinister, the most repulsive, and the one that arguably has left the deepest scars in the country. This is due to various factors. First, as already mentioned, and in stark contrast to the armed struggle carried out by both the extreme left and the extreme right in the 1970s, no organisation ever claimed responsibility for these attacks or declared their intended goals. On the basis of judicial evidence, it emerged that *stragismo*, at least until 1974, was part of a deliberate strategy to place the blame upon leftist groups, whereas extreme-right groups were in fact responsible for the massacres.

Second, judicial investigations also uncovered evidence showing that the extreme-right perpetrators of this kind of violence had been abetted, protected and shielded from the investigating magistrates by sections of the intelligence services and the armed forces. In short, unlike the armed struggle, this appears to have been a type of violence that was masterminded by forces radically different from and much more powerful than, its actual perpetrators (extreme-right activists).

Third, the goals remain unclear, and a source of endless conspiracy theories. The main interpretation postulates the existence of a strategy, the so-called Strategy of Tension, which aimed at creating an atmosphere of terror in the country so as to promote a turn to an authoritarian type of government. In this respect, recent judicial findings have pointed to a connection between *stragismo* and putschism, that is to say, the massacres allegedly were carried out in order to create the conditions for and open the way to an authoritarian coup d'état. *Stragismo*, therefore, at least until 1974, was part of a much wider conspiracy which included the neofascists but consisted of an umbrella coalition of anti-communist forces.

Fourth, it is also unclear to what extent (if any) different neofascist groups formed 'independent' organisations or were groups created by and for the benefit of other bodies, including intelligence structures. One of the most authoritative experts on the Italian extreme right, Franco Ferraresi, believed at first that the extreme-right groups had been independent creations, even though the role of the secret services and of 'other more or less visible forces, was crucial in shielding them from prosecution, and in some cases in keeping them operating' (1988: 105). Later, on the basis of judicial findings, he came to the conclusion that 'the hidden actors' degree of involvement was deeper' than originally envisaged (1996: 25).

Lastly, successive trials have uncovered at least part of the truth concerning *stragismo* and the Strategy of Tension, but have not succeeded in reaching clear-cut and irrefutable verdicts. This situation has left a bitter legacy of mistrust in the political institutions and/or the judiciary, of accusations and counter-accusations, of despondency among the surviving victims of the massacres and the relatives of those deceased, as well as victimisation on the part of the defendants and the extreme right as a whole. The reconstructions put forward by the latter in relation to *stragismo* are analysed in detail in Part II of this book.

## A civil war?

How are we to view the different strands of political violence which came to occupy the central stage in Italy in the 1960s and 1970s? Do they merit the definition of civil war? If so, can we compare Italy to countries torn by fratricidal conflicts and confronted by the need to rebuild trust and achieve lasting reconciliation?

Italians themselves are divided on these issues. According to various commentators, including Christian Democratic politicians Cossiga and Taviani, it is not possible to talk of a civil war with reference to the political violence discussed in the previous section. In their view, there was indeed a serious risk of a civil war reoccurring in Italy after the end of the Second World War. However, the risk was averted by the common will of the political elites. Each and every situation which could have led to a civil war was defused by the political leaders, who chose to exercise a restraining influence upon their respective followers.

In opposition to this prevailing interpretation, the vast majority of those who took part, in the late 1960s and 1970s, in the armed bands of the extreme right and the extreme left, talk openly of a civil war which raged across Italy in those years. Their position is understandable for a number of reasons. First, it allows them to claim the status of combatants and simultaneously to reject the derogatory label of 'terrorists', thus regaining personal dignity and self-esteem. Second, it diminishes their personal responsibility, as they are able to argue that they had very little choice, since they were socialised into a harsh political climate which required every activist to engage in violence. Third, confirmation of a status of civil war justifies their campaign for a general amnesty for all acts of violence carried out during the conflict. The campaign has gained some support from all sides of the political spectrum, on the grounds that amnesty does not necessarily require rehabilitation and that the fairness of many trials held in those years was not guaranteed. However, it is refuted by the majority of commentators, who argue that the 'civil war' was only in the minds of the extremists, since all the 'terrorist' groups put together represented only a small percentage of Italians, predominantly of a young generation, and did not enjoy any real following among the population at large. Many also believe that an amnesty would imply some condoning of the political violence of the 1970s.

An alternative, compromise reconstruction has been gaining momentum among a number of commentators. This sees the period of the Italian First Republic as characterised neither by the total absence of a civil war, nor by a full-scale armed struggle, but by the existence of an anomalous version of a civil conflict, defined alternatively as a 'creeping civil war' or a 'low-intensity civil war'. This concept achieved notoriety and obtained much publicity after the publication of two books, in the form of interviews with Giovanni Pellegrino, Chair of the Parliamentary Commission for the Failed Identification of the Authors of the Massacres (Fasanella and Sestieri with Pellegrino 2000; Fasanella and Pellegrino 2005). The same concept is now used widely in journalistic and academic reconstructions as well as by politicians (Ilari 2001; Pansa 2005; Bellini and Bellini 2005; Bermani

2005; Tassinari 2005; Bernardi 2006). According to Pellegrino's reconstruction, a full-scale civil war in Italy after the Second World War was always possible but constantly avoided thanks to the far-sightedness of the various political leaders. However, the political climate worsened considerably in the 1960s, especially after the 'Opening to the Left' and growing social unrest, and from 1969 onwards a civil war exploded, albeit with 'low intensity'. This was due both to the ideological hatred which pervaded the new generation of political activists, on the right and on the left, and to the deliberate exacerbation of these divisions on the part of occult strategists, whose nature and aims can only be understood through the logic of the Cold War (Fasanella and Pellegrino 2005: 52–63).

A more wide-ranging definition devised by experts could be applied to the Italian case, thus avoiding the highly controversial and emotionally charged expression of a 'civil war'. This is the concept of 'violent political conflict', which encompasses 'civil wars, bloody coups, massacres, democides, or riots' (Long and Brecke 2003: 7). According to the authors, 'a conflict is deemed to be violent when at least thirty-two people were killed within a one-year period as a result of the point of contention that initiated the lethal violence' (ibid.: 7). On the basis of this definition, Italy would have been in the grips of a violent conflict for three years running: 1978, when thirty-five people were killed for political motives (including Aldo Moro and his five bodyguards, assassinated by the Red Brigades); 1979, when thirty-six people were murdered; and 1980, with eighty-five dead and 200 wounded in the Bologna station massacre, and forty-eight more people killed for political motives (Boschi 2005).

However, the figures were almost as high in the preceding and following years, according to the chronology provided by Boschi. In 1969, apart from the seventeen people killed and eighty-four wounded in the Piazza Fontana massacre, there were three more deaths and roughly 100 woundings in various riots; in 1970, six people were killed and more than fifty wounded when a bomb exploded on a train (*Freccia del Sud*) and two people were killed in politically inspired riots. In 1971, three people were killed and fourteen wounded in various episodes of political violence; in 1972, eight people were killed; in 1973, four people died and forty-five were wounded in the bomb attack at the Milan police headquarters; two more people were killed as a result of political violence. From 1974 onwards, political violence escalated. In that year, eight people were killed and 103 wounded in the Brescia massacre, twelve died and forty-four were wounded when a bomb exploded on the *Italicus* train, ten more people were killed and many more wounded in various violent clashes involving extreme-right and extreme-left activists: a total of thirty deaths. In 1975, eighteen people were killed in various clashes; in 1976 and 1977, fourteen and thirteen people respectively died in similar circumstances. Fairly high figures were also recorded for 1981 (twenty-two people killed) and 1982 (nineteen people dead). It was only thereafter that there was a substantial drop in political killings, with three victims in 1983. These figures exclude the victims, on Italian soil, of 'external' political conflicts, such as the Israeli-Palestinian conflict, as well as the victims of suspected acts of sabotage or war unrelated to the intra-state political and ideological struggle, such as the downing of an Italian plane near Ustica on 27 June 1980, which killed all the passengers and crew.

According to other sources (della Porta and Rossi 1984: 18–19, 60–65), political violence in Italy was both more virulent and more widespread. The authors claimed that there were 350 deaths in the country in the period 1969–82, as a result of the political conflict waged by extreme-left and extreme-right organisations. That is an average of twenty-five deaths per year. The peak period was 1976 to 1982, with 281 people killed, an average of forty deaths per year. In addition, political violence was a diffused phenomenon, as evidenced by the fact that there were more than 11,000 violent episodes in the country in the period 1969–82, of which 47 per cent were attributed to the left, and 53 per cent to the right. The number of people killed, therefore, represented only the extreme manifestation of a more socially rooted conflict. On the basis of the study by della Porta and Rossi, it appears that right-wing violence was more prominent and caused a much higher number of victims in the early period, up to the mid-1970s, while left-wing violence developed especially from 1976 onwards, rapidly dwarfing its right-wing counterpart.

The attribution of the concept of 'civil war', albeit of an anomalous nature, or of the more neutral expression 'violent political conflict', albeit with a lower- than-average number of deaths, to the period following the social and political radicalisation of 1968–69 begs the question of whether Italy has carried out a process of peace building and national reconciliation in relation to this conflict, along the lines of many other countries torn by civil wars, and/or whether it should undertake such a process. These questions are also addressed in the volume.

## Italian neofascism after 1945

In all three types of political violence discussed above, neofascism figures as one of the protagonists, either acting independently or in alliance with other forces. It is therefore useful, before embarking on an analysis of its putative role in *stragismo*, to provide an outline of Italian neofascism after 1945, especially as regards its organisations, goals, beliefs and methods.

It goes without saying that the historiography of neofascism consists of three main strands: the works written by scholars, academics and intellectuals close to this political area, the studies produced by those who adopt a more neutral stance, and the works of those who are strongly opposed. Consequently, the interpretations put forward differ widely. It is possible, however, to recognise some common themes in all strands. One of these concerns primarily the condition of alienation and exclusion (and self-exclusion) in which the supporters and combatants of the Italian Social Republic found themselves at the end of the Second World War. 'Exiles in their Own Country' (*Esuli in patria*) is the title of a book published in 1995 by scholar and academic Marco Tarchi (himself an ex-member of the Movimento Sociale Italiano). Tarchi recalled the mixture of feelings – nostalgia, hatred, resentment, pride, self-victimisation – which pervaded the neofascists and led them to form a totally separate and 'foreign' body within the Italian nation. Whereas Tarchi tends to emphasise the condition of exclusion in which the neofascists were relegated by the winners, the same theme is brought to light by Francesco Germinario in his works (1999; 2001; 2005) in a way which emphasises instead the process of self-exclusion activated by the neofascists themselves. This was due to their deep hatred and contempt for the new Italian nation, coupled with a deep sense of constituting a chosen elite far superior to the vulgar masses, and strong bitterness (and bewilderment) for having been betrayed by these same masses. Such feelings were exacerbated by the realisation that a large part of the nation had betrayed the fascists in favour of those whom they considered criminals, barbarians, and by definition anti-nationalists, that is, the communists.

A second theme common to most histories of neofascism concerns the existence of two main political strategies within Italian neofascism. The first strategy was carried out by the Movimento Sociale Italiano, set up in 1946, especially after the appointment of Arturo Michelini as General Secretary in 1954. It consisted of a gradual rapprochement with the moderate right and the political centre, in the name of law and order, discipline, hierarchy, and of course anti-communism. It did not, however, mark a change in the party's ideology and it was motivated primarily by opportunistic reasons (Ignazi 1989: 440). This strategy led the party, in the early 1950s, to recognise NATO (North Atlantic Treaty Organization), and, on various occasions, to lend its votes in Parliament in support of Christian Democratic governments. In 1960, it also led to the formation of the Tambroni government, with the external support of the MSI. The government collapsed after a wave of demonstrations and strikes, organised mainly by the Communist Party, in several Italian cities, most notably in Genoa, where the MSI was holding its annual Congress. There were violent clashes in the streets and a number of people died as a result, some of whom were shot dead by the police. The scale of the protest brought the collapse of the Tambroni government, opening the way for the subsequent strategy of rapprochement between Christian Democracy and the Socialist Party, which led to the formation of more stable centre-left coalitions. This put paid to any hope the MSI might have entertained of moving closer to the governing forces.

The second strategy was carried out by a series of groups to the right of the party and consisted of revitalising the revolutionary and anti-democratic fascist tradition, under the influence of a charismatic thinker, Julius Evola, whose ideas of revolting against the decadent modern world seemed particularly apt for a community of people who looked to the past and were alienated by the present. Among these groups, made up of young and radical activists, was Centro Studi Ordine Nuovo ('Study Centre New Order'), set up by Pino Rauti in 1956, and Avanguardia Nazionale ('National Vanguard'), set up by Stefano Delle Chiaie in 1959. The former group especially was influenced by Evola's 'spiritualist', hierarchical, elitist, racist, anti-modern and anti-Western ideas. In his 1934 *Rivolta contro il mondo moderno* ('Revolt against the Modern World'), Evola had theorised a critique against modernity which represented a phase of decadence and spiritual degradation, both in its liberal-democratic and in its communist guise, and advocated a return to Tradition, as embodied in the premodern world and non-Western societies. In his vision, Reaction and Reactionary were positive terms, with the return to a golden past representing the only way forward. In 1953, Evola's *Gli uomini e le rovine* ('Men Among the Ruins') appeared. Against postwar defeatism, he postulated the need for a new select elite of warriors, bent on self-sacrifice and on emulating the spirit of the Waffen SS and Codreanu's Iron Guard. He also advocated a new authoritarian European Order, which would resist Westernisation and reject both superpowers. Rauti was directly inspired by Evola's thoughts, and the latter often contributed articles to *Ordine Nuovo*, the group's magazine (Evola 2001).

After the publication, in 1961, of *Cavalcare la tigre* ('Ride the Tiger'), other fringe neofascist groups were inspired by Evola's ideas, including Franco Giorgio Freda, one of the main defendants in the trials for the 1969 Milan massacre (Rao 1999: 111), who in 1969 published *La disintegrazione del sistema*. Freda attempted to move beyond Evola's traditionalism by reviving a 'Third Way' approach and advocating revolutionary ideas, together with a positive appreciation of Maoist China (Freda 1969; Stellati 2001). One of Evola's most influential ideas concerned *apoliteia*, an existentialist rejection of the modern world which did not mean 'renouncing politics or even acts of violence, as long as it is done in a spirit of "love of action in itself"' (Griffin 2000: 41). According to various commentators, this encouraged a total rejection of 'normal' politics, exaltation of individualist political actions and even nihilism. Whether it also provided theoretical justification for terrorist violence, not least in Freda's reelaboration of the myth of the 'political soldier' and the 'warrior', is one of the issues which the various trials on *stragismo* endeavoured to establish.

The positioning of Italian neofascism vis-à-vis the Western alliance also merits attention. On the surface, there was a clear strategic split within this political area concerning the attitude to adopt towards the superpowers. On the one hand, the MSI had openly, if with some difficulty, accepted the Western alliance, including NATO (Chiarini 1990; Neglie 1994). Indeed, according to a recent study (Parlato 2006), various future leaders of the MSI had established close links with the American secret services even before the official formation of the party, aware that the Cold War gave them the chance to play the anti-communist card to their advantage. On the other hand, the radical groups to the right of the party officially remained fiercely opposed to both superpowers and to the ideologies they promoted, in line with Evola's position. While this is uncontested, there is little consensus, however, over the hypothesis that many radical neofascist leaders themselves collaborated with the Western block, seen as the lesser of two evils, and specifically with its intelligence services, albeit in an underhand fashion and often unbeknown to their followers. This aspect is crucial to an understanding of the role played by the more extreme neofascist groups in *stragismo*, and will be assessed in some detail in the course of this study.

By contrast, there is considerable consensus regarding the later evolution of Italian neofascism. After 1968, in fact, radical neofascism was influenced by the youth and students' movement, while the MSI changed its strategy after appointing Giorgio Almirante as General Secretary in 1969. The youth rebellion encouraged a generational split within neofascism, and was later to inspire the creation of new groups (Lotta di Popolo, Costruiamo l'Azione, Terza Posizione, Nuclei Armati Rivoluzionari [NAR]), which were heavily critical of the 'historical' groups like ON (Ordine Nuovo) and AN (Avanguardia Nazionale), believing that they had been implicated in the Strategy of Tension and had collaborated with state structures. They were also very critical of the MSI, judged to have betrayed all revolutionary ideals and have become a truly conservative party. Some of the new groups, such as Terza Posizione, clearly inspired by Freda's ideas, advocated a middle way between fascist and Maoist ideologies, and even an alliance between the extreme right and the extreme left in a common fight against capitalism and Western imperialism. As for the older radical groups, Pino Rauti and his Centro Studi Ordine Nuovo in 1969 decided to reenter the MSI. This decision caused a split and the formation of a new group, Movimento Politico Ordine Nuovo ('Political Movement New Order'), which continued to operate outside the party, under the leadership of Clemente Graziani, until it was proscribed in 1973. As for AN, it was proscribed and disbanded in the mid-1970s.

Almirante launched a dual strategy, partly continuing to pursue collaboration with the parties of the democratic right, and partly showing solidarity with, and support for, the radical neofascist groups. The strategy reached a critical point when the party was faced with an escalation of political violence and constant fighting in the streets between extreme-left and extreme-right groups. This was the time, in the late 1970s, when a series of deaths among the youth members of the MSI, in Rome and other places, led some groups, notably Terza Posizione and the NAR, to take up arms. Neofascism had thus become a protagonist in the armed struggle, and the MSI was increasingly perceived by the public as complicit in this new radicalism, thereby losing its image as a party of law and order and consequently also losing votes (Ignazi 1994: 49). A few tentative attempts, made in the 1980s, to change the image of the party and its political isolation did not lead to any significant changes.

It was only in the 1990s, with the fall of the Italian First Republic and the consequent collapse of Christian Democracy and the Socialist Party, that the MSI could at last be 'unfrozen' to become a player in the new bi-polar party system. After Almirante's death in 1988, Gianfranco Fini became leader of the party, but was soon replaced by Pino Rauti, under whose secretaryship, in 1990-91, the party remained loyal to its fascist ideals. Following disastrous election results, Fini was reelected leader and he developed a strategy of political and ideological reorientation. In 1994, the MSI was replaced by Alleanza Nazionale, and a year later, at the Fiuggi Congress, the new party embarked on the path of renouncing the old fascist ideology. In open dissent with this decision, the most radical wing within the MSI, led by Pino Rauti, formed an alternative party, the Movimento

Sociale-Fiamma Tricolore (MS-FT), thus also indirectly conferring credibility on the democratic credentials of the new party. However, the transformation of the MSI into a fully postfascist party has been slow and patchy (Tarchi 1997), and the jury on the final outcome is still out. According to one of the most accredited experts, Ignazi (2003), the party was (still) on the threshold of exit from the extreme right at the beginning of the new century. More recently, Ignazi (2005: 348) claimed that Alleanza Nazionale was no longer a radical-right party, but a moderate-conservative one. One of the crucial criteria for ascertaining whether AN has exited the radical right concerns the attitude of its leaders and middle ranks regarding fascism and its legacy. This book contributes to this debate by exploring the attitude of the party regarding radical neofascism and its legacy, and comparing it with the attitude prevalent among the groups to its right which still subscribe to a fascist ideology.

## Research questions

Two sets of research questions underpin this study. The first set of questions concerns the current state of judicial investigations and trials on the massacres. In Italy, many trials related to crimes of *stragismo* were held while the Cold War was still raging and various state and political actors had an interest in preventing sensitive information from reaching the magistrates (not least because they themselves were implicated in these crimes). In the 1990s, following the collapse of the Italian First Republic, investigations on specific massacres were reopened, thanks to the dedication of individual magistrates, a new attitude of collaboration on the part of the intelligence services, the availability of new witnesses who were prepared to testify to the Courts and confess to their involvement in past crimes, and, on a more general level, the new political climate and the fall from power of many protagonists of the First Republic.

In the light of these new 'favourable' political and judicial conditions, can it be said that criminal justice has been achieved and that the truth has finally been established about the country's violent past, particularly with reference to the murkiest events related to *stragismo* and the Strategy of Tension? Have recent investigations and trials confirmed or disproved the role of neofascist organisations in *stragismo* and their connivance with state and intelligence structures, already established in previous trials, albeit tentatively in some cases? Who are the new witnesses for the prosecution and why have they decided to confess to their participation in past crimes? Have the culprits, in the form of both perpetrators and instigators, been successfully prosecuted, found guilty and punished? If not, what are the implications for the country's transition to a fully fledged, as opposed to an imperfect, democracy, as well as for the restoration of trust in its political and judicial institutions? These questions are explored in Part I, where it will be shown that the role of neofascist groups in *stragismo* has been forcefully reasserted by the criminal Courts, even at their highest level. Despite these findings, criminal justice has only partially been achieved and the truth about the massacres has only patchily been revealed. In this context, the judicial truth is of little use to the victims of the massacres, both because very few people have been convicted as culprits, and because they (and the witnesses to the trials) are often used as pawns in a political game, still lacking proper public recognition of the injustices that were inflicted upon them.

The second set of questions, addressed in Part II, concerns the extent to which the judicial verdicts have been acknowledged by all political parties, including those on the right who were most closely related to the organisations found responsible for *stragismo*. In the light of the literature on conflict resolution and national reconciliation, the book examines the nature and aims of the reconstructions of post-war violence put forward by representatives and sympathisers of Alleanza Nazionale and the groups to its right. Adopting a narrative psychology perspective, the book also analyses the self-narratives of three prominent leaders of neofascist groups operating in the 1960s and 1970s, with a view to ascertaining their contribution, if any, to the establishment of the truth concerning their own individual responsibilities, as well as those of their groups, in the three types of political violence outlined above. A related question concerns the extent to which the narratives and self-narratives put forward by the right present a pluralist reconstruction of the past and allow for different views and interpretations or construct a uniform, overarching 'master narrative'.

Part II shows that Alleanza Nazionale has not been able to distance itself from the extreme right and to acknowledge the judicial truth as regards Italian neofascism. Among the right it is as if the judicial truth simply does not exist, given that it is either dismissed and ridiculed, as being the product of a partisan and left-leaning judiciary, or altogether ignored and 'erased' in their own reconstructions. Indeed, it is the legitimacy of the judicial process itself which is refuted by the right. As for the role of the radical right in *stragismo*, this is presented, contrary to judicial findings, as having been a scapegoat for other forces, ranging from state and intelligence structures to Christian Democracy and to the left parties, above all the old Communist Party. One of the effects of these reconstructions is to deprive the real victims of the political conflict and the massacres of proper recognition of their status, given that the condition of victimhood has been appropriated by one of the groups responsible for the conflict.

In short, the prevailing attitude among both the radical and the postfascist right in relation to the trial verdicts and the role of neofascism in *stragismo*, is one of nonreconciliation. Deep-seated feelings of resentment, the conviction that they are made to figure as the only villains in the plot while the ex-communists are allowed to escape blame and condemnation for their part in the political conflict, a burning sense that there were real victims on their side, too, who still await criminal justice, and the inability to let go of longstanding myths and values largely explain widespread attitudes of intransigence within Alleanza Nazionale. In some cases, moreover, and this is much more in evidence among the radical-right groups which still adhere to fascist ideals, these feelings are put to the service of a rather more sinister aim, that of safeguarding the reputation of neofascism as a revolutionary movement untainted by any crimes or underhand deals, and of promoting a new militancy.

The analysis of the judicial process and of the prevailing attitude among the radical and postfascist right clearly shows that the old extreme right has not been able fully to transform itself into a mainstream postfascist, democratic party, and that the country at large has not succeeded in achieving either lasting reconciliation or successful amnesia as regards its divided and violent past. In this context, the concluding part of the book takes into consideration the issue of whether, now that criminal proceedings appear to have run their course, a process of truth telling and reconciliation would be desirable and ought to be undertaken in the Italian case.

# Part I

Villains? The Judicial Truth

# Introduction to Part I

*Stragismo*, as discussed in Chapter 1, refers to a bombing campaign which started in the late 1960s and lasted for several years, causing a high toll in terms of the number of people killed and wounded. Initially, investigations targeted extreme-left, especially anarchist, groups (the so-called 'red trail'), since the available evidence appeared to point in their direction. Later investigations started to probe an alternative path, the so-called 'black trail', which pointed the finger at extreme-right groups as the culprits for the massacres, albeit acting in ways that would pin the blame upon the extreme left. In connection to this discovery, investigating magistrates also brought to light the existence of a strategy, which became widely known as the Strategy of Tension, whose aim was to create an atmosphere of subversion and fear in the country so as to promote a turn to an authoritarian type of government. Since the strategy was mainly directed at containing communism in Italy (especially in the light of the formation of centre-left governments from 1963, and increasing unrest on the part of students and workers in 1968 and 1969), it was an essential part of this strategy that the threat of political subversion should be seen as coming from the left, not from the right. This explained to many why much of the early evidence had appeared to point in the direction of anarchist groups. Indeed, when investigations started to target the extreme right, various state forces mobilised in order to obstruct their progress and to prevent information from reaching the magistrates, thus severely hampering the judicial process.

The chapters that make up Part I examine *stragismo* and the Strategy of Tension in the light of judicial findings and trial material, especially in connection with the latest trials, concerning the December 1969 massacre at Piazza Fontana, Milan, and the 1973 attack against the police headquarters, again in Milan. The chapters are organised 'from the bottom up': that is to say, the analysis starts with an in-depth examination of the role of Italian neofascist groups, and other organisations acting 'on the ground' (Chapter 2). It then proceeds to assess the role of various national and foreign bodies, including the intelligence services, the armed forces, the *Carabinieri*, and the police (Chapter 3). Finally, Chapter 4 discusses the interpretations of both *stragismo* and the Strategy of Tension as put forward by well-informed individuals who have incorporated the findings of the recent trials in their reconstructions of events. Before we analyse the judicial material, it is important to provide a brief account of the judicial process itself, and the reasons why it has proved so convoluted, with the latest trial on Piazza Fontana concluding as recently as 2005, and the one on the Brescia massacre still pending.

# The long and tortuous search for the culprits

The longest and most convoluted of all judicial investigations and trials concerning bombing attacks and other acts of *stragismo* – which collectively are seen as constituting the so-called Strategy of Tension – was the one concerning the bombing attacks of 12 December 1969, when various explosive devices went off in Milan and Rome. One of these, planted at the Banca Nazionale dell'Agricoltura, in Piazza Fontana, Milan, resulted in seventeen people dead and eighty-four wounded. Police investigations at first identified the culprits as Giuseppe Pinelli and Pietro Valpreda, two anarchists who belonged to the Milanese group 22 marzo ('22 March'). While being interrogated at Milan police headquarters, Pinelli died, officially committing suicide by jumping out of one of the windows. This event was to inspire Dario Fo to write his famous play *Morte accidentale di un anarchico* ('Accidental Death of an Anarchist'), first performed in December 1970. It also marked the beginning of a campaign of hatred directed against the officer considered responsible for Pinelli's death, Commissar Luigi Calabresi, himself assassinated three years later.

In 1972, after new investigations on the part of Treviso magistrate Giancarlo Stiz, neofascists Franco Freda, Giovanni Ventura and Pino Rauti were arrested. The latter was at the time a national leader of the MSI, having been founder, in 1956, of the extreme-right group Centro Studi Ordine Nuovo. The first two were leaders of the Padua-based cell of Ordine Nuovo. Initially charged with being the organisers of bombing attacks at Milan's Fiera Campionaria and Central Station on 25 April 1969, as well as various attacks on trains on 8 and 9 August 1969, the Padua group was later also charged by Judge Stiz with the massacre of 12 December 1969. On 21 March 1972, as required by law, the investigation was transferred to Milanese magistrates, headed by Judge Gerardo D'Ambrosio, who on 24 April discharged Pino Rauti and on 28 August charged Freda and Ventura with the Piazza Fontana massacre.

On 23 February 1972 the first trial began, initially with the anarchists as defendants. Later, both Valpreda and Pinelli on the one hand, and Freda and Ventura on the other, stood as defendants, despite the obvious mutual incompatibility between the 'red' and the 'black' trails. On 13 October 1972, for 'reasons of law and order', the trial was transferred from Milan to Catanzaro, in the deep south, in a move which was interpreted in many quarters as an attempt to stifle any further investigations into the 'black trail', and especially into the suspected links between the neofascists, intelligence and military structures, and politicians. These suspicions were compounded by the fleeing abroad of Marco Pozzan, a friend of Franco Freda, on 15 January 1973, and of Guido Giannettini, an informer of the Italian secret services (then named SID – Servizio Informazioni Difesa), on 9 April 1973. Both were potentially crucial witnesses, and both were helped to flee Italy by the SID itself, as will be discussed in Chapter 3. Ten years after the crime, the trial concluded in February 1979 with a life sentence for both Freda and Ventura, as well as Giannettini, while Valpreda was found not guilty on the grounds of 'insufficient evidence'. On 20 March 1981, the Court of Appeal ruled that Freda and Ventura were also not guilty for lack of evidence. On 11 June 1982, the Supreme Court, the Court of Cassation, declared void the sentence of the Court of Appeal and ruled in favour of a new trial, which was to take place in Bari. The new trial involved only Freda and Ventura, since the Court also established that Giannettini should no longer be prosecuted. On 1 August 1985, the new Court confirmed that Freda and Ventura were not guilty on the grounds of 'insufficient evidence', a verdict which was later confirmed by the Court of Cassation on 27 January 1987. The two neofascists, however, were condemned to sixteen years in prison for the attacks at Milan's Fiera Campionaria and Central Station of 25 April 1969, and on various trains, on 8-9 August 1969.

In 1987, the same year as the Court of Cassation ruled that neither the anarchists nor the neofascists were guilty of the Piazza Fontana massacre, albeit with recourse to a 'not proven' verdict, Milanese magistrate Guido Salvini reopened investigations, on the basis of fresh findings. The new investigation, which became publicly known only in 1991, resulted, first in 1995 and later in 1998, in a series of charges against the Venice-based cell of Ordine Nuovo, led by Delfo Zorzi and Carlo Maria Maggi and the Milan-based extreme-right group La Fenice, led by Giancarlo Rognoni (as well as the Padua-based cell of Ordine Nuovo, even though neither Freda nor Ventura could be put on trial for a second time). One of the main witnesses in the new trial, Carlo Digilio, was also a self-confessed culprit, in his capacity as both expert on weapons and explosives and adviser on such matters to Ordine Nuovo in the Veneto region. In June 2001 the Court found the defendants guilty of coorganising the massacre and sentenced them to life imprisonment. On 12 March 2004, the Milan Court of Appeal reversed the first sentence and found the defendants not guilty, although it acquitted both Maggi and Zorzi only with reference to Article 530, comma 2, of the Italian penal code, that is, on grounds of insufficient evidence. This sentence was later confirmed by the Court of Cassation. However, the Court also ruled that there was sufficiently strong evidence to establish that Freda and Ventura were indeed guilty of the Piazza Fontana massacre, as found in 1979, even though they were no longer judicially liable. In addition, both the Court of Appeal and the Court of Cassation confirmed the initial guilty verdict for Carlo Digilio, and concluded that the massacre was to be attributed without doubt to the extreme-right group Ordine Nuovo, thereby clearing the anarchists Pinelli and Valpreda of any involvement in this crime.

Another important investigation and trial concerned the bombing attack at Bologna central station of 2 August 1980, which resulted in eighty-five people dead and more than 200 wounded. The trial started on 19 January 1987 and ended with a first verdict on 11 July 1988. The Court sentenced to life imprisonment Valerio Fioravanti, Francesca Mambro, Massimiliano Fachini and Sergio Picciafuoco. Fachini was a member of the MSI and Ordine Nuovo, Picciafuoco was a common criminal who was considered close to extreme-right activists, and Valerio Fioravanti and Francesca Mambro were leaders and founders of the NAR

(Nuclei Armati Rivoluzionari). In addition, the Court condemned for obstruction of justice Licio Gelli (Head of the Masonic Lodge P2), Francesco Pazienza, General Pietro Musumeci and Colonel Giuseppe Belmonte. All were sentenced to ten years in custody. The Court also sentenced Valerio Fioravanti to sixteen years' imprisonment, Francesca Mambro and Massimiliano Fachini to fifteen years each, Gilberto Cavallini to thirteen, Roberto Rinani to twelve years, all for membership of an armed group. This verdict was reversed by a Court of Appeal two years later. In 1992, the Supreme Court upheld the guilty sentences for Mambro, Fioravanti and Picciafuoco, while Fachini was found not guilty. Three years later, on 23 November 1995, the Court of Cassation confirmed a sentence of life imprisonment for Valerio Fioravanti and Francesca Mambro, cleared Massimiliano Fachini and condemned Licio Gelli, Francesco Pazienza, Pietro Musumeci and Giuseppe Belmonte for obstruction of justice. Picciafuoco was also cleared definitively in 1997.

In 1986, another member of the NAR, Luigi Ciavardini, a minor at the time of the massacre, was also accused of being one of the perpetrators. In January 2000, the Juvenile Court of Bologna cleared him of charges. Subsequently, on 9 March 2002, he was found guilty by a court of appeal and sentenced to thirty years in jail, but in 2003 the Court of Cassation annulled this verdict. In 2004 a different Appeals Court confirmed he was guilty of involvement in the massacre. The final decision by the Court of Cassation, on 11 April 2007, upheld the guilty sentence.

More recently, in 2005, the Bologna case was reopened by a magistrate, Paolo Giovagnoli, on the basis of new evidence which seemed to incriminate Ilich Ramirez Sanchez, better known as Carlos, an international professional terrorist closely linked to extreme Middle Eastern (mainly Palestinian) political groups. The reopening of the investigations followed a concerted campaign, organised mainly by politicians and intellectuals of the right, but supported also by representatives of all political tendencies, directed at proclaiming the innocence of the three neofascists charged with the massacre. For their part, Fioravanti, Mambro and Ciavardini have always maintained that they had nothing to do with this act of *stragismo*. Thus far, however, the new investigations have not led to a retrial.

Other important judicial investigations and trials on acts of violence and *stragi* considered to be closely connected to the Strategy of Tension concerned the attack on the Milan police headquarters of 17 May 1973, which killed four people and wounded another forty-five, and the bomb attack which took place at Piazza della Loggia, in Brescia, on 28 May 1974, resulting in eight people dead and 102 wounded. The trial for the first crime concluded initially (on 11 March 2000) with a sentence of life imprisonment for Gianfranco Bertoli as the perpetrator of the attack, and Carlo Maria Maggi, Giorgio Boffelli and Francesco Neami (of Ordine Nuovo) as well as Colonel Amos Spiazzi (of the Nuclei for the Defence of the State) as coorganisers. Gianfranco Bertoli was a self-declared anarchist who later was found to have been in close contact with extreme-right members of Ordine Nuovo in Venice and Mestre, Maggi and Boffelli were respectively leader and member of the Venice-based cell of Ordine Nuovo, and Neami belonged to the

Trieste-based cell of the same organisation. Amos Spiazzi was the leader of the Verona branch ('Legion') of a national organisation known as Nuclei for the Defence of the State, which depended on the army and recruited civilians and ex-military personnel for anti-communist purposes (see Chapter 2). The Court of Appeal subsequently ruled that Maggi, Boffelli, Neami and Spiazzi were not guilty of the crime, and that Bertoli had organised and executed the attack entirely of his own accord. On 11 July 2003, the Court of Cassation dismissed the latter sentence in highly critical terms and declared it void, thereby asking for new investigations and a new trial with reference to the three suspected organisers of the attack, who belonged to Ordine Nuovo. At the same time, however, the Court ruled that key witness Carlo Digilio was not to be considered credible and that his testimony should not be taken into account. The new Court of Appeal ruled on 1 December 2004 that the defendants were not guilty, albeit on grounds of 'insufficient evidence' (Article 530, comma 2 of the Italian penal code). Nevertheless, similarly to the verdict for the Piazza Fontana bombing, the Court also ruled that the attack was without doubt to be attributed to the extreme-right organisation Ordine Nuovo, and most probably to its Venice-based cell, whose leader was Carlo Maria Maggi.

In relation to the Brescia bombing, two investigations took place. One of these led to the charging of a small group of Brescia-based extreme-right elements, among whom was Ermanno Buzzi. The trial started in 1974, led to a first sentence which found the defendants guilty, a second sentence by the Court of Appeal in 1982 which reversed this judgment, and finally a ruling on 25 September 1987 by the Court of Cassation in favour of the defendants. In between the first two sentences Ermanno Buzzi was strangled, in jail, by two extreme-right terrorists, Pierluigi Concutelli and Mario Tuti. The second investigation ended with the charging of a number of Milan-based extreme-right activists, among whom was Giancarlo Rognoni, leader of the group La Fenice. The trial ended with a verdict by the Court of Cassation, on 13 November 1989, which ruled the defendants not guilty, albeit – once again – on the grounds of insufficient evidence.

A related story involved prosecutor Mario Arcai, who in 1974 was investigating the Movimento di Azione Rivoluzionaria (MAR), a subversive group the magistrate suspected of being involved in the 28 May massacre (see Chapter 2). Soon after, when the name of Arcai's son appeared in a list of neofascists suspected of the bombing, the magistrate was transferred elsewhere for 'incompatibility', and his investigation came to an end. A new trial on this massacre is still pending. However, given that the main witnesses are the same people who testified at the recent trials for both the 1969 Piazza Fontana massacre and the 1973 attack at the Milan police headquarters, it is doubtful whether a significantly different verdict will result from this latest judicial process.

Finally, an investigation and trial which revealed crucially important aspects of the Strategy of Tension, specifically in relation to systematic cover-ups on the part of the armed forces and the *Carabinieri*, concerned the car bombing carried out in Peteano (Gorizia) on 31 May 1972, which killed three *Carabinieri* and injured a fourth. Initially, the investigators followed a 'red trail', which quickly proved unfounded. Later, a group of common criminals was charged with the crime and put on trial. In 1979 they were all found not guilty. In 1984, neofascist Vincenzo Vinciguerra, already in prison for another politically inspired crime, confessed to having perpetrated the Peteano attack as an act of war against the state. Without turning collaborator, he nevertheless helped investigations, while denouncing the manner in which various state apparatuses had covered up the true culprits (including himself) and tried to blame others instead. This episode is discussed in Chapter 3.

The trial against Vinciguerra, his neofascist friend and partner in crime Carlo Cicuttini (at the time on the run in Spain) and various *Carabinieri* for obstruction of justice first ended in 1987 with a sentence of life imprisonment for the two neofascists, and between three and ten years' imprisonment for the *Carabinieri*. The Court of Appeal established in 1989 that the two neofascists were guilty and the *Carabinieri* were innocent. In 1990, the Court of Cassation annulled this sentence and requested a new trial, which ended in 1991, confirming the sentence to life imprisonment for Vinciguerra and Cicuttini and sentencing the *Carabinieri* to three years and ten months, a verdict later reaffirmed by the Court of Cassation in 1992.

## Assessing the outcomes of the judicial process

To sum up, after more than thirty-five years since the events of 12 December 1969 and following costly and lengthy judicial investigations and trials, the only tangible results appear to be a handful of confirmed culprits, a few minor prison sentences against officers of the *Carabinieri*, the armed forces and members of the Masonic Lodge P2 for obstruction of justice, and no clear-cut explanation of the exact nature, aims and organisers of the Strategy of Tension. The sentences appear to have followed a fairly regular pattern, with the lower Courts finding the defendants guilty, the Appeal Courts reversing their verdicts and finally, after several years and various obstructions of justice, not least on the part of those same state bodies which should have supported the work of the magistrates, the Court of Cassation ruling the defendants not guilty, albeit with recourse to a 'not proven' verdict. This pattern can be attributed to a combination of factors, the most important being:

- Repeated cover-ups on the part of certain sections of the armed forces, the *Carabinieri* and the intelligence services. Cover-ups took the form of giving false information, hiding important information, helping crucial witnesses/perpetrators escape abroad, failing to follow up vital leads and/or to take on board unwelcome evidence.
- In the most recent trials, taking place so many years after the events, the difficulty of obtaining fully reliable and detailed information from ageing,

sometimes ill, witnesses, and the death of other potential informers. Carlo Digilio, for instance, one of the two crucial witnesses (as well as a defendant) for the latest trial on the Piazza Fontana massacre, appeared to suffer from memory losses as a result of a stroke he had had in 1995. His confusion over dates and events undermined his testimony and resulted in the Court of Appeal's decision, later confirmed by the Court of Cassation, that he should not be considered a credible witness. Many other witnesses who could have corroborated the stories told by Digilio and others had already died.

- Again in the most recent trials, the difficulty of retracing places, such as hiding places for weapons and explosives. In the Piazza Fontana trial, Carlo Digilio had described at some length a place where explosives had been kept by the Venice-based group of Ordine Nuovo, but when he was taken to the village where he was confident he could recognise the exact spot, he found it changed 'beyond recognition' and failed to identify its location.

To these factors one needs to add that Italian law, like Scottish law, allows three alternative verdicts in a criminal trial, one of which is the verdict of not proven. While being on a par with a verdict of not guilty in terms of its effects, it is often used by judges to indicate that they have reasonable doubt as to the defendant's guilt. Some of the Courts deliberating on acts of *stragismo* used the verdict of not proven quite explicitly and deliberately in this sense, especially in view of the fact that they all agreed on the identification of the extremist group which had carried out the crimes. Conversely, there are specific ambiguities surrounding the behaviour of some Courts, as exemplified by the extraordinary verdict of the Court of Appeal in the trial for the 1973 attack at Milan police headquarters, which was declared void by the Court of Cassation, on the grounds that the evidence had been 'bent' by the judges in order to demonstrate a preexisting theory. Commenting on this decision, Milanese magistrate Ferdinando Pincioni, responsible for the supplementary trial requested by the Court of Cassation, stated that it constituted a very severe indictment of the professional conduct of the Court of Appeal judges (interview with the author, 20 October 2005). He also raised a question mark over the decision, by the Court of Cassation, to request a new trial while simultaneously preventing the reconvening Court from considering the evidence of key witness Carlo Digilio. In the magistrate's view, Digilio had proved a credible witness and the new Court would have reached a clear verdict of conviction had his testimony been taken into account.

At a more general level, considerable criticism has been levelled in Italy and abroad at the exceptional system of justice instituted in the late 1970s and early 1980s, especially with Law No. 15 of 6 February 1980, which included Article 270 bis, referring to crimes of association for terrorist ends or with intent to undermine the democratic order, and Article 280, referring to atrocities for terrorist ends or with intent to undermine the democratic order. In addition, Law No. 304 of 1982, later replaced by Law No. 45 of 13 February 2001, established the legal category of 'collaborators of justice', the so-called *pentiti* ('repentant witnesses'), thus allowing suspects assisting the police and the judiciary and denouncing their former comrades to plea for reduced sentences. This law has often been criticised for resulting in short prison sentences for serious offences and for encouraging the spread of false information by former terrorists, eager to acquire the status, and enjoy the benefits, of 'collaborators of justice'. While the legislation proved effective in bringing about a reduction in the number of terrorist acts in the country and contributing to the ultimate collapse of this political phenomenon, its morality was put into question.

A number of trials against presumed terrorists, carried out under this emergency legislation, incurred special condemnation and became the target of a vigorous campaign by Italian and European intellectuals, politicians, and part of the media. The trial against Adriano Sofri is a case in point. Sofri was a founder and leader of the extreme-left organisation Lotta Continua ('The Struggle Continues'), set up in 1969. Together with another leader, Giorgio Pietrostefani, he was arrested and charged in 1988 for instigating the murder of police officer Luigi Calabresi, killed in Milan on 17 May 1972 and considered responsible by the extreme left for 'suiciding' Pinelli. A third activist, Ovidio Bompressi, was charged with the actual murder. Their main accuser was Leonardo Marino, himself an ex-member of Lotta Continua, who, troubled by his conscience, confessed to his own involvement in the crime, and also implicated the other three. After a series of trials, and two verdicts annulled, in 1997 the three activists were found guilty and Sofri was sentenced to twenty-two years in prison. In October 2000, the Court of Cassation confirmed this verdict. The case was taken to the European Court of Human Rights, which in 2003 ruled that the application lodged on behalf of Sofri and others was inadmissible. With reference to two judges, Judge Pincioni (the same who ruled in the case against Bertoli) and Judge Della Torre, the Court considered that there was no evidence to cast doubt on the former's subjective impartiality and that there was nothing in the case file to suggest that Della Torre's assessment of the facts had been arbitrary (Registry of the European Court of Human Rights, 2003). Despite this judgment, a wide spectrum of opinion remained convinced that Sofri was innocent, questioning the credibility of Marino's testimony, and campaigned for his early release through a presidential pardon.

With reference to the trials against presumed extreme-right terrorists, similar doubts have been raised, as already mentioned, concerning the validity of the judicial process against, and the guilty status of, Valerio Fioravanti and Francesca Mambro, leaders of the neofascist group NAR, sentenced to life imprisonment for the Bologna station bombing. In 1994, a group of politicians and intellectuals, mainly from the right but including representatives of the left, set up a committee named 'What if they are innocent?', and started a campaign to have them cleared of this crime. Unlike the Calabresi murder, for the Bologna station massacre a new investigation is under way, which may eventually lead to the incrimination of different people with radically different political ideologies and roots. It is also the case, as will be seen in greater detail in the following chapters, that the Bologna massacre may constitute an anomalous act of terrorism, in the sense that it was not part of the Strategy of Tension as this is commonly understood, and may have pursued a different agenda.

As regards the other trials on *stragismo*, there have been no equivalent claims of judicial partiality or unfair outcome concerning the defendants in Italian public opinion, other than among the right. On the contrary, much public opinion supported the view that these trials had suffered from repeated obstructions of justice on the part of state bodies and intelligence services, which accounted for the missing evidence. Unlike some of the trials whose verdicts are being contested, these trials, especially the most recent ones on the Piazza Fontana bombing and the attack at the Milan police headquarters, relied on a wide range of testimony, including that of independent witnesses alongside 'repented' ex-neofascists. In addition, the final verdict of acquittal clearly indicated that the Courts had given full consideration to the available evidence and to the rights of the defendants. It is also interesting to note that most of the neofascist and postfascist right campaigned against the granting of a presidential pardon to Adriano Sofri, defending the legitimacy of his trial. In their view, as will be seen in Part II, the extreme right in Italy was criminalised by the judiciary, while the extreme left was treated much more leniently. For this reason much of the right has resisted the temptation to question the legitimacy of all the trials concerning acts of political violence and terrorism, calling instead for bringing all the extreme-left perpetrators to justice, including those who were granted asylum in France, like Cesare Battisti, found guilty of murder and sentenced to life imprisonment in 1985, or who escaped to other countries, like Achille Lollo, found guilty of a murderous arson attack and sentenced to eighteen years' imprisonment in 1987.

Finally, from the point of view of discovering the truth and uncovering the perpetrators of the *stragi*, the assessment of the criminal process is not as bleak as its seemingly meagre results might suggest. Thanks to judicial findings, today it is possible to identify fairly accurately which specific groups were responsible for which *stragi* and why, even though the trials were unable to identify 'beyond any reasonable doubt' the individual culprits other than in a few cases. Yet these cases are in themselves revelatory, since all the known perpetrators belonged to neofascist organisations, among which the most prominent was Ordine Nuovo. Franco Freda, Giovanni Ventura, Carlo Digilio, Vincenzo Vinciguerra and Carlo Cicuttini all belonged to this organisation. Nico Azzi, charged and later sentenced for a (failed) bomb attack on a train, carried out on 7 April 1973, belonged to the Milan-based group La Fenice, which had close contacts with the Veneto cells of Ordine Nuovo. Whether or not the Bologna massacre was perpetrated by international terrorists rather than home-grown ones, the fact remains that all the other *stragi*, and especially those carried out between 1969 and 1974, have been attributed by the Courts to neofascist groups. In addition, despite the very lenient sentences approved by the Courts against members and officers of the intelligence services, the armed forces, the *Carabinieri* and the police, it is also true to say that many cases of cover-ups have been identified and disclosed, to the extent that it is now fairly clear which state bodies were involved and which groups they protected. The trials have even provided some important clues as to the role played by Italian and international political forces in the Strategy of Tension and in *stragismo*. In short, the judicial trials have produced substantial and illuminating material for establishing the role of neofascism in *stragismo* and for helping to reconstruct the historical truth concerning the entire Strategy of Tension.

This more positive assessment of the judicial process, however, is no consolation to the relatives of the victims of the massacres, who fought for so many years to achieve justice for the hundreds of people who were killed or badly injured. Furthermore, although the trials have uncovered much of the truth, the whole truth remains unknown, so much so that even the most recent investigations met with reticence on the part of many potential witnesses, and uncovered a persisting climate of intimidation and connivance, as we shall see in the following chapters. Finally, the at best partial success of the judicial process, and the exposure of much wrongdoing on the part of military, intelligence and political actors, have led to continuing mistrust in, and undermined the legitimacy of, state institutions, despite the collapse of the First Republic in the early 1990s and the many hopes entertained at the time for a renewal of the country's political system. This leaves open the question of whether the criminal process was the most effective, or indeed the only tool for dealing with these politically inspired crimes and whether it should be complemented by different approaches, related to what is known as 'restorative justice'. These issues are taken into consideration in the Conclusion to Part I.

# CHAPTER 2
# The Role of Italian Neofascism in *Stragismo* and the Strategy of Tension

## Introduction

As we saw in the Introduction to Part I, the evidence amassed in successive judicial trials has in many instances not proved sufficient to secure the conviction of individual suspected culprits, all of them members or sympathisers of neofascist groups. Despite these obvious setbacks in terms of securing clear-cut verdicts on the role of individuals, successive judicial trials have uncovered a wealth of data on the activities of various neofascist organisations. Much of the evidence unearthed in the investigations was judged incontrovertible even by the Courts which finally reached 'not guilty' verdicts. In this section, the most relevant judicial findings will be analysed and assessed; only those which were endorsed by the Supreme Court will be used in order to reconstruct the role played by Italian neofascism (or at least by some of its segments) in both *stragismo* and the Strategy of Tension.

Let us start with the cases as reconstructed by Milan prosecutors Guido Salvini and Antonio Lombardi, available through the *Sentenze-ordinanze* produced by Salvini and dated 18 March 1995, 3 February 1998, 2 and 18 March 1998, and the *Sentenza-ordinanza* produced by Lombardi, dated 18 July 1998. As Salvini noted in the opening parts of his *sentenze*, his reconstruction had been made possible thanks to the information provided by neofascist and ex-neofascist witnesses Sergio Calore, Angelo Izzo, Gianluigi Radice, Vincenzo Vinciguerra, Guelfo Osmani, Edgardo Bonazzi, Carmine Dominici, Giuseppe Albanese, and above all Carlo Digilio and Martino Siciliano, the two key witnesses in the Piazza Fontana trial. The former, as already mentioned, was an expert in weapons and explosives and a member of the Venice-based group of Ordine Nuovo. As Salvini pointed out, he turned collaborator after reentering Italy in 1992 from Santo Domingo, after an absence of seven years, and was faced with a sentence of ten years' imprisonment. At that point, he decided to come to an agreement with the prosecutors and 'confess' in exchange for the preferential terms accorded by law to all collaborators. Martino Siciliano was also a member of the Venice-based cell of Ordine

Nuovo (although, in his role as middle-rank activist, he was kept in the dark regarding Digilio's personal details, as the latter was referred to by ON leaders only as 'Zio Otto' or 'Ziotto'). Siciliano, as stated by Salvini, oscillated for some time between accepting the offers of money and work in Russia or Japan made to him by defendant Delfo Zorzi (who himself lives in Japan, where he obtained nationality), and 'confessing' his own role and that of his comrades in the massacres of the 1960s and 1970s. He then decided to confess all, partly out of 'sincere remorse for the tragic events which he, with his militancy ... had contributed in part to make possible' (*Sentenza-ordinanza* Salvini, 3 February 1998: 25), but also partly because of his fear that his ex-comrades might decide physically to eliminate him if he ever went to Russia. This fear proved fully justified when it emerged, from a recorded telephone conversation between two close collaborators of Delfo Zorzi, that the 'Siciliano problem could be solved with a 9-calibre gun' (ibid.: 30).

As Salvini emphasised (and this will be discussed in some detail in Part II), the fact that a considerable number of neofascists had agreed to testify was in itself a very significant breakthrough, given that principles (however misguided) of 'honour' and 'loyalty' were paramount among 'comrades', and for this and other reasons (including fear of retaliation and revenge against themselves and/or their close relatives) they had always proved extremely reticent and very reluctant to reveal anything to the judicial magistrates.

What, then, emerged from the testimony of these and other witnesses, as well as from the archives of the intelligence services (including a forgotten archive of the Ministry of the Interior, discovered by the historian Aldo Giannuli, researcher for prosecutor Salvini and consultant to the above-mentioned Parliamentary Commission on the Failed Identification of the Authors of Terrorist Massacres)? First and foremost, the new evidence brought to light, in much greater detail than had been known before, the composition as well as the illegal/criminal activities of various subversive organisations, many of them neofascist and neo-Nazi ones. This is especially true in the case of the operations carried out by Ordine Nuovo at national and regional level, especially in the Veneto-Trentino-Friuli Venezia Giulia regions, collectively known as the Triveneto. Furthermore, the new evidence revealed that Ordine Nuovo retained a clear identity and unity of purpose even after its split in 1969, which was 'merely apparent' (*Sentenza-ordinanza* Salvini, 18 March 1995: 34).

## Ordine Nuovo (ON) ('New Order')

In the late 1960s and early 1970s, in the area of the Triveneto, Ordine Nuovo could rely on the following cells and activists:

- In Trieste, a cell including Francesco Neami, Claudio Bressan and Manlio Portolan;

- in Venice-Mestre, a cell led by Carlo Maria Maggi and Delfo Zorzi, including Paolo Molin and Giancarlo Vianello;
- in Verona, a cell led by Elio Massagrande, Marcello Soffiati and Amos Spiazzi;
- in Treviso, a group led by Roberto Raho;
- in Padua, the group led by Franco Freda, which included Massimiliano Fachini and Aldo Trinco;
- in Trento, a cell including Cristano De Eccher;
- in Udine, a group including the Vinciguerra brothers, Carlo Cicuttini and Cesare Turco;
- in Milan, a group known as La Fenice ('The Phoenix'), set up in 1971. It published a magazine with the same name. The leader of this group was Giancarlo Rognoni, his closest collaborator was Nico Azzi, and other activists included Pietro Battiston, Mauro Marzorati, Francesco De Min and Pierluigi Pagliai. While based in Milan, the group was extremely close to the Ordine Nuovo cells of the Triveneto.

Each cell comprised a small number of activists and, to ensure a high degree of secrecy, the cells were in contact with each other only through their leaders. The leader of the Venice-based cell, Carlo Maria Maggi, also acted as the regional coordinator of Ordine Nuovo for the Triveneto and as such he was higher-ranking than all the other leaders in the area. He reported directly to the national leaders, especially Pino Rauti and Paolo Signorelli.

All these cells had large quantities of explosives and other weapons available, were able to rely on Carlo Digilio to train them in their preparation and use, and theorised about the need for terrorist attacks. According to Siciliano, from 1966, and even more intensively from 1968, the Ordine Nuovo cells of Venice-Mestre were getting ready for a 'qualitative step forward', amassing weapons and explosives and preparing to become one of the leading structures for a new terrorist strategy (*Sentenza-ordinanza* Salvini, 3 February 1998: 55). As far back as 1966, at a cinema hall in Mestre known as the 'White Room', Siciliano had attended a meeting which marked the setting up of Ordine Nuovo in the Triveneto. The meeting had been chaired by Pino Rauti; among the participants were Digilio, Maggi, Molin, Zorzi, Freda, the Vinciguerra brothers, Neami, Portolan, Soffiati and Besutti. After the meeting, there had been a restricted gathering, also chaired by Rauti, and attended by Maggi, Romani, Molin, Zorzi, Freda and Siciliano. Here the discussion had revolved around the risk that the Italian Communist Party might take over power and the need to prevent this risk by relying on the support of the armed forces. It was decided that Ordine Nuovo should keep its official members to a minimum. There was also talk, especially by Freda, of the need to create a specific type of member, defined as the 'soldier', who would carry out military actions 'with bombs and attacks against both state structures and the population ... so as to determine a reaction on the part of the civil population' (Sentence of the Second Section of the Court of Appeal of Milan, 12 March 2004: 159).

Siciliano also recalled that, in the spring of 1969, a meeting took place in Padua in the Ezzelino bookshop owned by Giovanni Ventura, which was attended, among others, by Maggi, Zorzi, Molin, as well as Siciliano himself. As he recalled, during the meeting 'one of the Padua members, most probably Freda, remarked that a useful strategy would consist of small demonstrative [explosive] attacks which would cause minor damage ... I remember however that Freda said that we should not have scruples if, despite their being demonstrative attacks, a few civilians were hit' (*Sentenza-ordinanza* Salvini, 3 February 1998: 120). According to Judge Salvini, the presence of both Freda and Maggi at that meeting was proof of the 'operational synergy' between the Padua-based and the Venice-Mestre-based cells of Ordine Nuovo, something that had not emerged in previous judicial investigations and trials given a lack of witnesses and collaborators (Sentence of the Second Section of the Court of Appeal of Milan, 12 March 2004: 120).

Among the first violent actions carried out by these cells was an arson attack against the Communist Party section of Campalto, near Mestre, on 9 October 1968, performed when the section was shut and empty. Among the culprits on that occasion were Siciliano himself, Delfo Zorzi and Giampiero Mariga, all members of the Venice-Mestre cell. The cells were also responsible for two bomb attacks, one against the Slovene School at Trieste, and another at the border with Yugoslavia, in Gorizia, both carried out in October 1969, which had no consequences because the explosives failed to detonate. The culprits were Siciliano, Delfo Zorzi and Giancarlo Vianello, from the Venice-Mestre cell, while logistical help had been supplied by members of the Trieste-based cell, including Francesco Neami, the explosives by Carlo Digilio, and the car by Carlo Maria Maggi.

Siciliano likened these early, relatively minor, episodes to a kind of dress rehearsal, in terms of the means and the people employed, in preparation for more serious terrorist plans, an explanation fully shared by Judge Salvini (*Sentenza-ordinanza* Salvini, 3 February 1998: 92). More serious bomb attacks did indeed follow, in the form of explosives placed on ten trains on 8 and 9 August 1969, for which Freda and Ventura were found guilty in 1979 and sentenced to sixteen years' imprisonment, a verdict later confirmed by the Supreme Court, as we saw. According to Carlo Digilio, these attacks were in fact a coordinated effort on the part of all the Ordine Nuovo cells of the Triveneto. Digilio recalled that Maggi, at a meeting which had taken place in September 1969, had clarified that the attacks had been carried out by all available activists from the cells of Mestre, Trieste, Rovigo, Vicenza and Verona (*Sentenza-ordinanza* Salvini, 18 March 1998: 35).

With reference to Ordine Nuovo's role in the Piazza Fontana bombing, the investigations of Milan prosecutor Salvini were able to rely on further testimonies on the part of a witness who had already made important revelations at the first trial against Freda and Ventura but had also proved somewhat reticent. This witness was Tullio Fabris, an electrician who had worked occasionally for Franco Freda and who had originally testified that he had acquired on behalf of Freda fifty timers and five metres of nickel-chrome (later used as resistor for the Piazza

Fontana explosive). He had also testified that, in September 1969, Freda had told him that the timers had to be placed inside metallic boxes (as indeed was the case in the bombing of the Banca Nazionale dell'Agricoltura, in Piazza Fontana) and had asked him to procure some of these.

Interrogated by Judge Salvini in November 1994, Fabris explained that at the time of the first trial he had not disclosed any more information because he had received various threats and feared for his life. One of these threats had been made in his own shop by two people, one of whom was Massimiliano Fachini (from the Padua cell), while the other he did not know but later saw on television and recognised as Pino Rauti (the national leader and founder of Centro Studi Ordine Nuovo) (*Sentenza-ordinanza* Salvini, 18 March 1998: 4–5). After agreeing to testify further, Fabris disclosed that he had taken part in three meetings with Freda and Ventura in Padua, in October and November 1969, and that on these occasions he had trained them in the use of the primers and the timers. At the third and last meeting, they had performed two practical tests, which had proved successful, to the satisfaction of both Freda and Ventura (ibid.: 6–7). Fabris added that Freda had often talked of an important event that was to take place in December 1969, explicitly linking this important event to his requests for information and training in electrical matters; and, finally, that Freda used to refer to an imminent 'coup d'état', or, at any rate, a 'destabilisation' of the Italian political situation. Immediately after the Piazza Fontana bombing, Fabris recalled, he became certain that Freda and Ventura were two murderers, even though at first he refused to believe it (ibid.: 9).

With reference to the same event, both Martino Siciliano and Carlo Digilio provided vital new information. Siciliano testified that, a few weeks after the bomb attacks of 12 December 1969, he had spent New Year's Eve with Zorzi and Vianello, and the former had said that the attacks had been carried out by Ordine Nuovo of the Triveneto region (*Sentenza-ordinanza* Salvini, 18 March 1998: 18). Carlo Digilio testified that Zorzi had admitted to him, in a meeting in Mestre in January or February 1970, that he had taken part in the Piazza Fontana attack, stating that this action had played an important role because it had 'strengthened the Right and hit the Left in the country' (ibid.: 22). Digilio had also testified that Marcello Soffiati, of the Verona-based cell of ON, had revealed to him that Zorzi and other members of the Mestre group had taken part in the Milan attacks, using the car owned by Maggi. Maggi himself had stated, in the presence of Digilio and others, that Ventura had coordinated the 12 December attacks in northern Italy, while Zorzi had personally selected the men who would carry them out (ibid.: 38). Digilio also referred to an important meeting, held in Padua in 1969, mentioned to him by Ventura, which was attended by members of the Padua, Venice-Mestre and Treviso cells, as well as the national leader of ON, Pino Rauti. Ventura had told him that at this meeting a decision was taken to carry out a new series of attacks, following the ones against the trains of 8–9 August 1969 (ibid.: 40).

As well as being responsible for the first act of *stragismo* that was to cause the death of numerous innocent victims, Ordine Nuovo, and specifically the Venice-Mestre cell headed by Carlo Maria Maggi, was charged with organising various terrorist attacks in 1973–74, including the attack at the Milan police headquarters, in Via Fatebenefratelli, on 17 May 1973. Despite attracting much less attention than the better-known Piazza Fontana bombing, this attack and the related trial were extremely important, according to Ferdinando Pincioni, the magistrate responsible for the final sentence on this *strage* on 1 December 2004 (a sentence later confirmed by the Court of Cassation). In his view, the episode can be viewed as a typical example of the Strategy of Tension, in so far as it presented all the usual ingredients associated with this strategy: an anarchist as the ostensible culprit, Ordine Nuovo as the organiser, other groups linked to the armed forces and the secret services both instigating terrorist attacks and obstructing the course of justice, and a coup d'état or the formation of an authoritarian government as the final aim (interview with the author, 20 October 2005). It is worth examining in some detail the judicial findings on this episode.

On 17 May 1973, in Milan, a man (later identified as Gianfranco Bertoli) threw a bomb into the courtyard of the police headquarters, where Christian Democratic Minister Mariano Rumor was attending a ceremony in honour of Police Commissar Luigi Calabresi, murdered on 17 May 1972. It transpired that Rumor was the real target of the attack, but also that Bertoli had mishandled the operation, killing four bystanders and injuring forty-five others. Under interrogation, Bertoli stated that he was an anarchist and that he had planned the attack entirely on his own, as a gesture of revenge in memory of the anarchist Giuseppe Pinelli, for whose death he blamed Calabresi. He also claimed that he had carried the explosive all the way from Israel, where he had lived uninterruptedly for two years, to Milan, which he reached, via Marseilles, in the afternoon of 16 May. The next day, at around 8 a.m., he had learnt, while reading the *Corriere della Sera*, that a ceremony for Calabresi would take place at the Milan police headquarters that same morning. He then took the underground and reached Piazza Duomo, from where he walked to Via Fatebenefratelli, carrying out the attack at around 11 a.m. Under interrogation, Bertoli continued to insist that nobody had told him anything beforehand, that he had foreseen that a ceremony of some kind would indeed be organised in Milan on that day, as it was the anniversary of Calabresi's death, and that he had found out the exact details in the *Corriere*.

In the words of Judge Pincioni, 'Are we kidding? If someone lies, and does it so blatantly, it means that he has to cover up a different reality, i.e., those who gave him that task' (interview with the author, 20 October 2005). Pincioni added that Bertoli was the ideal culprit for that crime, as he was a (self-proclaimed) anarchist but was also very close to members of the Venice-based cell of Ordine Nuovo (as testified by numerous witnesses, including Martino Siciliano), he did not have a regular job, drank very heavily and was easily persuadable. Since it was almost certain that the culprit would be caught (as the bomb had to be thrown at a specific target, rather than planted surreptitiously beforehand), it was absolutely

necessary, in line with the Strategy of Tension, that that person should be identi-
fied as a left sympathiser. Indeed, the *Sentenza-ordinanza* of Milan Prosecutor
Antonio Lombardi concluded that the attack had been physically carried out by
Gianfranco Bertoli, but under instruction from the Venice-Mestre cell of Ordine
Nuovo, whose members had psychologically indoctrinated and technically
trained their chosen 'anarchist'.

The key witness for the prosecution, Carlo Digilio, recalled that Bertoli had
been kept segregated for several days, in May 1973, at a flat in Via Stella, in
Verona, where Neami (from the Trieste cell of ON) and Soffiati (from the Verona
cell) gave him plenty to eat and drink and instructed him, 'with a kind of proper
brainwash', on how to carry out the attack and what to say in case he was caught:
that is, that he was an anarchist who had acted alone. They also used to tell him
that he would be seen as a hero and a great man. Maggi himself used to come and
go from Via Stella in those days, and was perfectly aware of the purpose of those
sessions; indeed he had personally chosen Neami as the most appropriate person
for the task of indoctrinating and subjugating Bertoli. According to Judge Pincioni, Digilio had told the truth, and his testimony was borne out by the fact that
he was able to describe Bertoli in minute detail, including his various nervous tics
and the fact that he wore moccasins rather than shoes (interview with the author,
20 October 2005). However, as we saw, the Court of Cassation had deemed his
testimony not credible, thus preventing the second Court of Appeal from con-
victing the three defendants of Ordine Nuovo.

Judicial investigations also met with a clear attempt at cover-up on the part of
the intelligence services, similarly to what had happened during investigations
into the Piazza Fontana bombing, the Peteano attack, and indeed for all the other
bloody massacres that had taken place in Italy. This brings us to the most important aspect of the Strategy of Tension, that is, the relationship between Ordine
Nuovo and military and intelligence structures, and the role played by the latter
in devising and promoting the Strategy itself, as well as in covering up the culprits
after each massacre. Before we venture into the meanderings of the military and
political ramifications of the Strategy of Tension, let us look at two other organisations which were almost certainly involved in *stragismo*: the Nuclei per la Difesa
dello Stato ('Nuclei for the Defence of the State'), which operated in close contact with Ordine Nuovo, at least in the Veneto region, and the Movimento di
Azione Rivoluzionaria ('Movement for Revolutionary Action'), often known simply as MAR, led by ex-partisan Carlo Fumagalli, which was especially active in the
Valtellina, in Lombardy.

## The Nuclei per la Difesa dello Stato and the MAR

Parallel to, and partially overlapping with, the organisation of Ordine Nuovo
were the Nuclei Territoriali di Difesa dello Stato or NDS ('Territorial Nuclei for
the Defence of the State'), which operated under the direction of the army, and

had as one of their goals the implementation of a so-called *Piano di Soprav-
vivenza* ('Survival Plan'), consisting ostensibly of resistance or guerrilla actions in
the event of a Soviet invasion. Another plan, the *Operazione Patria* ('Operation
Fatherland') appears to have been more accurately a project of coup d'état in the
event of a significant increase of support for the Italian Communist Party. The
Nuclei were divided into Legions (up to thirty-six in all) and each Legion con-
sisted of civilian and ex-military personnel who could be relied upon as staunch
anti-communists and be trained and eventually utilised by the army. The fifth
Legion, active in Verona, was led by Major (later Colonel and then General)
Amos Spiazzi, who, by his own admission, started to recruit neofascist and neo-
Nazi elements, so much so that he practically incorporated the Verona group of
Ordine Nuovo into the Nuclei.

Another group in close contact with (indeed subordinated to) the Nuclei was
the Rosa dei Venti ('Point of the Compass'), previously investigated by Padua
magistrate Giovanni Tamburino and charged with subversive activities and with
planning a coup d'état. Among the members of this group in Padua were Eugenio Rizzato, who had been part of the fascist Republic of Salò, Sandro Rampazzo
and Virginio Camillo. Spiazzi revealed that the Nuclei were set up in 1966-67 and
that they reported directly to the intelligence services (then called SID), but
denied that they had been involved in acts of *stragismo*. However, Spiazzi admitted that the Verona-based group of Ordine Nuovo (closely linked to the fifth
Legion he himself led) was responsible for a bomb attack at the Palazzo dell'A-
gricoltura, in Verona, on 22 April 1969.

In the investigations and subsequent trials for the Piazza Fontana bombing and
for the 1973 attack at the Milan police headquarters, Amos Spiazzi and his fifth
Verona Legion emerged as key players, since, in the testimony of numerous witnesses, Spiazzi had organised meetings at which training in the use of explosives
was provided, and had made explicit references to the need for 'demonstrative'
terrorist attacks to be attributed to left-wing elements. These attacks should
preferably not have caused injury. However, in the event that casualties did occur,
they were to be considered the price to pay in order to win the momentous conflict that was under way (against communism).

One of these witnesses, Enzo Ferro (in 1970 a conscript at the Duca Monto-
rio barracks, in Verona, where Amos Spiazzi was located), recalled that Spiazzi had
tried to recruit him for the Nuclei and had used him as courier on several occasions. After he moved to Trento, he had been repeatedly approached by the equivalent organisation in that city, headed by Colonel Michele Santoro. In 1977,
Ferro had decided to reveal what he knew to a magistrate, in view of a number of
terrorist attacks which had taken place in Trento itself. His testimony remained
dead letter, and he himself was 'paternally' advised by a *Carabiniere* not to persist
in his behaviour (*Sentenza-ordinanza* Salvini, 18 March 1995: 106–7). During
one of his statements to Salvini, on 5 June 1992, Ferro disclosed that he had
received a clear warning, as two months earlier his car had been destroyed in a
premeditated attack. He then refused to make any further revelations.

Another witness, Giovanna Crisetig, ex-partner of Virginio Camillo of the Rosa dei Venti, testified, in 1974 and again in 1992, that in the early 1970s Camillo kept weapons and ammunition for the group in his workshop, that the weapons were often procured by Spiazzi, and that Camillo was often asked by Rizzato and others to transform his workshop into a weapons factory. She also stated categorically that the Rosa dei Venti group took orders from Spiazzi, as he was clearly the leader while the others were his subalterns. Furthermore, she told the magistrate that Camillo, commenting on Spiazzi's activity, had remarked that it would soon lead to a coup d'état (*Sentenza-ordinanza* Lombardi, 18 July 1998: 55–57).

Finally, a key witness, Roberto Cavallaro, a close collaborator of Amos Spiazzi, had testified to a Rome magistrate, as far back as 17 February 1975, that Spiazzi had told him and a member of Ordine Nuovo, most probably Massagrande, that ON was in his view the only organisation capable of 'creating a state of real tension' in the country, thanks both to its size and to its internal division into nuclei. On that same occasion, Spiazzi had referred to the need for the elimination of Rumor and other politicians, which in his view required an action by nuclei (*Sentenza-ordinanza* Lombardi, 18 July 1998: 65). Previously, on 4 May 1974, Cavallaro had been confronted with Spiazzi himself, and the two had had an exchange which is worth reproducing:

Cavallaro:  'Spiazzi told me more than once of the need to utilise the [neofascist] groups; he himself used to refer to cannon fodder or – euphemistically – to people who should be sacrificed.'

Spiazzi:  'I may have given some general directives but I exclude I went into details concerning the utilisation of these groups (Rizzato, Rampaldo or others). It is possible that Cavallaro has a better memory than mine …'

Cavallaro:  It is not true, Major, I took orders from you, tell the truth.'
(Sentence of the V Court of Assizes of Milan, 11 March 2000: 394–95).

It was established that Spiazzi had received a conspicuous payment from Attilio Lercari, on behalf of the owner of the industrial firm Piaggio, who sympathised with the extreme right, for the purpose of organising attacks and other drastic actions which would facilitate a coup d'état in Italy. According to Cavallaro, who had already testified to this end in 1975, Spiazzi belonged to an organisation which included officers of the army and the intelligence services: the top group comprised eighty-seven people, all linked to the Italian secret services (SID) as well as to foreign structures. According to Cavallaro: 'In Italy the strategic choice consisted of the Strategy of Tension; it started with attacks against objects, moving on to attacks against people … if there were no disorders in the Country the organisation would create them artificially … so as to create the possibility to reinstate order. The parallel groups were financed by the organisation' (*Sentenza-ordinanza* Lombardi, 18 July 1998: 68).

Cavallaro added that Spiazzi's role was to act as go-between, thus linking the operational (neofascist) and the directional (army and intelligence) groups. Indeed, according to Salvini, the aim was precisely that 'of absorbing the entire operational organisation of Ordine Nuovo into a parallel and occult structure, such as the Nuclei di Difesa dello Stato, controlled by the top military ranks of the time' (*Sentenza-ordinanza* Salvini, 18 March 1995: 272). In Verona at least, and most probably in the Veneto as a whole, this target appears to have been achieved. The ultimate aim was, according to numerous but also somewhat discordant witnesses, a coup d'état, a 'destabilisation' of the political order, or, more simply, a temporary declaration of a state of emergency and the creation of a quasi-presidential, Gaullist, system. The different interpretations concerning the likely aims of the Strategy of Tension are discussed in Chapter 4.

As for the Movimento di Azione Rivoluzionaria (MAR), it was set up and led by Carlo Fumagalli, who, during the Second World War, had fought with the movement of national liberation against the Germans and the fascists, himself leading an autonomous group of moderate 'white' partisans known as I Gufi ('The Owls'). He had been in close contact with the Office of Strategic Services (OSS, the forerunner of the CIA) and had been rewarded with a Gold Star medal by the Americans. In 1970 Fumagalli's new group, the MAR, became part of Italia Unita ('United Italy'), 'a centre-right alliance which was parallel to, but not in contrast with, the Fronte Nazionale led by Commander Borghese, and which favoured the advent of a strong, pro-American government' (*Sentenza-ordinanza* Salvini, 18 March 1995: 140).

Fumagalli's group was especially active in the Valtellina (Lombardy), where it was responsible for a series of explosions of electricity pylons. In addition, according to Vincenzo Vinciguerra (who, together with Stefano Delle Chiaie, leader of Avanguardia Nazionale, had been responsible for kidnapping and interrogating Fumagalli's right-hand man, Gaetano Orlando, in Madrid in June 1974), the MAR was responsible for an arson attack against a Pirelli factory in Milan, in the early 1970s, in which a worker lost his life (*Sentenza-ordinanza* Salvini, 18 March 1995: 141). Vinciguerra also testified that Fumagalli had contacts with another leader of the Nuclei for the Defence of the State, Colonel Michele Santoro. Fumagalli himself testified to Judge Salvini on two occasions, in 1991 and 1995, confirming that a coup d'état had been planned for April 1973 by his group with the support of the *Carabinieri* and the army. Relations between the MAR and the *Carabinieri* were especially close, particularly with Colonel Santoro. Indeed, it had been agreed that the *Carabinieri* would provide his group with the necessary weapons (ibid.). Salvini concluded that the story of the MAR constituted 'the most significant example of the organic links established in the 1970s between subversive organisations and top representatives of the army and the *Carabinieri*, and even of NATO' (ibid.).

Another major neofascist organisation we need to consider before assessing the role of military and intelligence structures is that of Avanguardia Nazionale.

## Avanguardia Nazionale (AN) ('National Vanguard')

Avanguardia Nazionale, founded by Stefano Delle Chiaie in 1959, was not among the groups charged with the Piazza Fontana massacre in the recent retrial. However, its role in *stragismo* was reasserted in the *sentenze-ordinanze* produced by Judge Salvini with reference both to the bomb attacks carried out in Rome on 12 December 1969, which produced no victims, and to other massacres carried out in the South of Italy. The most important of these was a bomb attack carried out against the train *Freccia del Sud* at Gioia Tauro on 22 July 1970, which caused the death of six passengers and injured fifty-four others. According to Salvini, his investigations as regards the role of AN were greatly helped by the critical reflections of Vincenzo Vinciguerra on the activities of the group led by his longstanding friend Stefano Delle Chiaie, with whom he had shared years of clandestine militancy in Spain. As Salvini explained, Vinciguerra had been an activist first in ON, later in AN, and had for long believed that the latter had not been involved in the Strategy of Tension or connived with intelligence structures. However, since 1992, Vinciguerra had started to change his views, coming to the conclusion that,

> Throughout the period starting at the end of the 1960s and lasting until the beginning of the 1980s, the division between ON and AN had been more tactical and apparent than real so much so that, according to Vinciguerra, the two organisations had shared out the task of carrying out the attacks of 12.12.1969, with Ordine Nuovo taking responsibility for those against the banks and Avanguardia Nazionale for those against the War Memorial in Rome. (*Sentenza-ordinanza* Salvini, 18 March 1995: 223)

On the basis of the testimony of Vincenzo Vinciguerra, it was also possible to attribute to this group a series of seven attacks against trains or railway tracks carried out near Reggio Calabria during the night between 21 and 22 October 1972. Vinciguerra had claimed that the timers used for the explosives on this occasion were the same as those used for the Piazza Fontana massacre and indeed were part of the same stock acquired by Franco Freda in 1969. Another crime perpetrated by AN, specifically under instructions from Stefano Delle Chiaie, was the attempted murder of Bernard Leighton and his wife, two prominent opponents of the Pinochet regime in Chile. Both were seriously injured in Rome on 6 October 1975. According to Vinciguerra, AN had carried out this crime as a favour to Pinochet, who had direct contacts with and the full support of Delle Chiaie. Similar testimony was provided by Michael Townley, ex-agent of the Chilean secret police DINA, who had been the organiser of the attack and later became a protected witness in the United States (Mayorga 2003: 37–53).

One of the few witnesses for the prosecution to come from within Avanguardia Nazionale, Carmine Dominici, also provided Judge Salvini with an important testimony on the activities of this group in the southern region of Calabria, from where Delle Chiaie himself originated and where AN's stronghold was based. Dominici gave details of the availability of explosives to the group, and related an important episode which had taken place in Rome in 1974, when Delle Chiaie had met with Massimiliano Fachini, leader of the Padua-based cell of Ordine Nuovo after the arrest of Franco Freda. On that occasion, according to Dominici, Delle Chiaie had given Fachini a considerable sum of money.

Salvini remarked that had this testimony been available in the late 1980s during the trial against Stefano Delle Chiaie and Massimiliano Fachini for their role in the Piazza Fontana massacre, a trial held after Delle Chiaie's arrest in Caracas in 1987, the verdict may well have been very different. At the time of the trial, in fact, there had been no evidence in support of an operational link between ON and AN, that is to say, in support of the hypothesis that the two groups were part of a single subversive structure. As a result, the Court of Appeal had acquitted both defendants in 1989, coming to the conclusion that the supposed links between Freda's cell and AN (as acknowledged by Giovanni Ventura himself during his interrogations) were not sufficiently proved (*Sentenza-ordinanza* Salvini, 18 March 1995: 238). The new evidence unearthed by Judge Salvini against Avanguardia Nazionale and its leader, however, did not result in a retrial since the deadline for bringing criminal charges against the alleged culprits had expired or, in other cases, a verdict of acquittal had already been reached, making it impossible for people such as Delle Chiaie to be subjected to a new tribunal.

An important episode upon which Salvini's investigations were able to throw considerable new light, which originally was not linked to *stragismo* yet could well have been part of a single, wider strategy, was the attempted coup d'état organised by Prince Junio Valerio Borghese, ex-leader of the X Mas naval sabotage unit for the Republic of Salò. Borghese was leader of another neofascist group, the Fronte Nazionale, and was in close contact with Stefano Delle Chiaie, to whom he was both a hero and a friend. During the night of 7 and 8 December 1970, Borghese led the famous operation, known as Tora Tora, which ostensibly aimed at a takeover of the Italian state. In his investigations on the Piazza Fontana massacre, Judge Salvini was able to rely on substantial new evidence produced by Captain Labruna, ex-agent of the Italian secret service, SID. The evidence consisted primarily of a series of recorded conversations which had taken place during 1973 and 1974 between Labruna himself and Remo Orlandini, a close collaborator of Prince Borghese, whom Labruna had convinced of his and his colleagues' trustworthiness. Most of these tapes had never before been handed over to the judiciary, despite their obvious relevance to a number of investigations and trials. This episode of obstruction of justice will be examined in the next chapter.

On the basis of this new evidence and of various other statements, Salvini hypothesised a link between the Piazza Fontana massacre and the Borghese attempted coup. According to various sources, in fact, the coup had been planned as early as 1969 and the bomb attacks of 12 December of that year most probably aimed at 'enabling the coup which had been programmed for the end of 1969, thanks to a surge of fear and disorientation created by repeated events which, like the bombs on the trains and in the banks, hit simple civilians' (*Sentenza-ordinanza* Salvini, 18 March 1995: 221). In short, in the opinion of Judge Salvini:

This obviously does not mean that all the leaders and activists of the Fronte Nazionale, involved in the coup project, were also complicit or conniving in *stragismo* but without doubt, at certain levels, the two projects ran on strategically parallel tracks.

It is also the case that in many areas the activists of Ordine Nuovo, and above all of Avanguardia Nazionale, formed the most important civil operational backbone the putschists in the Fronte Nazionale were able to rely upon. (Ibid.: 222)

## The final verdicts

Of the momentous evidence produced by judicial investigations and trials, especially the more recent ones on the 1969 bombing in Piazza Fontana and the 1973 attack in Via Fatebenefratelli, both located in Milan, which parts have been considered irrefutable and incontrovertible by the Supreme Court? With specific reference to the role of neofascist groups, what exactly has been judicially proven beyond any reasonable doubt; what has been considered highly plausible but not sufficiently proven; and what, finally, has been discarded as unfounded?

Starting with the Piazza Fontana trial, the Court of Cassation, as we saw, on 3 May 2005 confirmed the previous verdict of the Court of Appeal, issued on 12 March 2004. Of the two main witnesses for the prosecution, Digilio and Siciliano, the Courts deemed the former not credible in many parts of his testimony, even though his revelations were accepted as valid in relation to certain specific episodes, including the availability of explosives on the part of various neofascist groups. By contrast, the testimony of Martino Siciliano was considered fully credible, albeit not by itself sufficient to justify the conviction of the defendants (Maggi, Zorzi and Rognoni). Siciliano's convoluted behaviour as a witness for the prosecution was attributed to Zorzi's attempts to bribe him and prevent him from testifying, and was not taken as proof of his lack of credibility, as the defending magistrates demanded (Sentence of the Second Section of the Court of Appeal of Milan, 12 March 2004: 301–8). The Court also discarded as invalid the attempt, made by Zorzi's defending magistrates, to depict Siciliano as someone who had known the accused only superficially and who had played a very marginal role in the activities of Ordine Nuovo.

The Courts accepted as true most of Siciliano's revelations, including his depiction of Zorzi as a violent character, the organisation by Rognoni of a paramilitary training camp which operated near Lecco in October and November 1969, the existence of a secret deposit of weapons and explosives for use by the Milan-based group La Fenice, and the arson attack, carried out by Siciliano himself with Zorzi, against the Communist Party section of Campalto, near Mestre, on 9 October 1968 (Sentence of the Second Section of the Court of Appeal of Milan, 12 March 2004: 155–57, 166).

More importantly, the Court of Appeal also believed that Siciliano's testimony was 'fully credible' in relation to the 1966 'White Room' meeting and the subsequent restricted gathering, at which Ordine Nuovo in the Triveneto was set up, a secretive structure was agreed upon, and violent actions envisaging the use of explosives against civilians were freely discussed (2004: 164–66). In relation to these episodes, the Court of Appeal remarked that they had not been in any way refuted by the defending magistrates (2004: 164). The Court also ruled that the Ordine Nuovo cells of Venice-Mestre, led by Maggi and Zorzi, and the Padua cell, led by Freda, had subversive aims, were responsible for criminal and violent actions, theorised terrorist attacks against both structures and civilians, and had access to weapons and explosives. It ascertained that the Padua-based group of Ordine Nuovo led by Freda and Ventura was responsible for a series of crimes, among them the bomb attacks against trains, carried out in August 1969, and (on the basis of the recent testimonies) also the Piazza Fontana massacre. In particular, the Court judged the new testimony by Fabris against both Freda and Ventura to be fully credible, and reevaluated, in accordance with the prosecuting magistrates, a previous testimony by Guido Lorenzon, a friend of Ventura, who had revealed as far back as 1969 that the latter had confided to him his involvement in the massacre. The Court also ascertained that the Venice-Mestre, Trieste and Verona cells had close links with each other, and that the first two were jointly responsible for the October 1969 attacks in Trieste and Gorizia.

With reference to the existence of close links between the Padua and the Venice-Mestre cells of Ordine Nuovo, the Court ruled that these had been proven, particularly from 1970 onwards. However, there was a lack of evidence supporting the case, made by the prosecuting magistrates, that these two groups had collaborated with the explicit aim of carrying out jointly organised terrorist attacks in 1969 (Sentence of the Second Section of the Court of Appeal of Milan, 12 March 2004: 240). In the words of the Court of Appeal, 'it is not possible to state with the required certainty that the two groups jointly organised all the attacks carried out in 1969 and particularly those of 12 December 1969' (2004: 247). Similar conclusions were reached by the Court with reference to the relations existing between the Venice-Mestre cell of Ordine Nuovo and the Milan-based group of La Fenice. The Court of Cassation concurred with this judgment.

To sum up, the Court of Appeal and the Court of Cassation agreed that Digilio was not sufficiently credible, while Siciliano's narrative, although credible, did not always constitute irrefutable evidence, especially when it could not be corroborated by additional elements. This led the Court of Appeal to conclude in its sentence that: 'the general picture is that of the so-called "incomplete evidence": the unitary evaluation of those elements introduced by the two witnesses which have withstood a critical examination, does not allow a verdict of responsibility on the part of the two appealing defendants [Maggi and Zorzi] but nor does it allow the Court to clear them completely' (Sentence of the Second Section of the Court of Appeal of Milan, 12 March 2004: 328).

The Court therefore acquitted Maggi and Zorzi with a verdict of not proven, with reference to Article 530, comma 2, of the Italian penal code. It also acquitted Giancarlo Rognoni with a verdict of not guilty. The Court, however, established that Carlo Digilio was guilty of taking part in the organisation of terrorist attacks, including the one in Milan in December 1969, and of providing technical expertise and training to this end. Digilio was found guilty on the basis of his own confessions, which made it less vital for the Court to ascertain the irrefutable validity of the judicial evidence.

As for the Supreme Court, it agreed with the verdict of the Court of Appeal, while reasserting the responsibility of the extreme right for the Milan bombing. As its final sentence stated, 'That the responsibility for the massacre is attributable to segments of Ordine Nuovo is a non-controversial element.' Furthermore, the Court acknowledged that the reconstruction of events as put forward by the prosecution was highly plausible. Yet, as the sentence concluded,

> this hypothesis [that the Venice-Mestre and the Padua cells co-organised the Piazza Fontana massacre], certainly valid in theory and totally coherent also at a logical level (the tragic facts of 12 December 1969, in fact, did not represent the work of a crazy splinter group, but the fruit of a coordinated operational 'acme' embedded ... in a subversive, well developed, sedimented, programme, albeit one whose origins, boundaries and size remain obscure), has not found positive confirmation at the level of judicial evidence. (Sentence of the Court of Cassation, 3 May 2005: 14)

The final verdict for the 1973 attack at Milan police headquarters reached similar conclusions. Responsibility for organising the massacre rested without doubt with Ordine Nuovo. With the exception of Carlo Digilio, the other witnesses were considered credible and their evidence was, for the most part, not refuted by the defending magistrates. However, they did not amount to irrefutable cumulative evidence for securing the conviction of the defendants (Maggi, Neami and Zorzi). Hence, the final verdict of acquittal for this crime was also based on a not proven formula, that is, with recourse to Article 530, comma 2 of the Italian penal code, which refers to insufficient evidence. According to Judge Pincioni:

> An acquittal for insufficient evidence is not an acquittal, whether Maggi likes it or not, and in this sentence it is stated with certainty that they were the culprits and this is now definitive, nobody doubts it any longer. It [the massacre] is attributed with certainty to Ordine Nuovo ... most probably to the Venice-Mestre cell led by Maggi, but Maggi was not only leader of that cell, he was the coordinator of all the ON groups in the north. (Interview with the author, 20 October 2005)

The meaning is clear: if Maggi was the leader of Ordine Nuovo in the Triveneto and indeed in the north of Italy, considering the internal pyramidal and tightly compartmental structure of this organisation, it is most improbable that one of its cells acted independently of and without informing its superior leader. If we then consider together the two events of Piazza Fontana and Via Fatebenefratelli, we would have to believe that not just once, but on two crucial occasions a cell of Ordine Nuovo had organised and carried out a massacre without the explicit consent of its higher referents in the organisation, that is, Maggi (or, for that matter, Signorelli and/or Rauti). From a judicial point of view, such a hypothesis is at least conceivable and may constitute the element of doubt warranting a verdict of acquittal, but logically speaking one has to conclude that it makes very little sense.

Despite the acquittal of the defendants, the Court of Appeal located the massacre of Via Fatebenefratelli within the framework of the terrorist activities of Ordine Nuovo, as we saw, and, even more importantly, within the framework of the Strategy of Tension and hence of a wider and well-developed subversive strategy aimed at a coup d'état and/or the destabilisation of political institutions. On this aspect the final sentences for the two massacres were remarkably concordant, as they both agreed that those episodes did not constitute isolated incidents. This raises the issue of the involvement in *stragismo* of the armed forces and intelligence structures, both domestic and foreign, which will be analysed in the next chapter.

# CHAPTER 3
# The Role of the Armed Forces and Intelligence Structures

## Introduction: connivances and *depistaggi*

As stated in the Introduction, investigations and trials on the massacres were repeatedly obstructed by cover-ups and false leads (*depistaggi*), on the part of certain sections of the armed forces, the *Carabinieri* and the intelligence services. The measures adopted ranged from falsifying or concealing important information, to deliberately preventing crucial new witnesses from testifying to the magistrates and even to assisting suspected perpetrators escape abroad. In this section we will examine the most emblematic of these cover-ups, as brought to light by the investigations of Judges Salvini and Lombardi, as well as by the trial concerning the 1972 Peteano attack.

The available evidence points to the existence of close links between the Italian intelligence services and neofascist groups in the 1960s and early 1970s and to the obstruction of justice on the part of these same intelligence services during judicial investigations into the activities of the neofascist groups. This is not to say that there existed a single overarching strategy devised by the intelligence structures and carried out by the neofascist groups. Rather, the picture seems to be one in which some intelligence structures relied upon certain neofascist groups (and vice versa) at specific times and for specific purposes. What uniformly seems to be the case, however, is that the intelligence services were keen to protect neofascist groups and other occult structures, such as the Masonic Lodge P2, in order to prevent their activities or indeed their existence becoming known to the judiciary. In addition, the intelligence services acted to protect their own activities from judicial inquiries. In other words, the prevailing attitude was one of 'cleaning their dirty linen' in-house, rather than allowing the magistrates access to sensitive information.

While the behaviour of the intelligence services can be at least in part explained in the context of the Cold War and of a country which was seen to contain the 'enemy within', it cannot be excused in the light of the massacres of innocent civilians, especially when the likely involvement of neofascist groups and other secret structures in these massacres started to come to light. Any reluctance on the part of the intelligence services to disclose sensitive information should have been overcome to allow the judiciary to prosecute the perpetrators of these crimes in the name of justice and the rule of law. Instead, valuable information was hidden or destroyed and possible culprits were allowed to escape justice in the name of political expediency. Justification would probably be made by those responsible for such actions in terms of the superior interests of the nation and of the threat to its security by the communists. Whether such an excuse could ever prove sufficient in moral terms is a verdict that can only be made when (and on condition that) the whole truth is finally disclosed.

Furthermore, there is no doubt that the involvement of intelligence structures in acts of *depistaggio* has encouraged widespread and persisting mistrust in their activities, as their behaviour is open to the worst possible interpretations. All kinds of conspiracy theories, in fact, continue to circulate in Italy in relation to the secret services, and they are generally considered responsible for masterminding the entire Strategy of Tension, including the massacres. This may or may not be true; it may well be possible, as some interpretations maintain, that at least some sections of the intelligence services acted to prevent or minimise acts of terrorism. Nevertheless, even those sectors which opposed radical measures against the perceived communist threat appear to have operated in a context in which a range of subversive forces and groups, including neofascist organisations, were seen as valuable allies. Whatever crimes they had perpetrated, therefore, they could not be betrayed to the judiciary, not least since their betrayal would have triggered the disclosure of a complex and unpalatable web of networks whose secrecy had to be preserved at all costs.

Let us now examine the most significant episodes of obstruction of justice involving both the armed forces and the intelligence services.

## State structures and the Piazza Fontana massacre: the Casalini episode

As regards the role of the Italian secret services, the starting point for any analysis is the existence of two different intelligence structures operating in the late 1960s and early 1970s: the SID (Servizio Informazioni Difesa), previously called SIFAR, which worked within the military system, and the Office of Classified Affairs, which operated within the Ministry of the Interior. Each may have pursued its own strategy in relation both to information gathering and to security matters. It is important to note that the Head of the Office of Classified Affairs, Federico Umberto D'Amato, was a close collaborator of the American OSS (the precursor of the CIA) and of James Jesus Angleton, who in 1944 was in charge of a Special Counterintelligence Unit known as X-2. D'Amato's office, after the Second World War, had been filled with ex-combatants of the Republic of Salò (Fasanella and Sestieri with Pellegrino 2000: 28). It is also important to distinguish between two different political strategies within the SID itself. One strategy, supported by Vito Miceli, Head of the organisation from 1970 to 1974, and, as later discovered in 1981, a member of the Masonic Lodge P2, was, according to Judge Salvini,

> markedly right wing, if not nostalgic [of the fascist regime] … as would be revealed in the judicial inquiry on the Borghese coup, General Miceli was seriously involved in the conspiracy, put himself out to prevent the magistrates from being informed of the intelligence reports on the coup preparations from 1969 onwards, was a personal friend of many of the conspirators, so much so that the charge of simply abetting Borghese, which at the end of the inquiry replaced the hypothesis of participation in a political conspiracy, cannot but appear an underestimation of his real responsibilities. (*Sentenza-ordinanza* of 18 March 1995: 183)

By contrast, another strategy was linked to General Gianadelio Maletti – first Deputy Head, then Head of SID, following Miceli's departure and a brief stint by General Casardi. Maletti had as his main political referent Christian Democratic leader and Defence Minister Giulio Andreotti. This second approach aimed at strengthening the institutions of the state against the communist threat without recourse to a putschist strategy and/or extreme-right, openly fascist organisations. As Salvini pointed out, this strategy was more 'modern' than Miceli's and must be understood in the light of the international events of 1974–75, especially the fall of the authoritarian regimes in Portugal and Greece and the death of Francisco Franco in Spain. Such events obviously greatly undermined the chances of success, indeed even the credibility, of an extreme-right and/or military coup in Italy (1995: 184).

Despite his alternative strategy to Miceli's, Maletti, too, was responsible for obstructing the course of justice and hiding important information during the first Piazza Fontana trial held at Catanzaro. During his headship, the SID organised the flight abroad of crucial witness Pozzan and of informer Giannettini, planned an escape from jail for Ventura, and nailed Remo Orlandini, and through him several other conspirators, to their responsibilities in relation to the Borghese coup, yet also used this important information to 'deactivate' groups such as the Fronte Nazionale, as opposed to aiding investigations. Lastly, Maletti in person ordered the 'closure' of a new vital source of information for the investigating magistrates. This last episode is emblematic of the behaviour of the intelligence services vis-à-vis the judiciary, and for this reason is now examined in some detail.

As reported by Salvini, on 11 November 1980, during an official search of General Maletti's Rome apartment, carried out in the context of a judicial inquiry on the Masonic Lodge P2, some handwritten notes were discovered, including one dated 5 June 1975. Its content was as follows:

Padua case: Casalini wants to ease his conscience.
He started to admit having taken part in the 1969 attacks on the trains carrying explosives; the rest, together with the weapons, is kept in a basement in Venice. Casalini will speak again and is already picking on others the Padua group + delle Chiaie + Giannettini.
He is stating that they were all certain of the support of the SID.
Future action: close by June.
Talk to Defence Ministry pointing out all repercussions. Summon D'Ambrosio.
Charge *Carabinieri* (Del Gaudio) with proceeding. (*Sentenza-ordinanza* Salvini, 18 March 1995: 310)

The memo is fairly self-explanatory. Salvini explained it as follows:

A certain Casalini, member of the Padua cell [of Ordine Nuovo], perhaps pricked by his conscience, started to collaborate, that is to say, to become a 'source' for the *Carabinieri* in the city. He had already admitted responsibility for minor episodes and indicated that part of the weaponry of the group was kept in a house in Venice.

He intended to say more and was on the verge of approaching the more delicate issues, such as the links between the Padua cell, Stefano Delle Chiaie and SID collaborator Guido Gannettini, confirming the fact that these subversive structures were acting in the certainty of being covered by the SID ... In short, [it was decided to] deactivate the source as soon as possible, before it could damage the specific line of action adopted by the Services in agreement, evidently, with the highest authorities.

There is no other explanation for this note ... The Padua cell had to continue to be protected and no useful element had to reach the Catanzaro magistrates who just then were investigating the responsibilities of the SID and who in any case, a few months after the note was written, gave orders for the arrest of General Maletti himself. (*Sentenza-ordinanza* Salvini, 18 March 1995: 310–1)

Thanks to Salvini's investigations, in the early 1990s Gianni Casalini was able to testify to this episode, confirming the substance of the information contained in the memo found in Maletti's apartment. Captain Del Gaudio was also identified and interrogated by Salvini. It turned out that, like Maletti, he had been a member of the Masonic Lodge P2; hence he was clearly a trusted collaborator of the General at the time the latter had written his memo. It also turned out that Del Gaudio knew Gianni Casalini's father; therefore he may have been chosen by Maletti as the most suited person to bring pressure on the unwelcome witness. Del Gaudio refused to cooperate with the magistrates on this and other episodes and for this reason was sentenced to one year of imprisonment. As for D'Ambrosio, another magistrate, Felice Casson, had previously tried to identify him but had been told by the intelligence services in 1987 that no person with that name served in the *Carabinieri*. According to Salvini, this constituted another deliberate cover-up, since it was later discovered that an officer named D'Ambrosio served in the Army (as opposed to the *Carabinieri* special armed force), something the intelligence service must have been aware of. As far as Maletti was concerned, he had by then emigrated to South Africa and refused to reveal anything about his role in the affair (*Sentenza-ordinanza* Salvini, 18 March 1995: 312–13).

Notwithstanding the noncollaborative attitude of these key individuals, Salvini was able to reconstruct the dynamic of the incident. Initially (and ironically, as it turned out), the local *Carabinieri* in Padua had decided not to involve the SID headquarters in Rome (partly because of suspicions of their use of such information) and had instead informed the Investigative Office of the Milan *Carabinieri*, as was within their remit. However, unbeknown to them, the Office in question depended on the Pastrengo Division, stuffed with P2 members and found responsible, on numerous occasions, for serious acts of *depistaggio* as well as for procuring weapons to subversive groups. Indeed, based on the testimony of one of its ex-officers, it appears that this Division was an integral part of that section of the Italian military which favoured a coup d'état (Ruggiero 2006). The General Commander of the Pastrengo Division took it upon himself to charge a subordinate with the task of going to Padua and preparing a report on the case, which he then passed on to Maletti. When the latter got hold of the report containing sensitive and incriminating information, he proceeded to destroy it, since no copy was at the time handed over to the investigating magistrates, and no trace of it was found in the file named 'Casalini', which the intelligence services, when requested by Salvini, sent to the magistrate in the 1990s. In short, Maletti had been able to rely on alternative and trusted institutional channels in order to obtain the police report on Casalini's confession and prevent any further use of this source (*Sentenza-ordinanza* Salvini, 18 March 1995: 330–35).

When placed alongside other SID activities which were taking place in parallel to judicial investigations into the 'black trail' – including a plan to help Ventura escape from prison, various contacts, via Captain Labruna, between General Maletti and Massimiliano Fachini of the Padua cell of Ordine Nuovo, and the utilisation of Fachini himself in helping Marco Pozzan, a member of Ordine Nuovo and a potential witness, escape to Spain – the only conclusion that can be drawn is that the SID was deliberately obstructing the course of justice and was doing so by protecting the extreme-right groups. Salvini commented on his findings on the obstructive activities of the intelligence services as follows:

> The protection of the members of the Padua cell [of Ordine Nuovo] implemented through the flight of Pozzan and Giannettini, the planned escape of Ventura from jail, the 'closure' of the Gianni Casalini source and the contacts with Massimiliano Fachini, as emerged from the current investigation, constituted an activity that was absolutely necessary. If just one of the defendants had given in, this would have allowed the magistrates, step by step, to trace the highest levels of responsibility which had made possible the operation of 12 December and the repercussions from this would perhaps have been even incompatible with the preservation of the status quo in the country, which is the basic objective of any intelligence service at any time. (*Sentenza-ordinanza* Salvini, 18 March 1995: 184)

## The SID and the 1973 Milan massacre: establishing Bertoli's leftist credentials

Judicial investigations concerning the 1973 attack against the Milan police head-quarters also met with a clear attempt at cover-up on the part of the intelligence services. Two days after the massacre, General Maletti, Head of SID, sent one of his collaborators, Captain De Marchi, to Israel to investigate Bertoli's activities. The captain prepared a report, exclusively for Maletti's eyes, in which it was stated that Bertoli was an anarchist who used to socialise with two brothers from Mar-seilles who belonged politically to the extreme left. In the words of Pincioni: 'Why did the secret services interfere? It had nothing to do with them' (interview with the author, 20 October 2005). Strangely, Maletti at the time had not com-municated this 'discovery' to the investigating magistrates; indeed, a note signed by Maletti himself, found in 1991, revealed that he had personally given orders not to make use of this piece of intelligence. Many years later, in the early 1990s, prosecuting magistrate Antonio Lombardi was able to ascertain that the infor-mation hastily gathered by the captain was false, as the two brothers who had befriended Bertoli in Israel, far from being left-wingers, had been members of a French organisation which was the equivalent of Ordine Nuovo (*Sentenza-ordi-nanza* Lombardi, 18 July 1998: 134–35).

In addition, it emerged that Bertoli had acted as informer in the pay of the secret services. Representatives of the latter, when confronted with the evidence, at first (in 1975) confirmed that Bertoli had had this role from 1954 up to 1960, but later (in 1991) had to admit that he had been in their pay also from 1966 until at least 1971 (*Sentenza-ordinanza* Lombardi, 18 July 1998: 78–84). Myste-riously, Judge Lombardi discovered in 1991 that the file containing information on Bertoli (who went under the name of 'Negro'), had been destroyed by the Commander of the Centro Controspionaggio (Counterespionage Centre) of Padua, Giuseppe Bottallo, in 1984–85, under instruction from the then Head of the Secret Services (1998: 81).

## State structures and the Borghese coup: the selected use of intelligence information

As discussed in the previous chapter, Borghese's close collaborator, Remo Orlan-dini, was lured by Captain Labruna, of the secret service SID, into revealing a series of details concerning the 1970 attempted coup. Most of the tapes with the recorded conversations, dating from 1973–74, were not handed over to the judi-ciary; rather, they were put to a different, political use, which is revealing of the complex web of interests and connivances which investigations into both putschism and *stragismo* have had to contend with.

On the basis of Salvini's investigations, and thanks to Labruna's testimonies, it has been ascertained that there had originally been about twelve to fifteen tapes, containing conversations with both Orlandini and Lercari. The latter, as we saw, was a representative of the industrial company Piaggio, whose owner was among those who were financing the coup. However, only four tapes were handed over to the investigating magistrates; the rest disappeared, with the exception of a set of copies of the tapes and the original written transcriptions, which remained in the hands of Labruna himself. It was only in the early 1990s that Labruna decided to collaborate with Salvini, partly because he wanted to redress his reputation as the main villain within the Italian intelligence services, and he produced copies of sensitive original information, including all the tapes with the recorded conversations with Orlandini.

At the time, the entire incriminating material had been handed over to General Maletti and Colonel Romagnoli, who, by the summer of 1974, had prepared a full report based on the information gained by Labruna. At the end of July of the same year, a meeting took place in the office of the Defence Minister, Giulio Andreotti, in the presence of Admiral Casardi (new Head of SID in succession to General Miceli), General Maletti, Colonel Romagnoli and Captain Labruna, as well as the General Commander of the *Carabinieri*, Mino. At the end of the meeting, the Minister had reportedly told the SID representatives to 'thin out the bundle' (*Sentenza-ordinanza* Salvini, 18 March 1995: 174). Accordingly, a new report was prepared which, in September 1974, was sent to the magistrates who were investigating the Borghese coup. Andreotti himself later testified that there were no other tapes in the possession of the intelligence services.

What were the aims of this operation and which parts of the recorded conversations were omitted from the 'thinned out' report? According to Salvini, the aims emerged fairly clearly from an analysis of both included and omitted content. The transcribed conversations, in fact, confirmed what many investigators had long suspected, that is to say, that there existed a wide and composite network of forces involved in this attempted coup as in other episodes of subversion. The most important revelations concerned the following:

- the existence of links between the Fronte Nazionale and the Masonic Lodge P2 and the involvement of the latter in the Borghese operation;
- the involvement of sections of the armed forces in the Borghese coup, through the Nuclei for the Defence of the State, as well as through the enlistment of various high-ranking officers;
- the full involvement of Avanguardia Nazionale in the organisation and implementation of the coup;
- confirmation that Avanguardia Nazionale had, at least until 1974, been close to the Office of Classified Affairs of the Ministry of the Interior, whose Head was Federico Umberto D'Amato (*Sentenza-Ordinanza* of 18 March 1995: 198);

- confirmation of the existence of an inner paramilitary core within Avanguardia Nazionale, 'dedicated to terrorist activities' (1995: 199);
- the support of the United States (or at least its intelligence structures) for the coup, as well as backing from NATO. (*Sentenza-ordinanza* Salvini, 18 March 1995: 176–80)

The information incriminating Borghese and the Fronte Nazionale was not withheld from the magistrates. This must be seen in the context of the new strategy, already discussed above, developed by Miceli's successors and consisting in cutting the links with the more ostensibly neofascist and 'nostalgic' forces which until then had been part of a wider anti-communist coalition. Interestingly, however, the role of Avanguardia Nazionale was played down in the final report.

By contrast, the information withheld from the magistrates concerned those forces whose identity and/or involvement needed to be protected from the public and the Courts. Among these forces were the Masonic Lodge P2 and the Mafia. In the case of Licio Gelli, the Head of P2, Orlandini had quite explicitly revealed that he was to have played a major role in the coup, since he would have had responsibility for organising a special unit with the task of taking prisoner the President of the Republic, Giuseppe Saragat (*Sentenza-ordinanza* Salvini, 18 March 1995: 186–89). Saragat, in fact, was considered a person who would have opposed a coup and refused to come to terms with the conspirators. Not only was any reference to Gelli and to his role omitted from the report sent to the magistrates, but Salvini was unable to find any information about him in the archives of the SID. He concluded that this was evidently the outcome of a deliberate decision to conceal his identity (*Sentenza-ordinanza* Salvini, 18 March 1995: 190).

In the case of the Mafia, the aim, according to Salvini, was less to protect the Mafia itself than to safeguard the identity of the person who had established links with the criminal organisation with a view to obtaining its collaboration in the coup. This man, Salvatore Drago, a Sicilian doctor working for the Ministry of the Interior, was very close to Federico Umberto D'Amato, the Head of the Office of Classified Affairs in the same Ministry, and was also a member of P2. Had his name appeared in the list of conspirators, it might have been possible to trace the links back to Gelli and his Masonic Lodge, and this had to be avoided (*Sentenza-ordinanza* Salvini, 18 March 1995: 208).

There was also no mention in the final report of NATO and the CIA, whereas Orlandini had provided details concerning the presence of coup conspirators at NATO meetings and the provision of considerable quantities of weapons to them by the organisation. As for the CIA, Orlandini had mentioned contacts with its representatives operating in Italy, such as a man named Hugh Fenwich (*Sentenza-ordinanza* Salvini, 18 March 1995: 208).

Finally, the names of various high-level officers of the armed and naval forces were also omitted from the report, so as to ensure that they continued to remain in their positions. Indeed, many of these were able in later years to pursue their careers and reach the highest ranks without being tainted by public knowledge of their previous involvement in an act of subversion (*Sentenza-ordinanza* Salvini, 18 March 1995: 208–9).

A second, related episode concerns another report on the Borghese coup prepared by SID agent and informer Guido Giannettini, and handed over to Captain Labruna in 1973. The report was later 'thinned out' by General Maletti, who destroyed an accompanying memo which set out the involvement in the conspiracy of Admiral Giovanni Torrisi, who had personally taken part in preparatory meetings for the coup with Salvatore Drago and various leaders of Avanguardia Nazionale. Maletti himself had then asked Labruna to lie in Court during the Catanzaro trial on Piazza Fontana, asserting that he could not remember where he had filed the document. Maletti had justified to Labruna his request, together with his decision not to produce the evidence, with the need to allow Admiral Torrisi to continue to pursue his career, especially in view of his imminent promotion to a higher rank (*Sentenza-ordinanza* Salvini, 18 March 1995: 195–96).

While the memo concerning Torrisi was destroyed, the report by Giannettini was kept by the SID, but it was still withheld from the judges. This is not surprising, given its content. Giannettini, in fact, had stated that the Office of Classified Affairs of the Ministry of the Interior had pretended, through Salvatore Drago and representatives of Avanguardia Nazionale, to support the coup, but in reality 'its aim was to sabotage the coup and then to condition the extreme-right and military groups involved in the conspiracy' (*Sentenza-ordinanza* Salvini, 18 March 1995: 196). In addition, Giannettini had written that 'Avanguardia Nazionale had been created a few years earlier by the Ministry of the Interior in order to weaken the MSI, and had joined Borghese's Fronte Nazionale' (ibid.: 196). In a previous statement, in 1990, Guido Giannettini had admitted that he was the author of the report, and confirmed that during the Catanzaro trial he had falsely stated that he could not remember having produced such a report, indeed he had categorically excluded its existence (ibid.: 197).

A final episode concerns the political use by the secret services of a report, written by a then leader of Avanguardia Nazionale, Guido Paglia, on the internal structure of this organisation. The report had been handed over to Captain Labruna in 1972, and passed on by him to his superiors. Paglia's report would have been especially useful to the magistrates since it gave detailed information regarding the existence of an inner paramilitary and terrorist core within Avanguardia Nazionale, complete with the names of those who belonged to these clandestine cells. The report, however, did not reach the magistrates. Rather, it was used to establish a contact between the SID and Stefano Delle Chiaie, then on the run in Spain. Labruna, in fact, met with Delle Chiaie in Barcelona on 30 November 1972. According to Salvini, by showing Delle Chiaie that the SID was in possession of the report yet had not used it to incriminate him, Labruna had been able to gain his trust, at a time when the Padua magistrates had started to pursue the 'black trail' for the Piazza Fontana massacre and there was a need to coordinate a defensive strategy (*Sentenza-ordinanza* Salvini, 18 March 1995: 198). In Salvini's words, the report therefore constituted: 'A possible weapon for blackmailing and for reciprocal trade-off with the group of Avanguardia Nazionale probably in view of the risky developments which were emerging at the end of 1972 for both the SID and for Stefano Delle Chiaie due to the extension of the investigations on the operation of 12 December 1969 in the direction of the black trail' (ibid.: 207). As regards the overall significance of the episodes, Salvini stressed the need to protect specific interests in the context of Italy's Atlantic alliance, and to prevent investigations into the existence of parallel military structures which 'relied on a secret supply of weaponry and on operative plans unknown to and uncontrolled by Parliament and the other institutions of the democratic system' (ibid.: 208–9).

## Concealing the culprits: the aftermath of the Peteano attack

As we saw in the previous chapter, the 1972 Peteano bombing attack, which caused the death of three *Carabinieri*, was carried out by Vincenzo Vinciguerra, member of the Udine cell of Ordine Nuovo. With the help of two other activists, Ivano Boccaccio and Carlo Cicuttini, Vinciguerra placed explosives in a Fiat 500, then fired a few shots at the car, and finally informed the *Carabinieri*, via an anonymous phone call (made by Cicuttini), of the 'fortuitous' finding and its exact location. When three *Carabinieri* arrived on the site and started to inspect the car, they were blown up. This episode was followed by another attack, in October 1972, this time involving Ivano Boccaccio, who was shot dead while attempting to hijack a plane at Udine airport, Ronchi dei Legionari. The remaining two culprits, Vinciguerra and Cicuttini, were then helped by Ordine Nuovo to escape to Spain, where Vinciguerra struck up a friendship with Stefano Delle Chiaie and became close to Avanguardia Nazionale, at least until he began to suspect that his new friend was linked to intelligence services and other 'suspect' forces.

Vinciguerra gave himself up in 1979, although it was only in 1984 that he spontaneously admitted to his crime, for which he was later sentenced to life imprisonment, a sentence he is still serving. His admission of guilt turned out to be the beginning of a difficult process of truth telling, in which the magistrates were his interlocutors. Vinciguerra's truth telling, however, should not be considered the same as confessing or turning witness for the prosecution, since he has never repented for his acts of violence, least of all for the Peteano attack which in his view was the only truly revolutionary act carried out by a fascist in postwar Italy. His declared aim was to fight against the state, and confessing, in his view, would have constituted 'an act of surrender to the state'.

By contrast, telling the truth signified for him the continuation of his fighting by other means, since the duplicity of both the state and his previous neofascist comrades could thus be fully exposed, and the ideals of true fascism safeguarded for posterity. In the years following his neofascist militancy, in fact, Vinciguerra had become convinced that practically all neofascist groups had acted in connivance with, but effectively subordinated to, Italian and foreign intelligence forces, in the illusion of achieving power through an 'unholy' alliance. This was especially true as regards Ordine Nuovo, but he gradually started to develop serious doubts concerning the role played by Avanguardia Nazionale, and even by the second-generation neofascist groups. His views will be analysed in some depth in Chapter 4, where the various interpretations of the Strategy of Tension which place the neofascists in the role of villains will be discussed.

What is particularly of interest in the Peteano case is the fact that there is a recognised and incontrovertible culprit who, as a known neofascist and member of Ordine Nuovo, caused the death of three *Carabinieri*, and also sufficiently strong evidence to prove that the intelligence services and the *Carabinieri* themselves did their utmost to cover up his crime and to channel investigations in other directions, away from the extreme right. This is one of the few cases, in fact, where officers of the armed forces were found guilty by the Courts and sentenced to some years' imprisonment for their obstructing actions. The facts concerning this episode of *depistaggio* are as follows.

Immediately after the Peteano attack, investigations focused upon the extreme-left group Lotta Continua, on the basis of confessions that a repented witness had allegedly made to Colonel Santoro in Trento (the same Colonel who, as we saw in the previous chapter, was denounced by Enzo Ferro as responsible for abetting right-wing extremists and promoting attacks in his area). These 'confessions' were later dismissed as false. The task of investigating the crime was conferred on the *Carabinieri*, and specifically on Colonel Dino Mingarelli, based in Udine, who was sent confidential information regarding the 'red trail' by General Palumbo, himself Head of the Milan-based Pastrengo Division and a member of the secret Masonic Lodge P2, as emerged after the discovery of the latter in 1981. Later, a different trail led to the arrest and incrimination of various local common criminals. All this time, the police were left out of the investigations and not even kept informed: their protests were to no avail.

For many years, the 'black trail' was altogether ignored, yet there existed serious circumstantial and forensic evidence pointing to members of Ordine Nuovo. The most important piece of evidence concerned the fact that at Ronchi dei Legionari Ivano Boccaccio had been found in possession of a gun, a 22-calibre Luger, which was the same type of gun which had been used to fire at the Fiat 500 in Peteano. Despite the fact that the same *Carabinieri* officers investigated the two crimes and that they knew that a 22-calibre gun had been used at Peteano, they never apparently established a link between the two events, thus allowing innocent people to be charged and the real culprits to escape justice. Worse still, they denied that any bullet cases had been found at the site of the crime. Indeed, at the time Colonel Mingarelli went as far as to report officially and publicly that it had not been possible to establish any connection between the attempted hijack and Peteano.

In 1985, Palumbo, Mingarelli and five other officers of the intelligence services and the armed forces were charged with falsehood and obstruction of justice. After a series of trials, Mingarelli and two other officers were found guilty of the charge of falsehood and sentenced to a few years' imprisonment, a sentence confirmed by the Supreme Court.

The full sequence of events is told by Vinciguerra in one of his books, aptly entitled *La strategia del depistaggio* (1993). The book reveals many other interesting facts, including the intervention of Captain Labruna of the intelligence service (then called SID) who allegedly had gone to Padua after the Peteano attack and the attempted hijack by Boccaccio, and had discussed these events with Massimilano Fachini of Ordine Nuovo, telling him to 'stop acting silly' (ibid.: 126). This shows that Labruna was convinced that Ordine Nuovo was responsible for this episode, even though he assumed that Vinciguerra had taken orders from Fachini. In either case, the SID clearly had no intention of aiding investigations in the direction of the black trail, but moved simply to warn Ordine Nuovo to stop carrying out such 'spontaneous' acts of violence.

Vinciguerra also recalled that soon after the hijack a *Carabiniere* went to Cicuttini's house, warning his parents of the likelihood of an official search. By then, according to Vinciguerra's memoirs, the *Carabinieri* investigating the case already knew of Cicuttini's involvement. They also knew, or strongly suspected, that he was the author of the phone call which, in May 1972, had lured the three *Carabinieri* to the place in Peteano where the booby trap had been prepared. Despite this, the investigators waited two weeks before issuing an arrest warrant, thus allowing Cicuttini plenty of time to escape abroad. According to Vinciguerra, the aim was precisely to avoid having to test Cicuttini's voice against the one recorded during the phone call, as this would have nailed him, and the other members of Ordine Nuovo, to the Peteano attack (ibid.: 134–36). Finally, in terms of the police, Vinciguerra is convinced that they had started to make their own investigations, but were stopped in their tracks by the Ministry of the Interior (ibid.: 123). In short, once the culprits were identified, the *depistaggio* in their favour began in earnest.

The significance of this episode is somewhat different from the previous two cases, albeit just as important. The affair indicates, as Vinciguerra argues in his book, that, at the time of these events, it seemingly did not matter whether an act of violence carried out by extreme-right activists had been agreed upon by state bodies in order to ensure the protection of the former by the latter. He himself had acted independently of any state or parallel body, yet he had discovered that he was still being shielded from criminal investigations. This has two possible implications. First, the intelligence services were obliged to shield him and his comrades, despite the fact that their acts were directed against *Carabinieri*, because they could not allow the actions of a few intemperate activists to expose the black trail and through it the existence of links, possibly even of a coordinated strategy, between state bodies and radical-right groups. Alternatively, they were protected because their actions, albeit not 'sanctioned' by state bodies, could still be used to incriminate the left, that is, in support of the Strategy of Tension. It is even possible that both types of reasoning contributed to determining the course of action adopted by the intelligence services and parts of the armed forces.

## American and Italian intelligence structures and stragismo

Carlo Digilio, one of the two main witnesses in the trial against Maggi, Zorzi and other members of Ordine Nuovo for the Piazza Fontana massacre, provided Judge Salvini with important new information regarding the existence of close links between this organisation, top-ranking officers of the armed forces, as well as NATO and American intelligences services. He revealed that neofascists such as Maggi were in contact with General Magi Braschi, who was close to NATO and had been one of the speakers at a Conference organised in May 1965 in Rome by the Istituto Alberto Pollio, a think-tank close to the armed forces. The main focus of the meeting, which was a private gathering, even though the papers later appeared in a little-known publication, was on the communist threat and on the need to counteract this threat through various means, especially unorthodox warfare. The speakers included neofascists such as Pino Rauti alongside high-ranking representatives of the military. This is the meeting where, in the opinion of many experts as well as magistrates, not least Salvini himself, the Strategy of Tension was first theorised. By contrast, as we shall see in Part II, both neo- and postfascists continue to claim that it was no such thing, and that the publication of its papers proves that it was not a secret gathering with sinister aims.

Carlo Digilio also revealed that he and Marcello Soffiati had both worked for Ordine Nuovo and had also acted as informers for American intelligence units which were based in the FTASE command in Verona, which was the equivalent of the NATO command in southern Europe. Digilio recalled that his American contacts in the FTASE base consisted, first, of Captain David Carret of the US Navy, and later, since 1974, of Captain Theodore Richards. Digilio stated that he had kept both officers fully informed of the terrorist attacks that the Ordine Nuovo cells were planning and/or had carried out, including the attacks of 12 December 1969, a few days before they took place. On one occasion, following these attacks, Captain Carret had told him that, despite the fact that there had not been a turn to the right in the country, the situation was under control and Ordine Nuovo would not be touched by investigations (*Sentenza-ordinanza* Salvini, 18 March 1998: 73). Digilio also revealed that he had learnt from Carret that Pino Rauti collaborated regularly with the CIA (ibid.: 280), so much so that he, Digilio, had been certain that Rauti would never be prosecuted, thanks to this collaboration, which was well documented. As for Maggi, Digilio had reported that the ON regional leader had repeatedly stated that the decision to carry out the attacks of 12 December had been taken 'at a very high level by people who directed the strategy even from Rome', adding that there was nothing to worry about since 'everything was under control' and 'those who had organised this strategy had also devised a way to direct investigations towards others.'

Digilio had also made reference to the activities of two Italo-Americans, Leo Joseph Pagnotta and Joseph Luongo, who, at the end of the Second World War, had started to set up a web of intelligence personnel for the United States and had recruited, in the name of a common anti-communist fight, ex-Nazi and ex-fascist officers as well as various other extreme-right elements. Both men had also established links with the Office of Classified Affairs of the Ministry of the Interior. Finally, another crucial person mentioned by Digilio was Sergio Minetto, who was himself a collaborator of the US-NATO intelligence structure, as well as a recruiter of extreme-right activists, in close contact with Maggi on the one hand, and Spiazzi on the other.

Further interesting information was provided by Vincenzo Vinciguerra. In 1993, during one of his interrogations, he told Salvini that, in November 1968, Delfo Zorzi, who had been briefly arrested for possession of arms and a small quantity of explosives, had been contacted by people working for the Office of Classified Affairs of the Ministry of the Interior. The latter had allegedly convinced Zorzi of the need to stop fighting an isolated battle against the communist threat, which would only land him in jail, and to work instead for a state apparatus which pursued similar aims to those of Ordine Nuovo. According to Vinciguerra, Zorzi had agreed to collaborate and to join forces with that state institution.

As for the general implications of the above revelations, the precise role of the American units referred to by Digilio is still unclear. At best, as Salvini remarked in his *Sentenza-ordinanza*, they did nothing to put a stop to the terrorist activities they had knowledge of, or indeed to denounce the authors to the competent authorities. At worst, they may even have aided the neofascists in carrying out their terrorist plans. As for the role of the Italian intelligence and military structures, Milan prosecutor Guido Salvini believed that the revelations by Digilio provided further confirmation that

> The occult structure of Ordine Nuovo was not the expression of a few subversive fanatics but, at least tendentially, had clear military and institutional referents which, at the right moment, would be able to exploit the fear and disorientation caused by the terrorist attacks. (*Sentenza-Ordinanza* Salvini, 18 March 1998: 60)

It should be noted that the Court of Appeal for the Piazza Fontana trial (Sentence of the Court of Appeal of 12 March 2004: 280) ruled that no evidence had been found by the prosecuting magistrates in support of Digilio's testimony as regards his collaboration with the CIA unit within the FTASE base. Neither Captain Carret nor Captain Richards had been conclusively identified, and indeed Digilio himself had provided only confusing indications regarding their identities. This part of Salvini's investigations was therefore dismissed by the Court. It is interesting, however, that the Court of Appeal also doubted Digilio's testimony regarding Pino Rauti's collaboration with the CIA. Digilio, in fact, according to the Court, had based his revelation on a document – the so-called 'Winters document' – which allegedly contained a list of Italian citizens paid by the CIA. This document had been handed over to the *Carabinieri* by a journalist, Elio Ramondino, who in turn claimed to have received it from a US General called Oswald Lee Winter. The sentence by the Court of Appeal stated that this was an 'imaginary' person – i.e. nonexistent (*Sentenza Corte di Assise di Milano* of 12 March 2004: 642–43, Note 480). This apparently minor detail is fairly interesting, because such a man did exist, so much so that he appeared in a three-part documentary on Gladio, produced by the BBC and broadcast in 1992 (Timewatch). In the documentary, Colonel (not General) Oswald De Winter, a CIA-ITAC Liaison Officer for Europe, had revealed that there existed within NATO a secret policy which consisted in nonincriminating anti-communist extreme-right activists. In the same way as for 'General' Winters, therefore, the nonidentification of Captain Carret and Captain Richards does not necessarily mean that they did not exist. For the purposes of criminal justice, however, the Court of Appeal could not but dismiss this part of Digilio's testimony as constituting unsubstantial evidence.

## Conclusion

It would be impossible to underestimate the importance of the recent judicial findings in relation to acts of *depistaggio* and obstruction of justice. Admittedly, much of the information gained is not completely new. Previously, however, it was a question of relying mainly on hearsay, reported conversations, cryptic allusions, and, at best, extremely patchy documentation. By contrast, the numerous episodes analysed in this chapter are based on strong judicial evidence, and in large part corroborated by an insider of the Italian military intelligence service, Antonio Labruna. The latter, having strenuously denied, at the Catanzaro trial, any wrongdoing on the part of the SID in relation to *stragismo*, twenty years later admitted to an intense activity by this organisation, whose nature was often illegal and even criminal.

Why did the SID and part of the armed forces spend very considerable energy and resources in acts of *depistaggio*, at a time when, arguably, the security of the nation was at risk, not least from those same forces they were busy protecting? What was their role in *stragismo* and/or in putschism? These are questions which are still open to speculation, and will be addressed in the next chapter, in which the main interpretations of the Strategy of Tension based on the latest trial findings are discussed. Somewhat easier is the question related to the specific purposes of these various acts of *depistaggio*. On the basis of the examples provided above, three main aims can be identified.

First, as already stated, there seems little doubt that in the episodes reported above, the SID aimed primarily at shielding possible culprits from investigation and occult forces from exposure. Evidently, these were forces which were not considered a threat to the security of the nation but, on the contrary, were seen as contributing to the strengthening of the political and state system. Indeed, there is sufficient evidence to come to the conclusion that these forces were part of a wide, possibly fairly loose, coalition whose common denominator was anti-communism, which was perceived at the time as the main threat to the security of the nation. A common thread appears to link the radical neofascist groups, the intelligence services, part of the *Carabinieri* (especially the Pastrengo Division), the Nuclei for the Defence of the State, and the Masonic Lodge Propaganda 2, commonly known as P2. The latter became very important in the 1970s, after Licio Gelli, whom many are convinced was mainly a figurehead for other people and received orders from elsewhere, possibly the CIA, became its headmaster. Its precise role in the Strategy of Tension remains uncertain, even though there is no doubt that it acted as another 'parallel structure' in Italy during the Cold War. P2 included the leaders of the intelligence services, armed forces (especially well represented was the Pastrengo Division), and the police, as well as businesspeople and politicians (Flamigni 2005; Guarino 2006). It was notoriously implicated in financial and corruption scandals surrounding two banks, the Banco Ambrosiano, which crashed in 1982, and the Vatican bank IOR, which backed the Banco Ambrosiano and operated effectively as an offshore bank (Cornwell 1983; Raw 1992; Williams 2003).

Second, the episodes reported above, and particularly the use of the Orlandini tapes by the SID, seem to indicate that the weakest link in the chain of organisations that were part of the fight against communism were the neofascists. The tapes that were handed over to the judiciary, in fact, exposed the role of Borghese and his Fronte Nazionale in the 1970 attempted coup but concealed the part played by, indeed even the existence of, other, clearly more powerful, forces, such as the Masonic Lodge P2. It was only ten years later, in 1981, that a fortuitous discovery by investigating magistrates made this organisation known to the public, including a list of 953 members. In short, the neofascists were shielded from investigations as far as possible, but this seems in many cases to have been due to the need to protect other organisations. It is likely, as Salvini argued, that, following Miceli's replacement by Maletti as Head of SID, and the development of a more 'modern' anti-communist strategy, the collaboration of the neofascists was judged expendable.

What remains unclear, however, is the specific relationship existing between Ordine Nuovo and Avanguardia Nazionale, on the one hand, and the intelligence services, on the other. Had the latter, for instance, really been set up by the Office of Classified Affairs of the Ministry of the Interior? If so, was this the reason why the content of the tapes concerning AN was also 'thinned out'? Were these two organisations still considered politically and militarily useful by the SID and the armed forces and therefore continued to be protected in a way that the Fronte Nazionale was not? Or was it simply a question of expediency, in the sense that the role of Borghese and others was exposed, but in effect many extreme-right activists close to Borghese ended up simply being recycled under other organisations? Whatever the answers to these questions, there is no doubting, as we shall see in Part II, the deeply felt bitterness among both neo- and postfascists regarding the fact that in all the trials, including the most recent, they have been made to stand out as the (only) villains of both *stragismo* and the Strategy of Tension, whereas many other forces were implicated but escaped both the trials and the stigma.

Third, it is clear that the SID put whatever information was in its possession to a political use and was therefore an integral part in the complex web of ties, blackmailing and dirty dealings that characterised Italian politics in the 1970s. Since it is also the case, as evidenced by the Orlandini tapes episode, that the Heads of SID reported to top-ranking politicians and ministers, it has to be concluded that the latter were also fully implicated in these 'parallel' political dealings. This does not necessarily mean that state forces orchestrated *stragismo* and the Strategy of Tension, even though such a possibility cannot be ruled out. It does mean, however, that state forces played their own cards in the wider underhand game, quite ruthlessly and with scant regard for the criminal justice process.

Finally, and this is clearly related to the last point, recent investigations and trials have not succeeded in formally incriminating high-ranking officers in the intelligence services and the armed forces, or indeed top-ranking politicians. As for NATO, or indeed the CIA, some evidence was unearthed concerning the existence of links between the Nuclei for the Defence of the State and army officers close to NATO. However, despite Salvini's efforts in trying to uncover a possible role played by American forces, the leads provided by Carlo Digilio came to nothing, and the American officers whom he allegedly used to report to were not traced by the investigators. The precise role played by Gladio has also not been uncovered. This organisation came to light in the early 1990s, when it was disclosed that a secret anti-communist network had been operating throughout Western Europe. Its official aim was to fight in the event of a Soviet invasion, but it also had the all-important unofficial aim of fighting against the internal communist threat in those countries considered most at risk. It was hypothesised that Gladio was behind terrorist attacks in various European countries, including Belgium and Italy (Ganser 2005), but Salvini's investigations failed to unearth any specific links between this organisation and *stragismo*.

As argued in the Introduction, there can be plenty of reasons related to the superior interests of the nation and the threat to its security which, in the eyes of all those responsible for the acts analysed above, would have justified their behaviour; nevertheless, there can also exist no doubt that the overall casualties of such acts have been the criminal justice process, on the one hand, and the recovery of the truth, on the other. The implications of this situation are discussed in the Conclusion to Part I.

# CHAPTER 4

## Interpretations of the Strategy of Tension in Accordance with Judicial Findings

### Introduction

There are almost as many interpretations of the Strategy of Tension as there are scholars, journalists, magistrates and politicians who have commented on these events. This chapter looks at the principal explanations given by people who, in view of their formal role, whether institutional, professional or associational, have directly contributed to the discovery of the recent findings underpinning judicial investigations, as discussed in the previous two chapters, or have acquired specific and detailed knowledge of such findings.

These people include Judge Salvini himself, who granted a few interviews after the end of his investigations on the Piazza Fontana massacre, setting out his own account of what had happened in Italy in the late 1960s and 1970s. They also include Giovanni Pellegrino, ex-Senator for the Left Democrats (DS), and one of the Heads of the Parliamentary Commission on the Failed Identification of the Authors of Terrorist Massacres, often referred to simply as the 'Commission on the Massacres'. Set up on 17 May 1988 by Law No. 172, the Commission was given the task of investigating the reasons which had prevented the identification of those responsible for massacres and other acts of subversion since 1969. Pellegrino's role in the Commission and his efforts to conclude its works with a unitary and consensual report on Italy's violent and divisive past are discussed in Part II. Here, it should be noted that the Commission was able both to secure an input from judicial investigations and to rely on its own expert consultants – so much so that, by the end of its existence, it had produced a mass of empirical evidence on all three types of political violence outlined in the Introduction, based on documentation, hearings and interviews. Although it failed to produce a final unitary report, due to the constrasting opinions of the political party representatives who sat on it, the 'impartial' and professional role of Senator Pellegrino as Chair, between 1994 and 2001, was never questioned and indeed was praised by all participants.

Another expert whose interpretation will be taken into account in this chapter is Aldo Giannuli, historian, and author of numerous books on the political 'mysteries' of the Italian First Republic (Cucchiarelli and Giannuli 1997; De Palo and Giannuli 1989; Giannuli and Schiavulli 1991). He was consultant to both the 'Commission on the Massacres' and to Judge Guido Salvini, and, in 1996, responsible for discovering a 'lost' archive of the intelligence services, which contained a wealth of data on its activities during the Cold War. Giannuli was interviewed by the author in Milan in October 2005. His reconstruction can also be found in a report compiled for Judge Salvini and based on documents retrieved in the Central State Archive as well as in the archives of various Ministries (Giannuli 1997). Another explanation taken into consideration is that offered by left-leaning journalist Sandro Provvisionato, author of a number of books on Italy's political 'mysteries' and extremism, including two written in collaboration with Adalberto Baldoni, himself a (right-leaning) journalist who is currently a member of Alleanza Nazionale.

The views of the Presidents of two Associations of the Relatives of the Victims of the Massacres are also analysed in this chapter. One is Paolo Bolognesi, President of the Association of the Relatives of the Victims of the Bologna Massacre, and the other is Manlio Milani, President of the equivalent association in relation to the Brescia massacre. These associations have played a crucial role in ensuring that the massacres are not forgotten by the public, by promoting commemorations, conferences and debates, setting up specialist archives, lobbying for parliamentary inquiries and full judicial investigations, and representing the victims in the criminal trials.

Finally, the chapter will take into consideration the interpretation put forward by Vincenzo Vinciguerra, ex-member of Ordine Nuovo, self-confessed culprit for the Peteano massacre, (unrepentant) witness for the prosecution, and the object of a massive operation of obstruction of justice, as discussed in Chapter 3. Vinciguerra is serving a life sentence and has produced a number of publications where he has both outlined his account of the Strategy of Tension and denounced the inadequacy of judicial investigations and trials. Vinciguerra's reconstruction of *stragismo* is analysed in this chapter, rather than in Part II, because he considers the neofascists to have been accomplices in the massacres. He is therefore representative of that relatively small number of neo- and postfascists who are prepared to acknowledge the trial findings, while simultaneously arguing that the judicial process has allowed the masterminds behind the Strategy of Tension to remain untouched.

## Salvini's reconstruction

According to Salvini, the story of *stragismo* is no longer a story of unresolved 'mysteries', and the judicial trials, despite the unsatisfactory not-proven verdicts, have been able to establish the guilty status of Carlo Digilio and, in retrospect, also of Franco Freda and Giovanni Ventura, thereby clearly attributing the Piazza Fontana massacre to Ordine Nuovo (Lanza 2005). In his view, this massacre represented the culminating point of a strategy which aimed at promoting a coup d'état in the country, or at least 'the creation of a strong government, an authoritarian government' (*Il Resto del Siclo*, 16 April 2005: 3). In other words, *stragismo* and putschism were indeed part of a wider political project. The project also involved directing the blame towards Maoist and/or anarchist groups, which had previously been infiltrated by members of both Avanguardia Nazionale and Ordine Nuovo. This operation was promoted by the Office of Classified Affairs of the Ministry of the Interior, with the precise intent of directing the investigations away from the culprits of the various terrorist attacks. In this context, Salvini's interpretation, as he himself acknowledged, had many parallels with the one put forward by the extreme left immediately after the 1969 massacre, appropriately summarised in the expression 'state massacre'. As Salvini clarified:

> Instead of introducing repressive measures, the State, with a large part of its apparatuses, colluded with those who were planning the massacres, protected the culprits from being incriminated and, when necessary, helped the witnesses to escape. Hence this expression [state massacre], even if it can appear too strong, and if at the time seemed like a politically inspired twist, in reality has been confirmed by many new elements. On a historical-political level, therefore, it is profoundly true. (*Il Resto del Siclo*, 16 April 2005: 5)

Salvini sees the role of Ordine Nuovo as that of 'co-belligerent', rather than purely and simply that of hod carriers implementing someone else's political strategy, although its agenda was necessarily subordinate to those of other forces:

> Being unable to reach its objectives on its own, Ordine Nuovo, like other extreme-right organisations, could act as detonator of a pre-putschist phase which, however, to be successful, by necessity would have had to be taken forward by other forces, be they domestic military structures or anti-communist security structures of allied countries.
> Obviously such a strategy ... meant that the co-belligerents had to be previously informed of its basic operational aims as well as of the moments which were to act as detonators for institutional responses.
> It is not a coincidence that this strategy started to wane in the mid-1970s when, with the new institutional and European political climate, especially after the collapse of the right-wing regimes in Spain, Portugal and Greece, an openly authoritarian reaction had become anachronistic and inadmissible for Italy. (*Sentenza-ordinanza* Salvini, 18 March 1998: 49–50)

In terms of the political referents for the Strategy of Tension, Salvini seems to give credit to the confessions of those witnesses from the extreme right who had revealed that Christian Democratic leader Mariano Rumor, Prime Minister in December 1969, had been the person the putschists had relied on for declaring a state of emergency in the country. Salvini made it clear that, in his view, these revelations should not be interpreted as indicating that Rumor was among the organisers or masterminders of any subversive acts or indeed massacres. Rather, he was convinced that

The then Prime Minister, together with part of Christian Democracy, and above all the Social Democratic Party, were seen at the time as the terminal link which, with their decisions, would have brought to fruition a political-subversive strategy that, starting with a task force made up of elements such as Maggi, Zorzi and Freda, through various mediators, including the military, would have been able to influence decisions at the highest institutional levels. (*Sentenza-ordinanza* Salvini, 18 March 1998: 74)

In addition, Salvini gave credence to a reconstruction put forward by Fulvio Bellini, author, under the pseudonym Walter Rubini, of a little-known book published in 1978 with the title *Il segreto della Repubblica* ('The Secret of the Republic'), and recently reprinted (2005). Bellini testified to Salvini in 1997, confirming his version of events and revealing that his source for this book had been an English journalist who claimed to work for Reuters, but who in reality had most probably been working as an intelligence agent. As stated in his original book and restated in his subsequent testimony to Judge Salvini, Bellini hypothesised the existence of two main political strategies within Christian Democracy: a putschist line, or more precisely a strategy, favoured by the Americans, that envisaged the formation of a stronger (possibly presidentialist) form of government, on the one hand, and a more democratic strategy, supported by Aldo Moro, on the other. After the Piazza Fontana massacre and the mass public demonstrations that took place throughout Italy, Mariano Rumor, who had initially been in the 'American' camp, allied with Aldo Moro and determined the prevalence of the second strategy. However, a compromise was reached between the two political wings, which required the continuing concealment of the 'black trail' and exposure of the 'red trail' (*Sentenza-ordinanza* Salvini, 18 March 1998: 51–55).

Fulvio Bellini had also mentioned to Salvini two articles which had appeared in the British paper the *Observer* on 6 and 14 December 1969, which in the opinion of his English informer had amounted to a warning by the British government that it opposed a putschist strategy in Italy, thereby strengthening Moro and his allies in their defence of democracy. In a brief interview with the author, Salvini stressed the relevance of these two articles for understanding the Strategy of Tension and its national and international implications. Copies of the articles, made available through the *Observer*, have indeed confirmed their relevance to any reconstruction of *stragismo* and the Strategy of Tension. The first article, written by Leslie Finer, correspondent for the paper in Athens until he was expelled in February 1968, and entitled 'Greek Premier plots Army coup in Italy', revealed the existence of a 'planned military coup in Italy by a group of extreme right-wingers and Army officers – with the encouragement and assistance of the Greek regime and its premier, ex-Colonel George Papadopoulos' (*Observer*, 6 December 1969: 1). The article, based on a secret report, made reference to a certain Mr P., whom the article defined as 'the undercover representative of the Italian conspirators who had just returned from a meeting with Mr Papadopoulos in Athens' (*Observer*, 6 December 1969: 1). The report also mentioned the role of the armed forces and the *Carabinieri* in the coup, as well as activities by Italian students 'which will bear fruit shortly' (*Observer,* 6 December 1969: 2). The second article, entitled '480 held in terrorist bomb hunt', reported on the bombing attacks of 12 December 1969, and speculated as to which groups could be among the culprits. It then proceeded to offer its own interpretation, specifically using the expression 'Strategy of Tension', and claiming that its goal was indeed to exacerbate tensions in the country which would precipitate the political crisis and facilitate some kind of extraparliamentary intervention. In this context, the most likely explanation was that the attacks constituted,

> recognisable far-Right terrorism, but that even the 'moderate' Right stands to gain from it ... For the whole political line-up on the Right, from the Saragat Socialists to the neo-Fascists, the unexpected mildness of the 'hot autumn' threatened to puncture the fear of revolution they were counting on. Those who planted the bombs have brought that fear back to Italy. Even before the bombings, general public despair over any hope of politics' remedies had helped to bring about more and more unorthodox acting outside the regular political context ... the Right has been talking more and more confidently about extra-parliamentary 'solutions'. There has been talk of right-wing action groups, and of right-wing citizens' committees of public safety. (*Observer,* 14 December 1969: 2)

The article concluded that the situation in Italy was very volatile, but also that there did not seem to exist a serious possibility of a coup d'état, given that the Army had no tradition of political action and no wider appeal in the country, and the police did not seem to aspire to a political role. It is interesting to note that, after the content of these two articles was reported in Italian papers, there was much speculation as to the identity of Mr P., with the most likely candidates being Randolfo Pacciardi (suspected of favouring a presidentialist 'solution' to the Italian crisis), or indeed Pino Rauti, leader of Ordine Nuovo. These articles, as we shall see in Part II, are also widely mentioned in the reconstructions put forward by the right, but their significance is turned upside down, as they are taken as evidence of a 'plot' masterminded by left-wing editor Giangiacomo Feltrinelli and consisting in feeding false information to the left-leaning press – in this case the *Observer.*

Salvini's reconstruction has the merit of explaining much of the behaviour of the intelligence services after the departure of General Miceli. In particular, it would explain the subsequent role allegedly played by (some) intelligence structures to 'defuse' the Borghese coup and dispense with neofascist groups as 'co-belligerent' allies, as evidenced by the use of the Orlandini tapes, while simultaneously preventing judicial investigations from penetrating the murky subterranean network linking such disparate actors as neofascism, freemasonry, Mafia, and military and intelligence structures. Salvini's interpretation explains primarily the Strategy of Tension up to 1974–75, since he does not venture into a 'grand' explanation of Cold War politics in Italy. By contrast, both Pellegrino and Giannuli start from judicial findings but depart from them in order to provide much wider reconstructions of the Italian experience of the Cold War.

## Pellegrino's account

In two books (Fasanella and Sestieri with Pellegrino 2000; Fasanella and Pellegrino 2005), published in the form of extended interviews, Pellegrino examined the Italian experience in the light of the existence of a frontal contra-position between communists and anti-communists. Both groups were able to rely on paramilitary organisations but after the 1948 elections and the stabilisation of political relations, the 'white' (Catholic) armed groups were disarmed, while the communist ones (the so-called Gladio rossa) took on an increasingly defensive role. However, at the beginning of the 1960s, the changing international and domestic climate, leading to a new phase of détente between the superpowers and the formation, sanctioned by the Kennedy administration, of a centre-left coalition government in Italy with the inclusion of the Socialist Party (until then a close ally of the communists), was perceived as extremely dangerous by the more conservative political and military sectors. In this context, they started to develop a counter-strategy, which in Italy can be traced back to the famous meeting organised by the Istituto Pollio in 1965: 'Even if it did not amount to a true conspiracy, that meeting shows that the highest ranks of the armed forces, industrial sectors, part of the Judiciary and of the political class converged into a cultural milieu which without doubt formed the anti-chamber of a putschist plan' (Fasanella and Sestieri with Pellegrino 2000: 47).

According to Pellegrino, a putschist solution was seriously contemplated only between 1969 (with the massacres of 12 December) and 1970 (with the attempted coup by Borghese, which was a serious episode, as opposed to a farce). The Piazza Fontana massacre itself was most probably a 'mistake' since there are elements which suggest that the bomb should have exploded when the bank was closed and empty, as Christian Democratic politician Paolo Emilio Taviani had stated to the Parliamentary Commission on the Massacres (2000: 64). In Pellegrino's view, the massacres that took place between 1971 and 1974, including the one at Brescia, can be explained as a reaction on the part of the neofascists, angry about the betrayal of the putschist strategy on the part of the other forces, including the military. At Brescia, for example, the real targets appear to have been the *Carabinieri*, who were normally stationed in the galleried spot where the bomb exploded. However, on that day, unexpectedly it started to rain, and the *Carabinieri* moved elsewhere, while civilians took their place under the arcades. In short, the Brescia massacre was similar to the one in Peteano, in the sense that it targeted the military. As for the 1973 massacre at Milan police headquarters, its target was DC Minister Mariano Rumor, who was seen as a traitor by the neofascists. In revolting against their former allies, however, the neofascists contributed directly to their complete isolation and marginalisation.

In Pellegrino's view, the Strategy of Tension implied three different levels of actors and aims: at the lowest level, the perpetrators of the massacres, that is, the neofascists, wanted to implement a coup d'état; at a higher level, their instigators favoured instead the formation of a more conservative government; at the highest level, various international actors had their own reasons for, and pursued their own interests in, keeping the country in a state of instability and disorder (2000: 67). According to Pellegrino, the strategies pursued at this top level should not always be accounted for by the need to counteract a perceived communist threat in Italy. Rather, there may have been other agendas at play, including that of conditioning the country's foreign policy, especially in the Mediterranean, or indeed of preventing a convergence between Christian Democracy and the Communist Party.

Some of these issues are reexamined in Pellegrino's 2005 interview with Fasanella, where he more explicitly argued that the adoption of violence, both on the right and on the left, must be understood as a response to the perceived threat by the opposite side. Having said this, there is no doubt whatsoever that the Piazza Fontana massacre, as well as the 1973 attack in Milan and the 1974 attack in Brescia, were carried out by neofascists: 'That the [Piazza Fontana] attack was organised by cells of Ordine Nuovo with the backing of sectors of the state is uncontroversial. I can state this with absolute certainty on the basis of the immense mass of judicial material which was accumulated over the years and also, obviously, on the basis of the findings of our work at the Commission on the Massacres' (Fasanella and Pellegrino 2005: 64). Pellegrino also confirmed his views that there may have been an array of forces, both domestic and international, which were interested in preventing an agreement between DC and PCI leaders Aldo Moro and Enrico Berlinguer, so much so that the former was murdered in 1978 and the latter was the target of an assassination attempt in Bulgaria in 1973 (2005: 72–79).

Furthermore, his more recent book, significantly entitled *La guerra civile. Da Salò a Berlusconi* ('The Civil War. From Salò to Berlusconi') (2005) argued openly in favour of interpreting Italian contemporary history in the light of a continuing, albeit 'creeping' civil war, whose latest phase coincided with the fall of the First Republic, as evidenced by the bitter fight between politicians and (left-leaning) magistrates during the Clean Hands investigations and trials, as well as between supporters and opponents of Berlusconi after the latter's entry into politics. As will be examined in Part II, the need to put an end to this longstanding conflict, which to this day can be considered responsible for the country's anomalous status as an incomplete democracy, is one of the reasons why Pellegrino, as Chair of the Parliamentary Commission on the Massacres, tried to promote a unitary reconstruction of the past on the part of its members and favoured a process of truth telling and national reconciliation in the country at large.

## Giannuli's interpretation

For Giannuli the expression 'Strategy of Tension' is best understood with reference to a historical period and to an international, as well as domestic, political context. The period in question lasted from 1960 to 1973–75, that is to say, from the election of Kennedy as US President to the consolidation of a new phase in the Cold War, marked by the politics of détente. The Western political elites were split into two in relation to this new phase:

> The Strategy of Tension is the exact semantic opposite of the politics of détente [*distensione*]; it means that tension takes on a strategic value in itself for fear of a fall of tension in the fight against the communist world. Hence the relaunch of harsh forms of political confrontation, of a covered war, etc. This period marked a series of interferences in domestic affairs, it was the period of maximum concentration of coups d'état. (Interview with the author, 24 October 2005)

The Strategy of Tension went through four different phases: (a) a planning stage, 1960–65; (b) an initial implementation phase, 1966–68; (c) an acute phase, 1969–72; (d) a stage of decline, 1973–75 (Giannuli 1997: 258). In relation to the Italian context, the expression refers primarily to *stragismo*, which coincided with the last two phases of the strategy itself since it 'basically lasted five years – it is true that there were massacres both before [1969] and after [1974], but we cannot refer to a single strategy lasting half a century' (interview with the author). It is for this reason that in Italy, too, the Strategy of Tension ended in 1973–75; this is why the Bologna massacre followed a different logic and must be explained through different lenses – even though Giannuli does not exclude the possibility that the neofascists were implicated in this episode, albeit not necessarily the two found guilty by the Courts, Valerio Fioravanti and Francesca Mambro. Giannuli, like Pellegrino, talks of a latent civil war in the country in those years, with both the DC and the PCI having 'one finger on the trigger' and being deeply suspicious of each other, yet also preventing the more radical wings in their midst from precipitating the situation into open conflict. A third group, however, made up of sectors of the Social Democratic and Liberal Parties, as well as part of Christian Democracy, sectors of the intelligence services, the police, and the business elite, started to devise a project of civil war, through *stragismo*. Within this project, different forces had different aims, so much so that it would be more appropriate to use the expression 'Strategies of Tension' in the plural: 'its many actors were partly in conflict and in competition with each other, and often even cut each other out.' According to Giannuli: 'After 1974–75 the political tensions were discharged on the extreme wings on the left and on the right ... the PCI cut off not only the Red Brigades but also the workers' and students' radical movements, while the DC cut out the extreme right and even marginalised the MSI to an extent. At that point we entered a phase marked by a low-intensity civil war' (interview with the author, 24 October 2005).

As regards the role of the neofascists, the starting point is that, after the end of the Second World War, they were not prepared to disappear as a political subject. Their only hope was that the conflict between the USA and the USSR might reopen some space for them to reengage in political activism. In the meantime, the fascists had to decide which side they were on and they chose to ally with the Western world. Some fascists moved over to the other block, the Eastern block, but the vast majority decided to ally with the Americans and the British in the name of anti-communism (Giannuli 1997: 48–49). At the national level, for a long time the fascists played the card of acting as a lobby, with a view to exercising a possible role as partners in government with the Christian Democratic Party. During the 1950s, in fact, a few governments were formed thanks to the parliamentary votes of the MSI, including the Zoli and Tambroni governments, hence the prevailing policy was one of gradual integration. However, when the Strategy of Tension was launched at an international level, the neofascists started to believe that they could play a more important role. Until then, according to Giannuli, there had been a clear demarcation between the more moderate anti-communist strategy pursued by the Christian Democratic, Liberal, and Social Democratic Parties, and the more extreme anti-communism of the neofascists.

In 1960, however, the clashes in Italy over the Tambroni government, which the police had difficulty in controlling, demonstrated that the political conflict had taken on a violent character. The neofascists realised that this situation could be seen as requiring a new type of anti-communist militancy and that it offered them a new space for political activism. Later, when the 'civil war' project was born, the fascists started to believe that they could play an even bigger role if a new political system overseen by the military were to be established in the country. The successful coup d'état in Greece, whereby for the first time a European country went back to a fascist regime, fostered the illusions of the neofascists even further: no more than illusions, according to Giannuli, since the idea of a coup d'état was not widely supported in Italy. Rather, a different idea may have been nurtured, that of using the *fear* of a coup as a lever or even as a shield for Christian Democracy.

Giannuli was convinced that though all the neofascist groups were involved in the Strategy of Tension, nevertheless their aims and tactics did not necessarily coincide and they were often in competition with each other. The leader of the MSI, Almirante, in particular, did not believe that a coup d'état would be possible and preferred to follow a parliamentary strategy, while simultaneously trying to mediate between the putschist wing of the military and part of the political elite. In short, there were many different structures and projects at play which often intersected and obstructed each other. The Strategy of Tension failed, therefore, partly because of a mass democratic mobilisation in the country, but also partly due to the strategic inadequacy of its own masterminders. As for the specific role of the neofascist groups, Ordine Nuovo and Avanguardia Nazionale, Giannuli believed that the former was fully implicated in the massacres whereas the latter only marginally so. In particular, in his view the leader of AN, Delle Chiaie, became something of a scapegoat in the 1970s, when there was an attempt, on the part of state and military structures, to implicate him in the Milan massacre, so as to shift the blame away from ON. On his return to Italy in 1987, however, Delle Chiaie managed 'to save his skin', not least by sending a series of coded messages to high-ranking Christian Democratic politicians, in which he threatened to reveal everything during his trial. In the end he, too, was acquitted.

As regards links with external forces, Giannuli excluded the direct role of Gladio in the Strategy of Tension but emphasised the importance of the Nuclei for the Defence of the State, which in his view represented a structure set up with the explicit aim of fighting an 'internal' enemy, that is, the Italian Communist Party. To this end the NDS brought the radical neofascist groups under its own, as well as NATO's, protective umbrella. Indeed, 'the NDS, rather than an organisation proper, was a [political] operation, which aimed, on the one hand, at incorporating the extreme-right organisations in the clandestine defensive structure of NATO, and, on the other hand, at bestowing upon them the protection of the political-military secret concerning the Stay-Behinds' (Giannuli 1997: 261). By contrast, Gladio did not have direct links with political organisations and was set up officially to fight an external enemy. In short, there seems to have been something of a division of labour between Gladio and the NDS, with the former lasting for a longer period (1956–90) and focusing on a wider external threat, and the latter in existence only between 1966 and 1973, set up to respond to an immediate internal threat. According to Giannuli, there also remains a grey area concerning the exact role played by the CIA in the Strategy of Tension, as well as the attitude of the Eastern secret services towards neofascist and neo-Nazi groups.

Finally, when asked what he thought was the position of the neo- and postfascists today as regards the Strategy of Tension, Giannuli replied that in his view both constituencies were keen to erase a history which to them was extremely troublesome. They needed to legitimise themselves and they feared the dominance of the leftist version of events. For this reason, they had opted to turn the facts upside down, claiming that the prevailing interpretations of *stragismo* were nothing other than the product of a propaganda campaign orchestrated by the communists to hide the fact that they themselves were the real villains. With reference to the neo- and postfascists' own reconstructions, Giannuli stated that: 'it is like the stories of Superman, who had a parallel world where the truth was in reverse'. This is not to say that the neo- and postfascists really believed they could replace the leftist reconstruction with their own version; rather, they hoped that, by raising a huge cloud of dust, we would all conclude that history was only a matter of opinion. In effect, what they wanted was the opposite of a shared history, since they favoured as many 'unshared' reconstructions as possible.

## Provvisionato's reading

Sandro Provvisionato's thesis, as outlined in his interview with the author (14 October 2005), has many points of contact with those discussed above. In his view, the Strategy of Tension unfolded at the end of the 1960s and lasted for a decade. During this period, part of the extreme right, in accordance with the armed forces, attempted to develop the idea of coup d'état. There was a kind of transversal alliance which ranged from the extreme right to the democratic left, including sections of the Republican and Social Democratic Parties. This alliance lasted until 1969.

Both AN and ON took part in the Borghese coup, which was later ridiculed but was a serious affair. The general impression he had was that the coup was used to get rid of the more radical wing in a kind of settling of scores internal to the putschist alliance. Hence after 1969, when a definitive split between the more moderate and the more radical anti-communist forces took place, only the extreme-right groups continued to believe in the possibility of a coup solution in Italy. From then on, in fact, these groups were on their own, without the backing of the armed forces. It was only in the Veneto region that ON found some credibility in sectors close to the Americans, that is to say, in the FTASE command at Verona, the American base at Vicenza, and among some individuals linked to the CIA. By then, however, the neofascists were simply a workforce carrying out other forces' agendas, with no say in the matter. Provvisionato's reconstruction greatly limits the involvement of the neofascists in *stragismo* after 1970 to small groups of thirty or forty, a maximum of fifty people, even though, for ideological reasons, they could always rely upon a wider area of sympathisers.

As for the second-generation neofascists, they revolted against the older extreme-right groups and embraced the armed struggle. They were not ideologically inspired but were instead motivated by a need for revenge, against the left, the police, and the *Carabinieri*. In his view, these groups acted independently of, and were not manipulated by, other forces, including state structures. At a wider level, however, it was most probably the case that even the armed struggle, the 'civil war' of the 1970s, was fomented from outside, by whoever had an interest in promoting a climate of instability and disorder in the country (an interpretation similar to Pellegrino's).

Finally, the Bologna station massacre, according to Provvisionato, had been wrongly attributed to the neofascists. This massacre cannot possibly be accounted for with reference to the Strategy of Tension. To find a proper explanation for this *strage* and identify the real culprits, one had to look into the downing of an Italian civilian plane at Ustica, a year earlier, which may have been caused by a fight between Americans and Libyans. More recently, a newly discovered trail appeared to lead to the Palestinians as culprits for the massacre.

According to Provvisionato, nowadays the positioning of the neo- and post-fascist right regarding the activities of the radical groups in the 1960s and 1970s showed a clear-cut split between Alleanza Nazionale and the organisations to its right. This split, in his view, was more marked at the level of the party leaders, whereas among the middle and lower ranks many were still sympathetic towards radical neofascism, not least because they themselves had been members and activists of the more extreme groups. However, he also believed that the attitudes of the right towards first- and second-generation neofascists differed sharply, with enduring sympathy for the latter and greater distancing from the former, especially Ordine Nuovo and Avanguardia Nazionale. This reflected the old-standing rupture between the two generations, which had led the younger neofascists, in the second half of the 1970s, to reject everything the older neofascists had stood for, even contemplating their physical elimination.

## Bolognesi's and Milani's reconstructions

Paolo Bolognesi and Manlio Milani were interviewed by the author on 19 and 25 October 2005 respectively. For obvious reasons, given his personal experience and his role, Bolognesi focused mainly on the Bologna massacre, which in his view had without doubt been carried out by neofascists, including the two found guilty by the Courts, Francesca Mambro and Valerio Fioravanti. He stated forcefully that there had been no fewer than five judicial trials on the Bologna massacre, at which a vast mass of judicial material had been analysed. Various attempts had been made to sabotage the trials, with a number of false trails deliberately set up by the intelligence services and the armed forces, aimed at directing investigations abroad, towards the Libyans, the Palestinians or indeed various European terrorists. However, they all came to nothing, so much so that Mambro and Fioravanti were found guilty by the Supreme Court, the Court of Cassation, deliberating in plenary session in 1995.

Bolognesi was adamant that the two neofascists had not acted alone, since behind the massacre was the Masonic Lodge P2, a real occult power in Italy. This organisation had a clear political plan, as set out in the documents found after its discovery in 1981, and it also represented the interests of the USA. In his view, the latest attempts to reopen the case and to follow an international trail must be seen in the light of the older episodes of obstruction of justice; therefore as the last in a long series of *depistaggi* designed to create confusion. This was especially the case since Alleanza Nazionale and Forza Italia were together in government, and had a shared interest in erasing the role of both neofascism and the occult forces behind it, thereby turning Mambro and Fioravanti into innocent people unjustly persecuted by the magistrates.

Bolognesi was especially enraged by what he considered an unjustified campaign to turn the terrorists into victims while the real victims of the massacres were ignored by the state. This campaign brought together the right and a 'self-appointed' left which had fallen into the trap of harbouring a kind of romanticist belief in the innocence of those who were presumed terrorists, even when found guilty by the Courts. In his view, neither Mambro nor Fioravanti had told the truth regarding their role in the Bologna massacre (or indeed about what they knew in relation to the forces behind it), probably because they feared for their lives. Most terrorists had not told the whole truth for the same reasons, which gave the lie to their claimed status of victimhood and made it impossible to talk of reconciliation or forgiveness. As for the real victims of the massacres, it was only in 1980 that the state had approved a law introducing compensation for the victims, with a lump sum paid to the relatives of those who had lost their lives or who had survived but suffered from a high degree of disability. This had been followed by further laws, in 1990, 1998 and 2004. Despite this, throughout the years the state had treated the real victims of terrorism worse than the terrorists themselves, as bothersome beggars as opposed to claimants of justice, without any proper acknowledgement of their status as victims.

Milani's interpretation is largely in line with Pellegrino's, which in his view has had the great merit of locating the Italian political situation within the wider international dimension, within the conflict that raged not only between East and West in the context of the Cold War, but also North and South, including the Mediterranean. Starting with the Italian situation, the Strategy of Tension must be located in a phase which marked a transition to centre-left coalition governments, which in some political quarters was interpreted as a Trojan horse for letting the communists into power. Christian Democracy was divided between two wings and two strategies, the one favouring an institutional turn to the right, the other looking for an understanding with the parties of the left. At an international level, the division of Europe as sanctioned at Yalta had to be respected within as well as between countries, which meant that in Italy any rapprochement with the Communist Party had to be resisted. It was in this context that Italian neofascism was able to find a new political role. It was itself divided between an institutional wing (the MSI) and a radical wing, which at first tended to have conflictual relations, but later established increasingly close links (as witnessed by Rauti's reentry in the MSI in 1969). The Strategy of Tension was devised in 1965 at the famous meeting organised by the Istituto Pollio, after which date various bomb attacks were carried out in Italy. This was a putschist strategy inspired by anti-communism, culminating in the December 1969 bomb attacks.

Later terrorist attacks, however, were most probably inspired by a different logic, since by the early 1970s the putschist line had lost credibility and a search for a rapprochement between the DC and the PCI had started. These years marked the replacement of Miceli with Maletti at the SID, a series of arrests of extreme-right activists and the collapse of authoritarian regimes in southern Europe. The international climate should also be taken into consideration since, according to Milani, both the USA and the USSR were strongly opposed to any political understanding between the DC and the PCI and to the 'Historic Compromise' developed in the 1970s. In this context, the 1974 massacre at Brescia should therefore be interpreted as an attempt to put a stop to the dialogue between these two mass parties, rather than an attempt to implement a coup d'état in Italy. Milani stressed the fact that the Brescia massacre was the most politicised of all the bombing attacks, since the explosion took place during a mass democratic and anti-fascist rally. The other attacks, by contrast, had targeted civilians at random, in public places such as a bank or a train. Hence the symbolic meaning of the Brescia massacre is quite explicit.

What was extraordinary at the time – but tends to be ignored in most reconstructions – was the popular response to the attack, which 'blocked any possible violent response.' Local factories were occupied and guarded, as was the square where the bomb had exploded, and during the funeral ceremonies responsibility for law and order fell upon the people, while the police force was kept out. In short, there was a 'subversive' movement of a unique kind, in which the people both defended and challenged the state authorities. It was like saying: 'we denounce your responsibilities yet we also defend the institutions of the state beyond your role through our mass participation.' While there had been an incredible response to the Piazza Fontana massacre, which brought 100,000 people to the streets, thereby allowing the moderate wing of Christian Democracy to reject the putschist line, at Brescia the response exceeded all expectations, with three days of general strike and a democratic takeover of the institutions. It was this response, according to Milani, which made it clear that any attempt to utilise a bombing campaign in order to force the political situation in Italy would have resulted in a bloody and widespread civil war.

Milani concluded that in his view 'the right cannot ignore these facts which can be attributed to its violent history. This has been proved. The investigations into the Brescia massacre are taking place within this framework. The defendants are Zorzi and Maggi of Ordine Nuovo and Rognoni of La Fenice.' However, he was sceptical regarding the latest trial, because too many people were still refusing to reveal what they knew.

## Vinciguerra's reconstruction

Vinciguerra's reconstruction of *stragismo* and the Strategy of Tension is derived in large part from his own experiences as an extreme-right activist, both as a member of Ordine Nuovo and as an exile in Francoist Spain, where he met and became a friend of Stefano Delle Chiaie. It is also based upon his own experience as an object of a case of *depistaggio* on the part of the armed forces, a defendant in the trial on the Peteano attack, and a witness to prosecuting magistrates, one of whom, Felice Casson, he subsequently denounced as someone who was more interested in defending the state and its institutions than in disclosing the truth. Vinciguerra's positioning is therefore anomalous in respect to the others analysed in this chapter as well as defiant vis-à-vis his fascist ideals.

In an early book, published in 1989, Vinciguerra put forward his explanation for the Strategy of Tension, which is reminiscent of the articles which appeared in the *Observer* in December 1969. He defined the strategy as a defensive one against the communist threat in Italy. It was devised and justified at the meeting organised in Rome by the Istituto Pollio, where it was agreed that the communist threat could not be contained through an open coup d'état or by outlawing the Communist Party. Rather, what was needed was to push the communists towards forms of political extremism, which would have justified the state suspending constitutional rights and introducing emergency measures against the 'subversive' political forces of the left (Vinciguerra 1989: 152–55). This strategy could be carried out both through promoting and facilitating extreme-left groups and activities, and through infiltrating anarchist and Maoist groups, or indeed masquerading as leftist elements. The strategy was masterminded by the Americans in collaboration with the armed forces and with the subordinate participation of the neofascists.

In this context, Ordine Nuovo was simply a 'parallel organisation' working for American and Italian military forces (ibid.: 167–68), although this was not known to the great majority of its members (including himself). An accurate definition of the goal pursued by the Strategy of Tension would therefore be that of 'destabilising in order to stabilise' the political system, that is to say, the same political system that was already governing the country (ibid.: 169–70). In other words, there was never a serious risk of a coup d'état, for the simple reason that the neofascists were never in a position to take power away from Christian Democracy. It is true, however, that the neofascists were subordinate allies of the governing forces and for a time protected as such. This lasted until it was decided that a strategy of fighting all forms of extremism, from the left and from the right, was better suited to the Italian situation, at which point a 'fascist threat' was invoked.

In a second book, published in 1993, Vinciguerra focused upon the Peteano trial, with its various episodes of obstruction of justice, and on Judge Casson's investigations. In this book, he argued that the magistrate had failed to pursue the representatives of the Italian state for their role in *stragismo* and had opted instead for a distorted version of the Strategy of Tension. Specifically, Vinciguerra argued that there were three main interpretations of this strategy. The first, supported by Casson and by the communists, started from the presupposition that the strategy had been masterminded by 'occult forces', primarily the Masonic Lodge P2, in connivance with disloyal officers in the armed forces and 'deviated' secret services, as well as a mass of fascists and Nazis who had succeeded in infiltrating democratic institutions after the war. Within this reconstruction, the various episodes of *depistaggio*, including the one brought to light in relation to Peteano, can be explained through the activities of these occult forces and their accomplices in state institutions. The second interpretation, supported by ex-Prime Minister Giulio Andreotti, focused upon the *depistaggio* itself, justifying it in view of the need, for security reasons, not to expose the existence of 'stay behind nets' in Western Europe, known in Italy as Gladio. According to Andreotti, Cossiga and others, these covert armed networks, set up in various European countries with British help in the 1950s, had nothing to do with the Strategy of Tension but were vital for the defence of Western Europe from external aggressors. In short, the Italian state was guilty of partially obstructing the course of justice but only in the name of the superior interests of the nation, not because it had connived with the *stragisti*. The third interpretation, supported by Vinciguerra himself, explained the *depistaggio* in terms of the necessity of defending a state secret, which was not the existence of Gladio, but the Strategy of Tension itself, as a strategy devised and carried out by 'legitimate' (as opposed to 'deviate') military and intelligence state forces, under instruction from the political leaders of the country (Vinciguerra: 316–17).

Vinciguerra's third book, published in 2000, represented his farewell to his ex-comrades, whom he had come to view as traitors, whichever specific group they had belonged to. By then, he had also become convinced that most neofascists were in fact *stragisti*. In his words: 'You, comrades, handed over neofascism to the winners of the Second World War, to those who had defeated us. And yours, comrades, is called betrayal, conscious and deliberate' (Vinciguerra 2000: 141). Vinciguerra considers all neofascist groups to have been seriously implicated, under the umbrella of the MSI, including the second-generation groups of the so-called 'armed spontaneity' such as the NAR led by Fioravanti. They were all equally to blame: 'the only difference between you all – members of the MSI, Ordine Nuovo, Avanguardia Nazionale, "spontaneous" groups – lay in the state apparatus which used and directed you' (ibid.: 149).

It is in this context that Vinciguerra locates his decision to confess to the Peteano attack. The attack itself was directed against the state, for its grave responsibilities in *stragismo*. His 'confession' had also targeted the state. In an interview with Gigi Marcucci and Paola Minoliti, held in the Opera prison on 8 July 2000, Vinciguerra explained that his aim had been to 'put the state on trial.' Vinciguerra provided his own interpretation of his trial: 'I put the State on trial. I was not on trial. I did not consider myself the accused. Because for the first time and also the last, I believe, one could see an accused man who had to fight against everybody in order to assert his responsibility, when it would have been sufficient to keep quiet in order to be found not guilty' (Marcucci and Minoliti, 2000). However, the refusal on the part of the magistrates to pursue the truth and their determination to cover up for the state had prevented the latter from being fully exposed for its role in the Strategy of Tension. Vinciguerra sees himself as one of the few who continue to pursue the truth, in compensation to the victims of his own act of violence and to all those who died for the Strategy of Tension: 'I will continue to act in such a way that the death of so many people, from both sides, including the Peteano *Carabinieri*, will not continue to be in vain' (1989: 137).

## Conclusion

Of all the interpretations outlined in this chapter, there is not a single one which does not see the neofascists in the role of culprits as regards the bomb attacks which took place in Italy from 1969 to the mid-1970s. The majority also seem to agree that the neofascists acted at first as part of a wider coalition of forces intent on forcing some kind of institutional and constitutional change in the country, possibly even a coup d'état, while later they were discharged by their allies and acted out of revenge. However, interpretations differ as concerns the later massacres, especially the Bologna station attack, or regarding the nature and role of the forces which aided and protected the neofascists and most probably also masterminded the so-called Strategy of Tension. The various reconstructions also differ in terms of apportioning blame.

At one end of the spectrum we find Pellegrino's account, which tends to underplay the role of the Italian political elites – indeed these are praised for their restraint and foresight in critical times – and magnify the responsibility of both international actors and the neofascist activists themselves. This account can probably be best explained in the light of his attempt, as Head of the Parliamentary 'Commission on the Massacres', to promote a reconciliation process between the various political forces, as discussed in Part II. At the opposite end there is the account put forward by Vinciguerra, who put the blame squarely on the Italian (as well as American) establishment, without giving credence to the existence of mysterious forces acting in the dark, which were no more than a 'shield' invented to create a diversion from the 'real' state secret. He also blames the whole of Italian neofascism, whether in its parliamentary or radical guise. A third strand is that put forward by Bolognesi, which puts the occult forces, starting with the infamous P2, back on central stage, and for this reason sees most of the massacres, including the later ones such as Bologna, as masterminded by this organisation.

In between, there is a whole array of more or less nuanced reconstructions, which tend to distinguish between different state structures and political forces, as well as between different neofascist groups. As regards the former, the emphasis is placed on the Social Democratic Party, as well as the conservative wing of Christian Democracy, and on 'sections' of the armed forces and the intelligence services. As regards the latter, the role of the MSI in *stragismo* and the Strategy of Tension is reduced to that of a lesser player compared to the more radical neofascist organisations. These, in turn, are considered separately in some reconstructions – so much so that, in Provvisionato's version, the perpetrators of the massacre are reduced to roughly fifty individuals, albeit individuals able to enjoy some sympathy and support among the radical right. In any case, even Provvisionato's interpretation, which severely restricts the blame for the massacres to a small circle of activists, does not deny the fascist character of the culprits.

In conclusion, while all the main interpretations which take into account the judicial findings unanimously acknowledge that the neofascists were the perpetrators of the massacres, not all appear to see them as an indifferentiated body which is collectively to blame. Ironically, it is an ex-member of a neofascist group who blames Italian neofascism as a whole for having consciously betrayed its fascist roots and deceived so many young and naïve 'true believers'. It would be possible to envisage that a comparable array of interpretations characterise the Italian neo- and postfascist right today in relation to *stragismo* and the Strategy of Tension. Indeed, Provvisionato was of the opinion that there would be a clear-cut division between the more radical and the postfascist right, as well as between different generations, concerning their judgement of Italian neofascism. Giannuli, by contrast, was convinced that both neo- and postfascists were primarily concerned with opposing a uniform counter-truth to the judicial truth, or, alternatively, with countering the above interpretations with a plurality of others where the culprits originated from all sources but neofascism. As it turned out, Giannuli's prediction proved fairly accurate.

Despite the many openings provided by some of the interpretations examined in this chapter for a version of events which might find an echo on the right, there was a total rejection of all judicial findings among them. Rather than acknowledging the role of neofascist activists as perpetrators of many massacres, while also attempting to safeguard the reputation of the MSI and possibly even that of second-generation extreme-right groups, the right excluded the involvement in *stragismo* of any neofascist group or indeed any individual activist, other than that of unidentified and mysterious 'infiltrators'. In short, the right erected a clear barrier between their own narratives of the past and all the reconstructions outlined above, preventing any crossovers. The reasons for and implications of their uncompromising stance – defined as the 'politics of nonreconciliation' – are discussed in Part II.

# Conclusion to Part I

As analysed in Chapters 2 and 3, the judicial investigations and trials on the massacres have succeeded in uncovering much vital information regarding the nature and scope of the Strategy of Tension and the role played by various protagonists, above all the groups of the radical right. However, it is also the case that even the latest trials have largely failed to bring the culprits to justice, due mainly to the amount of time that has elapsed since the crimes themselves. Indeed, given that this was most probably one of the goals of the various episodes of obstruction of justice carried out by state institutions, it must be said that it has been fulfilled. One must also add that many of the protagonists continue to remain reticent, and that many potential witnesses continue to report the existence of a climate of intimidation and fear, which helps to ensure that only very few are prepared to come forward. According to historian Aldo Giannuli, researcher for Milan prosecutor Salvini and consultant to the Parliamentary Commission on the Failed Identification of the Authors of Terrorist Massacres, 'when you finally reach a verdict after thirty years the witnesses are dead or doddering, the evidence has disappeared and in the end you can always find a jury which is willing to acquit everyone' (interview with the author, 24 October 2005).

The criminal trials have also failed to unearth a comprehensively plausible truth in relation to *stragismo* and the Strategy of Tension, as evidenced by the continuing existence of a variety of interpretations based on the trial findings, as examined in Chapter 4. A general consensus regarding the full involvement of extreme-right groups, notably Ordine Nuovo, gradually gives way to diverse hypotheses concerning the role of state institutions and political actors, as well as international forces. According to Giannuli and Salvini himself, the shortcomings of the criminal justice process in this respect can be attributed at least in part to divisions within the judiciary. Indeed, Giannuli expressed the drastic view that 'the truth regarding the *stragi* was not part of the plans of the Italian judiciary'. This is not to say that individual magistrates were not committed to finding the culprits, but that the judiciary was not united in this, particularly since the police and the *Carabinieri* were themselves involved:

It is not a coincidence that in the trials concerning left-wing terrorism you have a very high percentage of convictions, in those regarding right-wing terrorism you have a much reduced percentage, and if you look carefully you find that those convicted belonged to the NAR not to ON and AN, and the sentences referred to individual murders not the massacres, for where there is an involvement of institutional bodies there is nothing doing. (Lack of) evidence does not come into it. (Interview with the author, 24 October 2005)

This raises a more general question regarding the relationship between truth and justice, and between 'retributive' and 'restorative' justice, particularly in countries which have experienced a violent political conflict. There seems to be a general agreement among experts that the full disclosure of the truth is a vital part of the process of achieving justice for past wrongdoings, while there is a fierce controversy raging around the merits and demerits of retributive versus restorative justice.

The former refers to criminal law proceedings and court trials, whereby the perpetrators are made accountable for their past actions and are punished in accordance. As Llewellyn and Howse (1999) pointed out, the advocates of criminal prosecutions stress the importance of trials to establish the supremacy of the rule of law, to ensure individual, not simply collective, responsibility for past crimes, to allow the full disclosure of the truth, to give victims redress for the harm they suffered. Others add the need to counter a culture of impunity and to instil trust in the (new) legal and political system.

Restorative justice, by contrast, refers to alternative processes of justice which typically bring together all stakeholders and focus on truth telling, reconciliation and healing. A typical example is that of the Commission of Truth and Reconciliation in South Africa, set up in 1995, which promoted the coming together of both perpetrators and victims of the apartheid regime, whereby the perpetrators confessed to their crimes in exchange for a wide amnesty and for the forgiveness of their victims. There are many advocates for this kind of justice, which is seen to promote peace and reconciliation and a general coming to terms with a divided past by all participants to a conflict. Indeed, there has been a proliferation of this type of commission in many countries emerging from violent conflicts or dictatorial regimes.

The debate over these two types of justice appears to have two main dimensions: a practical dimension and a moral one. Concerning the moral dimension, there are many who voice deep concern for what is seen as replacing the rule of law and the principle of individual responsibility and accountability with vague notions of 'reconciliation', 'forgiveness' and 'healing'. Studies of the South African experience, as well as the experiences of post-Cold War countries, have brought to light divergent opinions over the morality of restorative justice, particularly in relation to the victims (James and De Vijver 2000; Rotberg and Thompson 2000; Villa-Vicencio and Verwoerd 2000; Wilson 2003; Gibson 2004, 2005). As regards the practical dimension, the advocates of restorative justice emphasise the excessive length and costs of criminal proceedings, the difficulty of bringing the culprits to justice, especially in a climate where connivances and biases can influence court proceedings, or indeed when suspected perpetrators are still in positions of power. In this context, a restorative justice approach can be more successful in promoting the full disclosure of the truth and the restoration of state legitimacy.

Much of the controversy over the two types of justice involves having to choose between one or the other. However, some have argued that they should be considered complementary approaches (Hayner 2001; Minow 2000). Minow (2000: 238), in particular, has written about the limitations of both approaches, stressing, specifically in the case of state-sponsored political violence, the inability of many trials to bring to light the complicities and responsibilities of the wider institutional and political structures which made the crimes possible, because an emphasis on individual culprits often leaves these structures untouched. She argued for truth and reconciliation commissions working to complement the achievements of criminal trials, while recognising that even implementing a variety of approaches may fall short of a society's needs, since 'no response to mass atrocity is adequate' (ibid.: 235).

In the Italian case, it can be argued that the limits of the criminal justice process with regards to political and, most likely in the case of *stragismo*, state-sponsored violence, are very much in evidence. It is impossible to say whether more could have been achieved if the criminal process, at some stage after the end of the Cold War, had been discarded in favour of some kind of restorative justice approach. What does seem apparent is that criminal law proceedings have run their course and have gone as far as they possibly could as regards identifying the culprits, bringing them to justice, and uncovering the truth. The only way forward therefore seems to rest with novel approaches to truth and 'justice' that are external to the trials.

It is also important to establish how the victims themselves weigh the truth in relation to justice in the Italian case. Bolognesi, for example, was clearly not prepared to engage in a process of reconciliation or indeed forgiveness which did not have as a precondition a full engagement in truth telling on the part of the culprits. The latter had to take precedence over the former. Milani, on the other hand, was more open to various possibilities. This was partly because, while Bolognesi was convinced that at least some of the culprits for the Bologna massacre had been secured to justice, Milani faced a situation in which the perpetrators of the Brescia massacre remained officially unknown. In this context, he seemed to accept the need for a 'political truth' alongside the truth uncovered by the trials. In his words: 'The real state secret in Italy is that many know the truth but do not tell, even at very high levels. Not so much because they gave the orders [for the massacres] but because there were connivances, cover-ups.' In his view, the main limit of the lack of a full judicial truth, and of the ambiguous formula of acquittance applied to many defendants by the Courts, was precisely the persistence of an attitude of denial among many people for political reasons. Thus the culprits became alternatively extreme-right or extreme-left activists, according to the political affiliation of the commentators. This situation, in his view, necessitated an end to prioritising the 'reason of state'. Parallel to this, there was a need, for the sake of democracy, to 'invent something' that made it possible for people to tell the truth. Milani argued forcefully that the strength of any democratic system was based on truth, whereas in Italy the knowledge that the opposite was the case determined continuing mistrust in the institutions of the state.

It is in this context that Part II takes into consideration, within the framework of the literature on truth telling and national reconciliation, whether in Italy there have been any steps in this direction, and whether the political actors that have emerged from the collapse of the First Republic and of the old ideologies, have themselves attempted to contribute to the emergence of the truth through a critical reappraisal of the past. One of the ways, for example, in which the criminal findings can be reinforced and justice supported, thereby also restoring the legitimacy of the state, is through a wide acknowledgment of the truth the trials have uncovered so far, ideally by complementing it with missing 'bits of truth' concerning the role of political organisations and state institutions. This is especially the case for those parties which are the heirs of Italian neofascism, and above all those, like Alleanza Nazionale, which have officially renounced and even condemned their fascist past. As we shall see, this scenario is far removed from reality. The limitations of the criminal trials almost pale into insignificance when compared to the total absence of any meaningful process of national reconciliation, with the result that, among the heirs of neofascism, the criminal justice findings are rejected en bloc, the presumed culprits are turned into victims, the victims of the massacres are forgotten or relegated to a marginal position and the longstanding enemies of neofascism are turned into culprits. Their attitude challenges the rule of law and raises troubling questions concerning the value of pursuing criminal justice for politically inspired crimes through the Courts when there is no recognition of the legitimacy of their findings among political parties pledging allegiance to democratic principles and commanding the support of a considerable sector of the electorate and public opinion.

# Part II

## Victims? The Truth According to the Neo- and Postfascist Right

# Introduction to Part II

As we saw in Part I, the judicial process has only been partially able to establish the truth concerning *stragismo* and to ensure that the culprits be prosecuted and punished. It appears that retributive justice has now run its course, given the time elapsed since the crimes and the difficulty of finding reliable witnesses who are still alive and capable of testifying. This leaves open the question of whether a parallel process of truth telling and reconciliation has taken place in the country, with a view to complementing retributive justice with a form of restorative justice, as promoted in various countries experiencing a transition to democracy after going through a bloody conflict and/or an authoritarian regime. Restorative justice, as we saw, refers to a process in which the emphasis is on uncovering the truth about past crimes, rather than on securing justice through the Courts. Indeed, at times the pursuit of criminal justice is consciously abandoned in favour of truth revealing. Truth, in turn, is seen as leading to reconciliation. Conversely, there can be no lasting reconciliation without truth: 'Until people know where responsibility lies for atrocities committed and are given information such as the location of missed loved ones, obstacles to reconciliation will remain' (Borris 2002: 168). This is a highly controversial and sensitive issue, yet many countries throughout the world which were experiencing a transition to democracy after the end of the Cold War had recourse to different combinations of retributive and restorative justice, often involving Truth Commissions. According to Wilson (2003: 369), 'roughly 20 such commissions … were established between the 1970s and the present day, with the majority (15) established in the latter years of the Cold War (1974–1994).'

In Italy, since the end of the Cold War, there has not been a comparable process of truth telling and national reconciliation; only a few abortive steps were taken in that direction, for a number of reasons. To start with, the anomalous character of the political conflict during the period of the Cold War (in between a fully blown-out and a 'congealed' conflict), the similarly anomalous character of the fall of the First Republic and the transition to a Second Republic (in between an in-depth process of renewal of a static model of democracy and a simple institutional readjustment), and the unclear link between the two sets of events (the violent conflict had ended well before the end of the First Republic), contributed to relegating the question of national reconciliation well down the list of priorities of the new political parties that emerged out of the collapse of the old political system. Once the Communist Party had transformed itself into the Democratic Party of the Left (PDS), and the Movimento Sociale Italiano had become Alleanza Nazionale, they acquired democratic credentials, even though doubts were expressed in relation to the latter (Ignazi 1994; Tarchi 1997; Chiarini and Maraffi 2001). Each of these two parties was able to take part in government, the PDS in 1996–2001, the Alleanza Nazionale in 1994 and again in 2001–2006. Thanks in no small part to their political 'unfreezing', Italy for the first time witnessed an alternation of parties in government, which seemed to indicate that the transition from a consensual to a competitive model of democracy had been fully completed.

## Persisting divisions

Despite this achievement, according to many commentators, the country remained deeply divided socially, politically and ideologically. At first, however, it was the issue of persistent divisions of a territorial nature that rang alarm bells, due to the unexpected rise of the regionalist and secessionist Northern League Party (Biorcio 1997; Cartocci 1991, 1994; Cento Bull 1992, 1993; Curi 1997; Diamanti 1993, 1996; Mingione 1993; Moioli 1990; Rumiz 1997; Rusconi 1993; Trigilia 1994). Later, it was the figure of Berlusconi, with his shady past, his conflicts of interest, his suspected involvement in corrupt dealings and his aggressive personality, which was identified as undoubtedly contributing to the persistence and indeed revival of deep political fractures and ideological confrontations (Andrews 2005; Bocca 2005; Colombo and Padellaro 2002; Ginsborg 2003, 2005; Lane 2005; Salerno 2006; Travaglio 2004; Travaglio and Gomez 2003; Veltri and Travaglio 2001). Given that both the League and Berlusconi represented new phenomena, they did not seem to require the country to confront its past in order to achieve more stable and less conflictual political relations.

In the meantime, however, the old divisions along the lines of fascism/anti-fascism and communism/anti-communism also resurfaced and the question of the need for national reconciliation and of how best to promote it started to be addressed. Nevertheless, this debate took place primarily in relation to the 1943–45 civil war, which, given the time scale involved, did not appear to warrant a protracted process of national reconciliation or indeed the establishment of a Commission for Truth and Reconciliation along the lines of the South African one. The process of historical revisionism with regards to anti-fascism and the 1943–45 Resistance movement goes back to the late 1980s, frequently involving non- and anti-fascist authors. In 1986, anti-fascist historian Nicola Gallerano published an essay in which he critically reconsidered the 'hegemonic anti-fascist narrative', focusing upon its growing crisis of legitimation. In 1988, right-leaning but non fascist historian Renzo De Felice (who in the 1970s had caused a full-scale controversy for emphasising, in one of his volumes on the history of fascism, the popular nature of the regime and the weakness of all opposition movements and parties), publicly proclaimed that anti-fascism should no longer be considered the founding myth of the Italian Republic, as it was both divisive and played into the hands of the communists. In 1991, anti-fascist historian Claudio Pavone published a widely praised scholarly history of the 1943–45 conflict, to which he applied the concept of a civil war, thereby opening space for consideration of the role and motivations of the losers, that is to say, those who had fought on the side of the Republic of Salò, while by no means establishing an equivalence between the two sides, least of all in moral terms.

After the crisis of the First Republic in the early 1990s, a flood of new studies and publications reopened the issue, this time deliberately blurring the difference between the participants in the 1943–45 civil war. In 1995, De Felice published a new book, again putting forward an uncompromising critique of the Resistance and anti-fascism, as well as identifying a fatal date for Italy in 8 September 1943, the day when the Italian government's armistice with the Allies was made public and national unity and identity were dealt an irrevocable blow (De Felice 1995; Bosworth 1998: 17–20). The same theme was re-presented and reelaborated by the historian Galli della Loggia the following year (1996). Personal memoirs by neofascist protagonists of the 1943–45 civil war were also widely read, especially Mazzantini's second autobiographical account of his role in the Italian Social Republic (RSI), dedicated to both the partisans who died for 'freedom' and the combatants for the RSI, who died for 'honour' (1995). Various atrocities committed by the partisans, but withheld from public debate, were reconstructed and discussed. Particular attention, often in a deliberately polemical manner, was paid to the so-called *foibe*, with reference to the massacre of Italians in the north eastern regions occupied by Yugoslav partisans (Spazzali 1990; Cernigoi 1997; Valdevit 1997; Salimbeni 1998; Papo De Montona 1999). By contrast, important studies on the Italian Social Republic and German occupation seemed to attract less public attention (Klinkhammer 1993; Battini and Pezzino 1997; Gagliani 1999; Ganapini 1999; Pezzino 2001).

This type of historical revisionism tended to be explicitly political, the more so when Berlusconi formed Forza Italia and set himself the task of building an effective coalition of the right with the inclusion of the neo- and postfascists. At one level, given that both the ex-fascists and the ex-communists were eager to establish their democratic credentials, historical revisionism appeared to be linked to a perceived need for reconciliation, through acknowledging one's own past responsibilities. Thus a few positive gestures were made from each side, officially to mark a rapprochement between former enemies. Among these gestures was the unreserved condemnation of fascism on the part of Alleanza Nazionale's leader and Deputy Prime Minister Gianfranco Fini in November 2003, during a trip to Israel, and the approval of a parliamentary law in March 2004, with the votes of the postcommunist PDS, which established a Day of Memory (*Giorno del Ricordo in Memoria degli Esuli e Vittime delle Foibe*) for the Italian civilian victims of Yugoslav partisans in 1943–45. The latter event, to which various ex-Communist Party leaders had paved the way with official declarations of acknowledgement of wrongdoing by their own side during the war, was hailed as 'the historical moment of reconciliation, of national pacification', by Alleanza Nazionale deputy

Mirko Tremaglia (INFORM, 31, 12 February 2004). The following year, on the day of remembrance itself, Gianfranco Fini made a speech in Trieste and declared that: 'We have started the road towards reconciliation and truth. We must not oppose truth to truth. There is only one truth which, once established, will allow us rapidly to move on'. (*Corriere della Sera*, 11 February 2005)

Despite these gestures, 'reconciliation' soon turned sour, as it appeared to many to have taken on the meaning of attributing equal moral standing to both sides of the 1943–45 civil war and/or promoting a general collective 'amnesia' as regards the past. An attempt on the part of the Berlusconi government to approve a bill granting recognition as legitimate combatants to those who fought for the Republic of Salò, confirmed many people's worst fears. Claudio Pavone spoke for many when he stated that the political right 'say they want pacification whereas the sentiment that inspires them is revenge.' He added that 'the signatories to the bill seem to subscribe to the thesis put forward by the extremists of the MSI. By their reasoning, the real Resistance in Italy in those years was carried out by the Republic of Salò, born out of a healthy rebellion against the traitors of 8 September' (*La Repubblica*, 18 February 2005). The bill was withdrawn in January 2006 in the face of widespread opposition and condemnation.

Rather than moving towards reconciliation, many acts of the Berlusconi government were judged to constitute a deliberate strategy to delegitimate and devalue anti-fascism (Focardi 2005a, 2005b; Giustolisi 2004; Luzzatto 2004; Mammone 2006; Santomassimo 2004). In the words of Focardi (2005b), 'in place of the memory of the Resistance there was an attempt to promote a "reconciled" national memory based on the presumed equal historical and moral dignity of fascists and antifascists. It is a matter of a hard struggle for cultural hegemony, which is fought on the contested terrain of historical memory.' In this context, the books by journalist Giampaolo Pansa (2003, 2005), on the killings of fascists by communist partisans after the war were heavily criticised by many left commentators for their a-critical stance in relation to the 1943–45 civil war. A book by anti-fascist historian Roberto Vivarelli (2000) on his personal experience as a combatant for the Italian Social Republic also proved controversial and was seen as another attempt to provide justifications for those who fought 'on the wrong side'. By contrast, journalist Paolo Mieli openly defended the right to historical revisionism in a volume published in 2001, which itself caused a lively debate. The 'war of memory', appeared to have taken central stage in political and scholarly debates (Ventrone 2006).

Not surprisingly, given the prevailing climate and the controversies raging over the 1943–45 civil war, the few voices raised by those who hoped for the creation of a 'Commission for Truth and Reconciliation' in Italy, along the lines of the one in South Africa, in order to achieve reconciliation for the post-1969 conflict, did not go very far. The proposal was initially put forward by Alleanza Nazionale Senator Alfredo Mantica (2001) in the *Commissione stragi* ('Commission on the Massacres') and was supported by Giovanni Pellegrino, Chair of the Commission between 1994 and 2001. Given his interpretation of the period of the Cold War in terms of a 'creeping civil war' whose legacy is still visible today, Pellegrino was one of the main proponents of the need for a process of 'Truth and Reconciliation', to be achieved through a 'shared memory' of the past, including the frank acknowledgement, on the part of the different political forces, of their own roles and mistakes during the period of the Cold War. 'Reconciliation', in his view, would also necessitate an end to any attempts to achieve justice through judicial trials, since justice presupposes getting to know the truth, and the judiciary does not represent the best way to arrive at the truth. In any case, 'judicial truth and historical truth often do not coincide' (Fasanella and Pellegrino, 2005: 155).

It is in this context that Pellegrino's role as President of the *Commissione stragi* can be properly understood, as, in the absence of a process comparable to the one carried out in South Africa and in other countries torn by fratricidal conflicts, he used his chairmanship to steer the Commission towards acting almost as surrogate for a 'Truth and Reconciliation' Commission. Originally set up by Law No. 172, on 17 May 1988, the Commission was chaired first by Senator Libero Gualtieri, of the Republican Party, and later, from 1994, by Senator Giovanni Pellegrino, of the Left Democrats. The Commission was given three main tasks: to assess the results achieved by the fight against terrorism in Italy; to investigate the reasons which had prevented the identification of those responsible for massacres and other acts of subversion since 1969; to assess new evidence in order to supplement the knowledge reached by the Commission of Inquiry into the massacre of Via Fani and the murder of Aldo Moro, which had been set up with Law No. 597 on 23 November 1979. According to D'Agnelli (2003), the two Chairmen marked two different phases in the work of the Commission. During Gualtieri's chairmanship, the main aim was to gather new information in relation to specific events with the help of technical experts, primarily magistrates, judges and police officers. By contrast, during Pellegrino's chairmanship, the aim was 'the construction of a comprehensive historical-political judgement' (ibid.: 3), and this was reflected in the choice of the collaborators, primarily historians and journalists, often chosen 'more for political reasons than for real research needs' (2003: 4). D'Agnelli remarked that parliamentary commissions of inquiry tend to aim at reaching a shared political and cultural judgement on recent historical events, and that this aim did appear achievable in the early years of Pellegrino's chairmanship, in a climate strongly conditioned by the fall of the Berlin Wall and the end of the ideological divide. The personality of the Chair also seemed to match the new goals of the Commission, since Pellegrino's political career was relatively recent and he had a reputation for speaking his own mind rather than adhering to the party line (ibid.: 3).

Pellegrino himself was convinced that within the Commission, which was not a judicial body and did not carry out the role of public prosecutor, the different political representatives could and should have worked together to overcome past divisions and promote a process of national reconciliation, through mutual recognition and a shared memory. His declared intention was to convince all members of the Commission to produce a final unitary report which would help the country come to terms with its past and heal still-open wounds. To this end, Pellegrino prepared a text as a basis for a unitary report (Commissione parlamentare d'inchiesta sul terrorismo in Italia e sulle cause della mancata individuazione dei responsabili delle stragi, *Proposta di Relazione Pellegrino*: 1996). However, by the year 2000 it had become clear that the divisions within the Commission would not allow such an outcome (Commissione parlamentare d'inchiesta sul terrorismo in Italia e sulle cause della mancata individuazione dei responsabili delle stragi, *Settima relazione semestrale sullo stato dei lavori*: 2000). Pellegrino himself had to acknowledge the complete failure of his aims; the Commission terminated its work in 2001, producing eighteen separate reports. In his own summing up of the situation, Pellegrino stated that the lack of consensus within the Commission reflected both the deep divisions between the political elites, as witnessed in the Italian Parliament, and the continuing fractures within the country at large. A further exacerbating factor was the imminence of the general elections (due the same year), which led the political parties to emphasise their distinctive identities and their differences. In this context, it had been illusory to assume that there could have been mutual reconciliation and an overcoming of bitter divisions (Commissione parlamentare d'inchiesta sul terrorismo in Italia e sulle cause della mancata individuazione dei responsabili delle stragi, 78th session, 22 March 2001). D'Agnelli (2003) also argued that the primacy of politics within the Commission, which in the early 1990s had appeared conducive to a shared judgement of the past, later determined the impossibility of an internal agreement, especially in the context of pressing electoral deadlines and a general failure by the political parties to reach an overarching consensus over institutional reforms.

While for Pellegrino the main obstacle to reconciliation was represented by party political interests and partisanship, his emphasis on a 'shared memory' of the past in turn turned out to be very controversial and was rejected by many historians, for whom the concept itself was highly problematic. Luzzatto (2004) interpreted their disquiet when he proudly reaffirmed the merits of a 'divided memory', which a common history cannot and should not suppress. Many also reacted negatively to the suggestion that 'justice' could be traded in exchange for 'truth', which appeared as both cynical and immoral, particularly from the point of view of the victims of the massacres.

Matters worsened considerably after the *Commissione stragi* was replaced, in 2002, by the Mitrokhin Commission, which examined the files concerning Italy brought to the UK by former KGB archivist Vasilif Mitrokhin, and subsequently made available to the Italian government. The new Commission, chaired by Forza Italia Senator Paolo Guzzanti, was set up by Prime Minister Silvio Berlusconi to investigate the links between the KGB and representatives of the left parties during the period of the Cold War. The new Commission soon became extremely controversial, under accusations that it was being used as a political instrument in order to discredit the leaders of the left, as opposed to ascertaining historical facts. At any rate, the Commission failed to produce any real evidence incriminating prominent leaders of the centre-left coalition. However, there are some who believe that the most compromising material may have been the object of political negotiations between left and right, which might explain the fact that the files examined by the Commission were never made public. In April 2006, thirty-four established Italian historians reacted to this situation by publicly asking for the files to be made accessible, in the name of 'ascertaining the truth concerning the past of the nation'. One of these, Salvatore Sechi, even expressed the opinion that the left parties were more interested in keeping alive the idea of 'political mysteries' than in providing the necessary evidence to solve them (Sechi 2006).

The polemics around shared memory, (instrumental) historical revisionism, and (lack of) justice, aggravated by the mutual distrust between the parties in government and those in opposition, and in particular the strong suspicion, on the part of the latter, that Berlusconi and his allies were intent on erasing anti-fascism as the founding value of the Italian Republic, all contributed to a negative evaluation of the concept and process of 'reconciliation', and the notion of a specific Commission to this end quickly became a nonstarter. In short, as O'Leary (2003) put it, 'the political mood has never existed to deal with the legacies of the *anni di piombo* ['years of lead']; there have only been partial or juridical attempts to clarify the history of those years.'

## The reconstructions of the Italian right

For the purposes of this book, however, the growing literature on conflict resolution and national reconciliation provides a useful lens through which it becomes possible to analyse the reconstructions of stragismo and the Strategy of Tension put forward by Alleanza Nazionale and the groups and representatives of the radical right. It is also possible through its lens to reassess the nature and depth of the transformation of the Movimento Sociale Italiano into the postfascist Alleanza Nazionale. It is not only the legacy of the fascist regime and the Italian Social Republic, in fact, that this party (as well as the radical right) has problems in coming to terms with, as has been shown in the excellent work by Francesco Germinario (1999, 2001, 2005). Just as importantly, the positioning of representatives and intellectuals linked to this party vis-à-vis the much more recent history of the Italian First Republic, specifically concerning the role played by neofascism in its murkiest deeds, can help to throw light upon the alleged distancing between Alleanza Nazionale and the groups to its right, its renouncing of fascist ideals, and its full acceptance of the democratic rules of the game. The literature on national reconciliation, in fact, emphasises many important aspects which go well beyond the highly controversial concept of a 'shared memory' of the past or the simplistic assumption that justice should be sacrificed for the sake of truth. National reconciliation implies above all that each party to the conflict has to change itself, its assumptions about the other(s) and its deep-seated prejudices. Second, each party must acknowledge its past deeds and adopt a critical stance towards its past actions and beliefs. In short, if we adopt a 'creeping civil war' perspective, and we also accept that one of the poles of the conflict was represented by the neofascist right, then we must also accept that this is one of the groups that should be involved in this difficult process of self-transformation.

Chapter 5 will consider the reconstructions of the Strategy of Tension put forward by representatives and sympathisers of Alleanza Nazionale and will assess the reasons why the party failed to take the opportunity of its participation in the Parliamentary Commission headed by Senator Pellegrino in order to distance itself from neofascist organisations and protagonists. Far from acknowledging that some at least of these organisations played a role in *stragismo*, Alleanza Nazionale representatives on the Commission seemed intent on turning the table on the traditional political enemies of Italian neofascism (above all the Italian Communist Party), placing the blame in turn upon the KGB, anarchist groups, left-wing editor Giangiacomo Feltrinelli and his paramilitary group GAP, the group MAR headed by ex-partisan Carlo Fumagalli, and, last but not least, Palestinian terrorists.

Why is a party which has seemingly abandoned its fascist ideology and is keen to achieve internal and external recognition as a legitimate and fully democratic party of the right, so preoccupied with shifting the blame away from extreme-right 'fringe' organisations and with safeguarding the reputation of notorious neofascists? The interesting aspect is precisely the fact that what is under discussion is not the involvement of the old Movimento Sociale Italiano (the precursor of Alleanza Nazionale) in the Strategy of Tension, as this would obviously have provided a strong motive for the party's attitude of total denial. The possibility that the MSI was implicated has indeed been raised on various occasions (though not in the main trials examined in Part I), but there are as many who believe that the party played an important role in curtailing the subversive activities of the radical groups operating to its right. One of these is Paolo Emilio Taviani, Christian Democratic Minister in successive governments, responsible for outlawing Ordine Nuovo in 1973. According to Taviani, some protagonists of the massacres came originally from the MSI but 'they had moved away from it, and had been expelled since the early 1970s' (Commissione parlamentare d'inchiesta sul terrorismo in Italia e sulle cause della mancata individuazione dei responsabili delle stragi, *Elenco Audizioni, Aggiornamento al 17 gennaio* 2001, 24th Session, 1 July 1997). Yet the heir to the MSI, Alleanza Nazionale, today appears concerned with shielding neofascist paramilitary organisations from any responsibility in the various acts of *stragismo*, even in the face of copious evidence produced by judiciary investigations and trials. The implications of the party's attitude for a policy of long-lasting national reconciliation, beyond the phase of conflict resolution, are also addressed in this chapter.

Chapter 6 will consider the self-narratives of prominent leaders of extreme-right paramilitary groups, who, either directly or indirectly, in many cases were charged and/or convicted for acts of violence, including acts of *stragismo*. The chapter will analyse not only their attitudes when confronted with charges of *stragismo*, and their own reconstructions of the Strategy of Tension, but also their reassessment of their past political militancy from the perspective of the present.

These personal testimonies are often used by the protagonists as an opportunity to reconstruct their lives as exemplary ideal-types, while, conversely, they can also represent a sincere attempt to revisit their past actions in a self-critical manner, thereby opening up space for other voices, including those of their victims. Given the complex and often contradictory psychological context within which these memoirs originate, the chapter makes use of narrative psychology and narrative analysis theory in order to investigate the motivations of the narrators, the 'truth' of their narratives, and the contrastive role these can play, either supplying ideological 'ammunition' for current and future generations to continue the struggle or promoting 'closure' through greater mutual understanding and a critical reassessment of their past actions and beliefs.

# CHAPTER 5
## Narratives of Victimhood: The Right's Reconstructions and Interpretations of *Stragismo*

### Introduction

What is meant by reconciliation and how is it achieved? While conflict resolution implies the formal termination of the armed struggle and/or other acts of violence, reconciliation requires a much deeper process, 'through which the parties in conflict form new relations of peaceful existence based on mutual trust and acceptance, cooperation, and consideration of each other's needs' (Bar-Tal 2000a: 355; 2000b). According to Bar-Tal, three key changes must occur within each group involved in the conflict in order to achieve reconciliation, concerning three sets of beliefs: 'beliefs about societal goals', 'beliefs about the adversary group' and 'beliefs about the ingroup'. As regards the first set of beliefs, they refer to 'the justness of one's own goals', and are always supported by a whole range of 'justifications and rationales, myths, symbols, and rituals to serve this epistemic purpose' (ibid.: 357). The second set of beliefs concerns the negative stereotyping of the adversary group, which is constructed as a 'homogeneous and unitary group', rather than made up of distinct individuals (ibid.: 358). The third set refers to the process of positive self-stereotyping, 'self-glorifying' and 'self-praising' (ibid.: 358).

For reconciliation to occur, each set of beliefs needs to be replaced by a new one. In terms of goals, what is needed is 'abolition … of the societal dreams and visions, expressed in specific goals that caused the intergroup conflict' (ibid.: 357). In terms of negative stereotyping, it should be replaced by a more balanced attribution of both negative and positive traits to former adversaries, as well as their 'personalisation', so that they are perceived as human beings, in contrast to the process of dehumanising that underpins political violence. Lastly, in terms of positive self-stereotyping, it should be replaced by new beliefs which 'illuminate the ingroup in a more objective light, especially with regard to acts related to the conflict, and hence should be more complex and even critical. The new beliefs should recognise the contribution of the ingroup to the outbreak of the conflict and its extension, as well as the misdeeds of the ingroup in the course of the conflict, including responsibilities for atrocities (if any)' (ibid.: 358).

Similarly, with reference to Northern Ireland, Liechty and Clegg (2001: 103) defined sectarianism as 'a system of attitudes, actions, beliefs, and structures', which 'is expressed in destructive patterns of relating.' Among these are attitudes and beliefs which always precede acts of physical violence, including 'hardening the boundaries between groups' and 'belittling, dehumanising, or demonising others' (ibid.: 103). The latter process involves caricaturing the other: 'in belittling, the caricature is aimed primarily at mockery, derision, or suggesting that the other is less than one's own group, and in dehumanising it is aimed at portraying others as not worthy of human consideration and respect. In demonising, on the other hand, it is aimed primarily at inducing fear and hatred of, or shock at, the tradition, practices, representatives, or beliefs of the other' (ibid.: 139). The authors also refer to the construction of a 'falsely homogeneous image' of both the ingroup and outgroups, which is constantly reaffirmed since 'to acknowledge differences of opinion or outlook is seen as weakening the group' (ibid.: 143). According to Liechty and Clegg, their definition of religious-political sectarianism has much in common with other 'isms' and can be used as 'an analytical tool' in order to identify the sectarian nature of actions, events, speeches and beliefs in different contexts and at different times. It goes without saying that for them reconciliation has to entail not just an end to the violence but above all 'changes in mental habits', particularly the adoption of 'bifocal vision' (ibid.: 339).

Kriesberg (1998: 329–31) argued that reconciliation entails a complex process which involves four aspects: truth, justice, forgiveness and security. Truth refers above all to taking into account the point of view of the other side. Justice relates to achieving redress but may imply foregoing a fuller justice as a price to pay in order to achieve full reconciliation. Forgiveness on the part of victims is also an important part of the process, as well as security, that is, expectations of a stable and long-lasting peace. Long and Brecke also emphasised the need to proceed through various stages: 'Reconciliation events restore lasting social order when they are part of a forgiveness process characterised by truth telling, redefinition of the identity of the former belligerents, partial justice, and a call for a new relationship' (Long and Brecke 2003: 3). The first phase, truth telling or recognition, refers to the acknowledgement of shame and anger by all parties involved in the conflict; the second phase 'involves a changed understanding of oneself and of the other party to a conflict ... Forgiving involves a self-transformation wherein the party sees itself as something other than the victim and achieves a more complete and balanced identity. Forgiveness is outwardly directed as well. Specifically, it requires constructing a new identity for the other, the enemy' (ibid.: 29). In other words, the process requires rehumanising the adversary, while still condemning their deeds. 'Third, the parties must forego the option of revenge ... Retribution for a wrong must be less than total' (ibid.: 30). Fourth, there have to be contacts between the different parties and 'a public expression of forgiveness, with the offer of a renewed but different relationship, what we call a reconciliation event' (ibid.: 30). It is only in this final phase that 'symbolic words and gestures help mark the trajectory, but not the end point, of the relationship' (ibid.: 150).

As can be seen from the above, reconciliation events, of the kind promoted (and even unilaterally imposed) by the Berlusconi government, represent only the final phase of a long and difficult process which requires first and foremost that each party looks at itself self-critically, and at its former adversaries in a more balanced manner, with a view to destereotyping and rehumanising them. In the absence of these prerequisites, reconciliation events can only be cosmetic or else, as in the case of some of the initiatives of the Berlusconi government, they smack of its opposite, that is, revenge and prevarication. The chapter which follows examines, on the basis of the reconstructions of the Strategy of Tension put forward by the neo- and postfascist right, the nature and scope of their revisitations of the past, with a view to assessing whether they have embarked upon – and/or how far they have proceeded along – the path of self-transformation.

## The reports submitted by Alleanza Nazionale to the *Commissione stragi*

An important source for understanding the reconstruction of the Strategy of Tension on the part of Alleanza Nazionale is constituted by the various reports submitted by Senator Alfredo Mantica and MP Vincenzo Fragalà to the Parliamentary Commission of Inquiry on the Failed Identification of the Authors of Terrorist Massacres and published in 2001. The questions asked, and comments made, by these same two representatives of Alleanza Nazionale during the hearings of the witnesses to the Commission, which took place between 1997 and 2001, also form a relevant supplementary source. Published works written by persons connected to this party, primarily in the form of books and articles (including newspaper articles), as well as interviews conducted by the author, complement the material examined in order to analyse the position adopted by the postfascist right. The same sources were consulted in order to understand the reconstructions put forward by representatives of extreme-right organisations who still adhere to neofascist ideals.

Of the eighteen reports submitted to the *Commissione stragi* in 2001, no fewer than nine contained the signatures of the two representatives of Alleanza Nazionale, Senator Alfredo Mantica and MP Vincenzo Fragalà. Most of these concerned the 1969 massacre at Piazza Fontana in Milan, while one addressed the bomb attack at Piazza della Loggia in Brescia, carried out in 1974. The main thesis put forward in these reports regarding Piazza Fontana can be summarised as follows.

The massacre was carried out by anarchists, including Pietro Valpreda and Giuseppe Pinelli, the two originally charged with the crime. On the basis of this interpretation, Pinelli had indeed committed suicide while being interrogated at the Milan police headquarters, because of his remorse for an action which had gone beyond the original intentions of the group. The initial investigations of the crime, which had followed a 'red' trail, were therefore the correct ones, whereas the later investigations into the 'black trail', under pressure from a public campaign orchestrated by the left, had simply created confusion. According to Gian Paolo Pelizzaro, a right-leaning independent journalist, consultant to the *Commissione stragi* and coauthor of some of the reports signed by Mantica and Fragalà, 'The inquiry on Valpreda was founded upon strong suspicions on the part of the Milan police, based on their knowledge of the activities of his anarchist group which quite openly pursued the political strategy of planting bombs' (interview with the author, 5 October 2005). Similar conclusions were apparently reached by the Red Brigades (BR) during a 'counter-investigation' it had carried out after the bombing, whose content was disclosed to the Commission by the two Alleanza Nazionale representatives (Mantica and Fragalà 2001c).

Admittedly, the anarchists at that time were unable to rely on any proper organisation; nevertheless they had links with other groups, both on the left and on the right. More importantly, the real Strategy of Tension was masterminded by Giangiacomo Feltrinelli, who was able to cement the fragmented galaxy of extreme-left and anarchist groups (not excluding a few highly disorganised extreme-right ones), by financing their activities, instructing them in guerrilla practices and establishing a huge international network, thanks to his far-reaching contacts and his fabulous wealth (Pelizzaro, interview with the author, 5 October 2005). Feltrinelli was obsessed by the idea of an imminent coup d'état, which required a widespread resistance and a counter-attack on the part of revolutionary forces. To this end Feltrinelli set up the GAP (Gruppi di Azione Partigiana – 'Partisan Action Groups'), in 1967–68, and promoted the creation of other extreme-left paramilitary groups, including the Red Brigades. Behind Feltrinelli was the KGB, which was interested in promoting guerrilla actions in the country, partly in order to keep up the pressure on and hence limit the growing autonomy of the Italian Communist Party (Mantica and Fragalà 2001b).

The arguments tend to become rather convoluted when it comes to Piazza Fontana, but they appear to amount to the thesis that Feltrinelli wanted to foment a climate conducive to (or at least exaggerate the threat of) a coup d'état, as he believed that such a climate would precipitate a left revolution: 'He started to write about the risks of a coup d'état much earlier, and argued in his writings that the Piazza Fontana massacre was meant to precede a coup, not by chance his group had very close links with the anarchist organisations which were placing the bombs' (interview with Pelizzaro by the author). He therefore either directed or sanctioned the actions of the anarchists. In this context, it was probably not a coincidence that Feltrinelli went into clandestinity a few weeks before the Piazza Fontana massacre (Mantica and Fragalà 2001b: 88). In short, Feltrinelli had a clear revolutionary strategy, the means to implement it, and the cynicism to take advantage of any useful tools: 'Feltrinelli utilised a logic typical of Marxist-Leninism, the ability to make use of everything society offers: If I need to hit a target I must make use of all possible instruments' (interview with Pelizzaro by the author). Furthermore, the source for the articles which appeared in the *Observer* on 6 and 14 December 1969, already discussed in Chapter 4, was identified by Mantica and Fragalà (2001a: 62–63) in Feltrinelli himself, thanks to his contacts with the left in Italy and Europe, while the purpose of the articles was a *depistaggio* in favour of the Italian extreme left.

The above reconstruction may have the merit of throwing new light on the links between the KGB and Feltrinelli's group, as well as other extreme-left organisations, primarily thanks to the material made available by Vasili Mitrokhin, a Soviet citizen who defected to the UK in 1992. According to the British Mitrokhin Inquiry Report:

> Vasili Mitrokhin was a KGB archivist who had access to papers which went to the heart of Soviet espionage activity during the cold war … The information which Mitrokhin brought with him was and is of enormous significance to the UK and its allies. It has provided a large number of leads to KGB activities in a period of at least 40 years before Mitrokhin's retirement in 1985. (Intelligence and Security Committee 2000)

The two representatives of Alleanza Nazionale on the *Commissione stragi* made extensive use of this material, and indeed it could have provided valuable new information in order to complement other available findings, not least those produced by judicial investigations and trials. The role of the KGB, the Stasi and other Eastern intelligence services in relation to Italian terrorism, especially as regards extreme-left organisations, clearly needs to be fully established. What happened instead was that the new sources were used by Alleanza Nazionale to put forward totally alternative interpretations which appeared to place the blame for virtually all terrorism upon the left. Not only were the GAP, the BR, Prima Linea and other well-known left paramilitary organisations guilty of terrorism in the form of acts of sabotage and the wounding and killing of individual politicians and state officers. To the left must also be attributed the Piazza Fontana bombing (via the anarchists) and the responsibility for masterminding the entire Strategy of Tension (whose brain was Feltrinelli). Add the KGB to this concoction and one ends up with a reconstruction whose advantages to the right are plain and obvious, for it makes the extreme right, the intelligence structures and the CIA both invisible and unjustly maligned. Its disadvantages in terms of foregoing the opportunity for a critical reassessment of its own past by one of the parties to the conflict are also quite plain.

Following the logic established for the Piazza Fontana massacre, the subsequent *stragi* were all explained by the Alleanza Nazionale representatives on the *Commissione stragi* in ways which cleared the extreme-right organisations of any involvement. For the 1973 attack at the Milan police headquarters, the culprit was Gianfranco Bertoli, a self-declared anarchist who, according to Alleanza Nazionale, had no ulterior motives and had clearly acted alone. As Fragalà declared in one of the sessions of the *Commissione stragi*: 'After twenty years they still accuse him of being a fascist, while he continues to declare himself an anarchist, and indeed the attack was a purely anarchist one' (Commissione parla-

mentare d'inchiesta sul terrorismo in Italia e sulle cause della mancata individuazione dei responsabili delle stragi, *Elenco Audizioni, Aggiornamento al 27 gennaio
2001*, 27th session, hearing of Francesco Cossiga, 6 November 1997). The trials,
as we saw in Part I, established a different truth; the only one which concluded
with a verdict fully compatible with Fragalà's interpretation was declared null by
the Court of Cassation, on 11 July 2003, with the damning motivation that the
judges had bent the evidence in order to prove a preconceived hypothesis.

The 1974 massacre at Piazza della Loggia, in Brescia, was attributed, on the
other hand, to the MAR, led by Carlo Fumagalli, an anti-fascist ex-partisan, who
was deemed to have joined forces with Feltrinelli before the death of the latter,
although each continued to pursue different aims. The thesis was explained in
another report submitted to the *Commissione stragi* by Mantica and Fragalà
(2001d). After stating that 'one by one the monster-trials on the *stragi* (from
Piazza Fontana to Bologna) have imploded miserably' (2001d: 416), the report
went on to praise the work of a magistrate from Brescia, Giovanni Arcai, who had
started to investigate the MAR but had later mysteriously been removed from the
investigation. This happened after his (neofascist) son had been unjustly (and
most probably instrumentally) accused of involvement in the massacre. As in the
case of Feltrinelli and the KGB, there may well be elements of truth in this reconstruction, including the suggestion that the bomb was intended to hit the *Carabinieri* as an act of revenge for their 'betrayal' of Fumagalli, whom they had
previously protected but later prosecuted. Another interesting aspect is a possible
link between Fumagalli and the extreme right, on the one hand, and Fumagalli
and Feltrinelli, on the other. Pellegrino himself appeared to take this hypothesis
extremely seriously, as indicating that extreme-left and extreme-right terrorism
may, at some point, have been directed by different external forces, such as the
CIA and the KGB, with an identical aim: to keep in place the postwar political
equilibrium established at Yalta (Fasanella and Sestieri with Pellegrino 2000:
130–34). However, in the report by Mantica and Fragalà, those elements which
could potentially contribute to a better understanding of the dynamics of this
massacre are mixed up with much less convincing aspects and with omissions,
demonstrating above all an overarching determination to 'erase' any possible role
played by the extreme right.

Finally, the verdict by the Supreme Court for the 1980 massacre at Bologna railway station is heavily contested by Alleanza Nazionale and the right. As we saw in
Part I, this is the only case in which doubts about the verdict seem to be shared by
a wide variety of forces, including some on the left. Once again, it was the
Mitrokhin papers which constituted the primary source for an alternative reconstruction to that which convicted Valerio Fioravanti and Francesca Mambro to life
imprisonment. According to this interpretation, the culprits for the massacre were
an organisation led by the Venezuelan terrorist Ilich Ramirez Sanchez, known simply as Carlos, together with the Palestinian Liberation Front, led by George Hab-
bash. The motive was a revenge act, to punish Italy for the imprisonment of Abu
Azeh Saleh, arrested in Bologna on 13 November 1979 for transporting two rocket

launchers, assisted by Daniele Pifano and two other members of an Italian left organisation. Saleh and the Palestinian terrorists were linked to Carlos; hence the ultimate culprits were the Palestinians, aided by the KGB. The interpretation can be found in various articles published by the monthly journal *Area*, some of which were written by Gian Paolo Pelizzaro, consultant to the *Commissione stragi* and coauthor of some of the reports submitted by Mantica and Fragalà (October 1999; December 2000; July–August 2005). The journal, edited by Marcello De Angelis, is the official mouthpiece of 'Destra Sociale', the Alleanza Nazionale faction which is headed by Gianni Alemanno, minister in the 2001 Berlusconi government. Another prominent leader, Francesco Storace, also minister in the Berlusconi government, left in 2006 to form his own current, 'D-Destra' and has since left Alleanza Nazionale altogether. Destra Sociale, which has its roots in the leftist strand of fascism and neofascism, advocates radical social reforms, communitarianism as opposed to individualism and liberalism, some form of workers' participation in industry, and a state role in the economy (Accame 1996; Alemanno 2002; http://www.destrasociale.org/). This is also the party current which most strongly opposed Gianfranco Fini's public condemnation of fascism during his trip to Israel in November 2003, and which for some constitutes an independent group within Alleanza Nazionale (Scaliati 2005: 212–16). Not least thanks to the relentless campaign by *Area*, investigations into the Bologna massacre were recently reopened.

What, then, of the numerous episodes of obstruction of justice, which have been well documented for almost every investigation and trial concerning acts of *stragismo*, including the Piazza Fontana massacre? The Alleanza Nazionale representatives on the *Commissione stragi* explained these episodes as attempts to shift the blame away from the real culprits and to pin it on the extreme right. Vincenzo Fragalà, in particular, made a point of asking various witnesses to the Commission repeated questions to this end. On 6 November 1997, he asked ex-President of the Republic Francesco Cossiga whether he possessed any knowledge that could throw light on the reasons why state or intelligence structures had 'utilised the massacres in order to criminalise the political right and victimise instead the left' (Commissione parlamentare d'inchiesta sul terrorismo in Italia e sulle cause della mancata individuazione dei responsabili delle stragi, *Elenco Audizioni, Aggiornamento al 17 gennaio 2001*, 27th session, hearing of Francesco Cossiga, 6 November 1997). On 16 January 1997, he asked Judge D'Ambrosio, who had investigated the Piazza Fontana massacre, why in his view those same forces which ostensibly had wanted to stop the Communist Party from coming close to government had been channelling investigations onto the wrong track 'so as to harm the right'. To which D'Ambrosio replied that 'there is nothing that is stronger than the facts and the facts, as far as the Piazza Fontana massacre is concerned, demonstrate exactly the opposite of what you said' (Commissione parlamentare d'inchiesta sul terrorismo in Italia e sulle cause della mancata individuazione dei responsabili delle stragi, *Elenco Audizioni, Aggiornamento al 17 gennaio 2001*, 6th Session, hearing of Gerardo D'Ambrosio, 16 January 1997). On 15 May 1997, Fragalà asked ex-Prime Minister Arnaldo Forlani if the DC and the government

knew how and why for over twenty years theories had been circulated 'of a strategy of tension which supposedly favoured the right while in reality this was used
to criminalise the right, and which supposedly had to prevent the Communist
Party from growing at the ballot box while it helped this party to become … a
party of Government, a party of the State with the Moro affair. How could this
take place without your knowledge?' (Commissione parlamentare d'inchiesta sul
terrorismo in Italia e sulle cause della mancata individuazione dei responsabili
delle stragi, *Elenco Audizioni, Aggiornamento al 17 gennaio* 2001, 18th Session,
hearing of Arlando Forlani, 15 May 1997).

The implications of these reconstructions for party political reasons can be
seen very clearly in the reaction of representatives of Alleanza Nazionale to the
final verdict in the Piazza Fontana trial. In an article significantly entitled 'Black
terrorism: so many bogus *pentiti*. Drug addicts, mentally ill persons, common
criminals: all found out as liars only after several trials', which appeared in the
party's newspaper, *Il Secolo d'Italia*, on 4 May 2005, Fragalà and Pelizzaro commented on the verdict, openly ridiculing the 'repented' witnesses for the prosecution, all of them ex-members of extreme-right organisations. In the article, it
was stated that Maggi and Zorzi had been 'fully acquitted' by the Court of Cassation (while in fact, as we saw in Part I, they were acquitted with recourse to a
'not proven' verdict). In addition, no mention was made of the fact that the
Supreme Court confirmed the ruling of the lower Courts that Freda and Ventura
were both to be considered guilty for the Piazza Fontana massacre, even though
they could no longer be prosecuted as they had been acquitted on the grounds of
insufficient evidence in 1987. With little respect for the truth, the article
affirmed, on the contrary, that 'the Piazza Fontana massacre is still without a
declared culprit'. Finally, the article stated that the two main witnesses, Siciliano
and Digilio, had both been found 'not credible' by the Court (as we saw, this was
the case only for the latter, whereas the Supreme Court had confirmed that Siciliano was to be deemed 'fully credible'). A second article in the same newspaper,
entitled 'Thirty-six years of inquiries and trials, red and black trails, without a single truth', listed the main trials, giving the reader the overall impression that they
had all come to nothing and had been a total waste of time and money.

What is puzzling about this article – as we shall see, the attitudes and interpretations it expresses are widely shared among right-leaning commentators – is
the virulence with which ex-members of extreme-right organisations who have
turned witnesses are rubbished and despised, and the eagerness with which
declared or suspected culprits are defended and exonerated. One would expect
representatives and sympathisers of a postfascist party to adopt precisely the opposite attitude, welcoming those who have decided to collaborate with the magistrates and distancing themselves from those who have been found guilty of the
most despicable crimes. But quite apart from the role various individuals may or
may not have played in *stragismo*, there is the issue of ideology to consider. One
would expect members and/or intellectuals close to Alleanza Nazionale not to
rush to the defence of people like Freda, Maggi and Zorzi, who professed (and

still largely profess) neo-Nazi and racist ideas, and to praise people like Siciliano, who have expressed regret for their past extremism. Ideology, however, seems to have been brushed aside with worrying ease.

As for the trial on the 1973 Milan attack, Fragalà welcomed the final verdict as vindication of the fact that the extreme right had been deliberately criminalised by left magistrates for massacres which 'from the very first moment, had markedly leftist authors and strategies.' As for Bertoli, he had never been believed when he proclaimed himself an anarchist, indeed 'for years it was attempted to pass him off as ... a pawn in a destabilising strategy attributed to the usual Maggi, Zorzi and other presumed activists of Ordine Nuovo' (Almanacco dei Misteri d'Italia, 2005). In the light of the trial findings, including the motivations for the final verdict of acquittal by the Court of Appeal and the Court of Cassation, outlined in Part I, these comments clearly indicate a seriously distorted representation of the judicial truth, and are emblematic of a collective mindset.

The above reconstructions do not bode well in terms of enabling Alleanza Nazionale to achieve a new and more balanced view of itself and its former adversaries or indeed in pointing to the emergence of less conflictual political relations. Despite the efforts of some of its leaders and above all its secretary, Gianfranco Fini, the party clearly sees neofascism as an innocent victim of both its old adversary, the left, and of state structures. The verdicts of judicial trials are all but ignored, indicating continuing mistrust of the impartiality of the country's justice process. Negative stereotyping of the 'other' and dehumanising are very much in evidence, indeed they are being applied not only to the left, but also to a new 'outgroup', made up of ex-neofascists turned witnesses for the prosecution. The latter are constructed as 'deviant' and 'subhuman': a ragbag of drug addicts, mentally sick people, criminals, social drop-outs and congenital liars.

Before we explore the factors accounting for these reconstructions, we need to consider other interpretations by right-wing political exponents and commentators, some of which differ quite substantially from – and are even antithetical to – the ones we have summarised so far. The reconstructions submitted by the representatives of Alleanza Nazionale to the *Commissione stragi*, in fact, do not constitute a shared overview, even though they have attracted the most attention and have been the ones used for party political reasons. On the contrary, there is a wide spectrum of opinions on *stragismo* and the Strategy of Tension among the political right, which makes it even more interesting to ascertain why the official line adopted by Alleanza Nazionale in the *Commissione stragi* was the one outlined above. More importantly, the different interpretations, as we shall see, mask different political preoccupations and exigencies within the right, and reveal the existence of controversial issues which cannot easily be reconciled into a shared version of events. These issues revolve around the set of beliefs concerning the 'ingroup', according to Bar-Tal's definition, that is, the representation of the neofascist right and of its identity. While positive self-stereotyping remains common to all these reconstructions, there is little agreement as to which specific traits should be attributed to Italian neofascism, in so far as few are perceived to be without risks or pitfalls.

## First-generation neofascist activists: naive pawns of *stragismo* or its blameless victims?

One of these controversial issues concerns the nature and role of extreme-right activists in both *stragismo* and the Strategy of Tension. While all the interpretations put forward by the right portray neofascism as victim of this strategy, they differ in their assessment of those activists who have been strongly suspected, and in some cases convicted, of involvement in the massacres. A typical illustration of this is given by the differing judgments expressed on Franco Freda, the main suspect for the Piazza Fontana massacre, who was acquitted of this crime in 1987 on the basis of insufficient evidence, but recognised as the culprit in the final verdict of the Supreme Court in 2005.

In line with the reports submitted by the representatives of Alleanza Nazionale to the *Commissione stragi*, Freda is defended as innocent by this party and by right-leaning intellectuals. In his interview with the author, Gian Paolo Pelizzaro, independent journalist and consultant to the *Commissione stragi*, coauthor of some of the reports submitted by the representatives of Alleanza Nazionale, put forward a number of arguments which, in his view, exonerated Freda. First, he was keen to define Freda as a 'theoretician' and someone without a precise political affiliation: 'in his political experience there are different types of political activism ... for instance Ventura had a past as a man of the left, Damacchio had been infiltrated into Freda's group by Feltrinelli.' Second, Freda was innocent; he had been 'used' by other forces: 'It is true that Freda's group was very agitated ... he did not plant the bomb, but the [Piazza Fontana] operation was orchestrated around him.' Third, Freda and the other suspected neofascists had been guilty only of naivety. Asked to explain his reconstruction, Pelizzaro went on to state the following:

> If I know that so and so are poachers and I do not belong to their group but I am interested in catching a particular fish which is illegal, and I do not want to do it myself because I do not have the tools or the ability etc. then since those people do this kind of things I insert myself in their group and I utilise them because they know how to do it. Alternatively, knowing that they are involved in this kind of activity, I do it myself as I know that suspicions will fall upon them because they are known and I am not.
>
> What I was trying to explain to you is that if you see the typology of what happened before Piazza Fontana, which is the work carried out by Judge Salvini – who up to a point has done an excellent job and has reconstructed in an impeccable manner the activity of those cells – you can see that they used to let off flares, silly things, totally ridiculous things, but at a certain point from this kind of things there is a move to more serious things. Ventura, those who were members of La Fenice, one has to know them to understand what greenhorns they were, if you talk to Rognoni ... (Interview with the author, 5 October 2005)

A similar portrayal of Freda was presented by Giorgio Pisanò, ex-combatant in the X MAS for the Italian Social Republic, Senator for the neofascist Movimento Sociale Italiano from 1972 to 1992, and leader of the movement Fascismo e Libertà ('Fascism and Freedom'), which he set up in 1991 as an alternative to Alleanza Nazionale, which in his view was too revisionist and 'postfascist'. A few years before his death, which occurred in 1997, Pisanò granted an interview to Michele Brambilla for his book *Interrogatorio alle destre* (1995), in which he defined Freda as an idiot who had fallen into a huge trap. In his own words, 'Freda is that idiot who procures the timers. But attention: Freda did not know that the timers would be used for a massacre … I went to any lengths to prove that Freda had nothing to do with the timers but that is the truth. Freda fell into a huge trap. He procured the timers without knowing what they were for' (Brambilla 1995: 54). Asked whether he believed that foreign agencies were also involved, Pisanò replied: 'But what foreign agencies, in the *stragi* there are only Italian imbeciles' (ibid. 1995: 54).

Pino Rauti, ex-leader of Centro Studi Ordine Nuovo, supported the interpretation that the neofascist 'hotheads' allowed themselves to be utilised by other forces. In an interview granted to Michele Brambilla for the same book (Brambilla 1995: 34), he declared that 'the [Italian] secret services utilised as pawns right-wing young men who played with explosives, with the idea of a coup, with clandestinity'. Asked whether these young men had been unaware of playing into the hands of the secret services, Rauti replied: 'I think so. Totally unaware' (ibid. 1995: 34).

A reconstruction that has some points of contact with Pelizzaro's but also differs from it in some important respects was put forward, in an interview with the author, by Marcello De Angelis, ex-leader of Terza Posizione and editor of the monthly journal *Area*, the official mouthpiece, as already mentioned, of a political current within Alleanza Nazionale. Since the interview, on 28 April 2006, De Angelis has been elected Senator for Alleanza Nazionale. In his view, all the trials on the *stragi* have come to nothing, since all the accused have been found innocent. With reference to the latest Piazza Fontana trial, he stated that

> This umpteenth trial concluded that Maggi and Zorzi were totally innocent, they were not involved, yet also [established] that the *strage* had been conceived in the context of extreme-right groups in the Triveneto. Even Freda and Ventura are brought up once again, so that it is said that these [Maggi and Zorzi] are not guilty so probably the culprits were Freda and Ventura. (Interview with the author, 6 October 2005)

While De Angelis's summing up of the verdict was more accurate than most, it was no less disparaging or dismissive.

In any case, in his opinion, the perpetrators of the various *stragi* in Italy were either professional terrorists, such as Carlos, or 'improvised misfits'. Asked whether they may also have been revolutionary extremists, he replied by attacking anti-fascism's negative stereotyping of fascists:

> A revolutionary extremist will attempt a revolution; he will not blow up an innocent person, that was an interpretative framework which lacked logic because it relied upon a widespread as well as superficial form of anti-fascism, since this was based on indirect knowledge, with the result that it seemed plausible that there could be people who either embodied absolute evil or were totally demented. (Interview with the author, 6 October 2005)

In his view, neofascist activists in Italy had been few and disorganised. In the north of the country especially, after Piazza Fontana, they were reduced to a handful of desperate and isolated individuals who may have attempted mad gestures but certainly not as part of a coherent strategy. Indeed, it is highly likely that they had been infiltrated. In this area of the country, characterised by the absolute predominance of the left and the disaggregation and collapse of the political right, there may have been a few anomalous acts of violence (such as those carried out by Nico Azzi and Vincenzo Vinciguerra), but in no way were they representative of the right as a whole.

Like Fragalà, De Angelis argued that state and intelligence structures deliberately set the investigators on the wrong track, to the detriment of the extreme right: 'All the *depistaggi* [wild-goose chases] from the first to the last were directed against the extreme right because when you organise a *depistaggio* you direct it in the opposite direction to that of the culprits.' Like many others, De Angelis also emphasised the 'fact' that the extreme right had been the real target of *stragismo*, whereas the left had been the beneficiary. He went beyond other reconstructions by stating not only that the right had been criminalised and persecuted, through mass and indiscriminate arrests, but above all that *stragismo* had prevented the political right from consolidating and had deprived it of a strong leadership.

In short, the neofascists are innocent on the grounds that (1) they did not have the means, the organisation or indeed the cynical mental attitude that would have allowed them to develop and carry out a coherent and coordinated strategy of bombing attacks; (2) they were not so stupid as to have pursued a strategy which had the sole result of strengthening the left and criminalising the right; (3) they were systematically the target of obstructions of justice on the part of the *Carabinieri* and other state forces, thus proving that the *stragi* were directed against them.

Compared to Pelizzaro's and Pisanò's, De Angelis's reconstruction put the emphasis more on the logic of the *cui prodest*, rather than on the naivety of many neofascist activists. In effect, the various reconstructions highlight some important and complex issues for the right, which cannot easily be reconciled into a unitary and uncontroversial interpretation. The first issue concerns the political naivety versus sophistication of neofascist activists (however exiguous their number). An interpretation such as Pelizzaro's runs the risk of depicting activists like Freda as (innocent but stupid) hotheads who allowed themselves, consciously but more probably unconsciously, to become pawns in the (cynical but cunning) political games of other forces. This reconstruction has the advantage of claiming the status of innocent victims for the neofascists even while acknowledging the plausibility of some of the findings of judicial investigations. However, the price to pay is that of reducing the neofascist activists to hopeless amateurs who were unable to see what was going on at their expense under their own noses.

De Angelis's reconstruction, by contrast, attempts to rectify this negative impression by stressing that in no way could the neofascists have devised a strategy that turned out to be so detrimental to their own political side. Their innocence is therefore predicated on their sense of honour and political astuteness, not on their naivety. The latter reconstruction has the merit of rehabilitating the political stature of the extreme right, but it collides head on with judicial findings, in so far as the Ordine Nuovo cells in the Triveneto have been found guilty of a series of bomb attacks, quite apart from their putative role in the Piazza Fontana massacre. If they were so politically aware, why did the members of these cells carry out terrorist attacks (against 'objects' rather than 'people', let us assume), thus playing into the hands of 'professionals' (according to the scenario presented by De Angelis) who were planning much more sinister actions? As we shall see, all the reconstructions put forward by representatives of the right (including those of perpetrators of political violence) oscillate between these two poles of interpretation without seemingly finding a satisfactory solution.

A somewhat more balanced interpretation was put forward by Giano Accame, writer, intellectual and one of the main representatives of the right, currently of Alleanza Nazionale, during an interview with the author (7 October 2005). According to Accame, it is possible that the Piazza Fontana attack was carried out by the extreme right with the intent of blaming the left or, more probably, by 'the police and the CIA using as manpower a mix of extreme-right activists and anarchists.' Subsequent massacres, however, probably followed a different logic, and may have been carried out by the left with the aim of blaming the right. One reason for this is that the extreme right would clearly not have persevered in carrying out a strategy that had already proved detrimental to their side. However, when asked whether he included Freda and Ventura among the culprits for Piazza Fontana, Accame still proved very reluctant to acknowledge their involvement. He first stated that they had both been acquitted and, similarly to Pelizzaro, recalled that many young neofascist activists had learnt to rely on a provocative but innocent method, that of using flares: 'noisy provocations, but they never caused any injury.' He then proceeded to dismantle Judge Salvini's investigations and to discredit his witnesses, with recourse to negative stereotyping and dehumanising. Salvini's accusations, in his view, were 'a total invention', so much so that Zorzi and the others had been acquitted. The police and the *Carabinieri*, together with Salvini, 'had gone and searched the prisons for right-wing elements convicted of drug abuse, manipulating them so as to obtain false convictions. It was ludicrous.' Martino Siciliano, in particular, one of the two main witnesses for the Piazza Fontana trial, was described by Accame as 'at the time a fat young man, tormented by his size, a drunkard; [his were] pure ravings, taken seriously by the Milan judiciary.' As for the judiciary: 'It acted under the pressure of prejudices which came from its being strongly conditioned by the left. This is the reality.'

Togliatti [leader of the PCI], who was a great leader, a very intelligent man, hav-ing become Minister of Justice, immediately after the war, had an intuition, that one of the three powers of the state, precisely the Judiciary, could gradually be taken over' (interview with the author, 7 October 2005).

Finally, as far as books published on Italian neofascism by authors sympathetic to, or ostensibly neutral towards, the right are concerned, the preferred recon-structions of the past appear to be ones in which the presumed role played by Freda and others in *stragismo* tends to be altogether ignored. Alternatively, this whole issue is relegated to a footnote, where their acquittal for the Piazza Fontana massacre is duly noted and their status as victims is implied. In this way the total irrelevance of both the massacres and the Strategy of Tension in any historical accounts of the extreme right is forcefully made, albeit at the cost of appealing only to the already converted and of refusing to come to terms with an 'incon-venient' series of events. It is doubtful whether a strategy of 'denial' and 'erasure' of the past can have any serious measure of success, other than perpetuating the 'ghettoisation' of much historical and journalistic work produced by the right or acclaimed by it (Germinario 2005: 126–28). One example of this can be found in journalist Nicola Rao's *Neofascisti* (1999), which deals informatively and at some length with Freda's ideology and political activities but reduces his involve-ment in *stragismo* to the following footnote: 'Arrested at the beginning of the 1970s under the charge of organising the massacre of Piazza Fontana, after a series of guilty verdicts and acquittals, [Freda] was definitively acquitted by the Court of Cassation in 1986, after more than 12 years in detention' (Rao 1999: 111). Rao's more recent version of this book (2006) was recommended by Alleanza Nazionale's youth organisation, Azione Giovani, as a text every activist should read and treasure. Another example is Arianna Streccioni's *A destra della destra* (2006), which also examines in some detail Freda's ideology, yet dismisses the issue of Freda's involvement in the Piazza Fontana massacre on the basis that 'our analysis is limited to the consequences … which those crimes directly or indi-rectly had upon the world of the radical right' (Streccioni 2006: 113).

A right-leaning consultant for the *Commissione stragi*, Virgilio Ilari, Professor of Military History, published a book in 2001, significantly entitled *Guerra civile* ('Civil War'). Its main argument is that the entire history of Italy has been marked by a partisan conception of the 'nation' and a series of civil wars, which make it impossible for a common memory to emerge. Indeed, in his view, the memories of the losers of these various wars run parallel to those of the winners, and the two sets of memories 'neither clash nor engage with each other; they ignore each other' (Ilari 2001: 24). After this promising start, the book proceeds to argue that the 'Strategy of Tension', the 'dual state' and the 'neofascist subversive activities' were nothing more than red herrings constructed by the left, and suggests that the massacres were part of a stabilising strategy aimed at promoting an anti-fascist alliance which included the communists: 'Anti-communist putschism and black subversive activities were more the pretext for cementing the historic compromise in the guise of "anti-fascist national unity", than a serious attempt to prevent that type of pacification' (ibid. 2001: 79) . In this context, 'it is possible that somebody believed it was necessary to sacrifice a few human lives [to this aim], with a witch-hunt against the putschists, if not even with the unpunished massacres at Brescia and on the train *Italicus*, which Senator Pellegrino defined as "anti-fascist massacres"' (ibid.: 79). The suggestion here is that these massacres had been perpetrated in order to make the fascists appear as the culprits. The reference to Pellegrino's definition is somewhat improper, since the latter, as we saw in Chapter 4, believed that the neofascists had carried out the attack at Brescia (though possibly not the one on the train *Italicus*), and that the state used its knowledge of their involvement to clamp down on their activities. Finally, Ilari argued that the only real threat to the strategy of rapprochement between the DC and the PCI, and hence the only serious 'terrorism' in Italy after the war, was that of the Red Brigades. However, the 'sacred' and untouchable history imposed by the left in Italy (ibid. 2001: 48), prevents this historical truth from emerging and was used instrumentally during the crisis of the Italian First Republic, in 1992-94, when the Christian Democratic state was put on trial by the left, in the latest twist of the ongoing civil war.

There are exceptions. One is Accame's *Una storia della Repubblica* (2000), an interesting history of the Italian First Republic, which succeeds in achieving a modicum of impartiality. However, his account of the Piazza Fontana investigations and trials strongly echoes Pelizzaro's reconstruction. In other words, it is suggested that the original 'Valpreda' trail was the most fruitful one, until 'some left-oriented magistrates thought they could identify the real culprits by following a "black trail"' (Accame 2000: 229). Subsequently, in the Catanzaro trial, 'the clues, albeit considerable, against both groups, were not sufficient to form incontrovertible evidence' and so 'they were all acquitted' (ibid.: 230). In a footnote, there is a somewhat ambiguous reference to the new trial: 'After more than thirty years a trial with defendants and witnesses still drawn from the circle of Venetian neofascism opened in Milan in February 2000' (ibid.: 230). The expression 'drawn from the circle' suggests that whatever the final verdict these people are to be considered isolated and marginal elements in relation to Italian neofascism. Significantly, Ordine Nuovo is not mentioned even once in connection to Piazza Fontana. Compared to what he wrote in this book, in his subsequent interview with the author, carried out in 2005, Accame was more prepared to acknowledge that Piazza Fontana may have been carried out by the extreme right but was also much more dismissive of the trial, as we saw.

Other interesting exceptions are the books by Adalberto Baldoni, journalist and writer, as well as member of the national executive of Alleanza Nazionale. I refer especially to *Il crollo dei miti* (1996) and *A che punto è la notte?* (2003), written in collaboration with left-wing journalist Sandro Provvisionato. The former deals at length with both extreme-right and extreme-left terrorism and is quite detailed concerning the investigations and trials for the Piazza Fontana massacre. The book has as one of its explicit aims that of contributing to a 'historical memory' for all those who 'lived those years militating on the right' (Baldoni 1996: 7).

In the Introduction, the author specifies that in order to achieve this aim, he also had to consider the role of the extreme left in Italian politics: 'this is not a casual choice, because I consider this work, as I have already said, effectively a *historical memory* of the Right whose isolation is at last ended' (ibid. 1996: 9). The book has various merits, not least its explicit aim of clearly and openly promoting a culture of dialogue as opposed to one of hatred and violence. Nevertheless, the prevailing message is one in which the extreme left figure invariably as the instigators and aggressors, and the extreme right as their victims. This is not to say that the latter did not make use of violence, but they did so in order to defend themselves. The Strategy of Tension is also presented as having been conceived primarily with a view to attacking and criminalising the right, particularly at a time when the neofascist party, the MSI, was growing at the polls. In short, the 'historical memory of the right' is still constructed in terms of self-victimisation, with the other groups figuring as the guilty parties.

Baldoni's 2003 book with Provvisionato represents, by contrast, a considerable effort at achieving a more balanced reconstruction of the past. While the two perspectives – left and right – tend to be presented alongside each other, rather than merging into a unitary account, nevertheless there is also evidence that each side has tried to open up to the views of the other. As far as *stragismo* is concerned, the book contains significant acknowledgements. It is stated, in fact, that the Valpreda trail was a 'false trail' (Baldoni and Provvisionato 2003: 38) and that the 'black trail' brought to light a connivance between Freda, Ventura, Delle Chiaie, Borghese and others, on the one hand, and the Office of Classified Affairs of the Ministry of the Interior, on the other (ibid.: 39). Gianfranco Bertoli, responsible for the 1973 Milan massacre, defined simply as a self-proclaimed anarchist in Baldoni's 1996 book, is now qualified as 'a very strange anarchist' (ibid.: 149). Finally, it is clearly stated that 'it is possible to identify extreme-right manpower in the *stragismo* which from 1969 onwards devastated Italy' (ibid.: 249). In his interview with the author, however, carried out in 2005, Baldoni largely sidestepped these issues, as will be shown in the next section. The coincidence of the interview with the latest verdict for Piazza Fontana, as well as the 'official' reaction of total dismissal of the verdict by Alleanza Nazionale, may have contributed to a more defensive position on the part of Baldoni.

Finally, another exception is a book based on an interview with Massimo Anderson, ex-leader of the MSI youth organisation, Fronte della Gioventù, and promoter, in the mid-1970s, of a postfascist party, twenty years ahead of the creation of Alleanza Nazionale. In the book (Anderson, 2003), the author gave an interpretation of *stragismo* which is close to Baldoni's, in the sense that he put the emphasis on the instigators, while not denying that some neofascists might have been among the culprits:

> If we stick to the identities of the perpetrators, nearly all now known, the attempt to diminish the responsibilities of the right and the left appears puerile ... Everything becomes more complicated, however, if we enter into the analysis of 'cui prodest' ... I

repeat: we cannot exclude that some circles of the radical right were infiltrated by elements of the Italian or foreign secret services, to make use of the more impressionable individuals. This hypothesis, however, if it puts into question the role of some individuals, does not explain the most serious issue, that of the masterminders. (Anderson 2003: 59–62)

What these oscillations seem to indicate is that we are at best in the presence of a few hesitant and tentative 'openings' to a more self-critical reconstruction of the past, but also that these have failed to make any significant inroads into the dominant homogeneous and justificatory 'memory' of the ingroup. Even more importantly, the 'ingroup' in this case is not to be identified solely with the radical right – that is, that part of the right which refused to accept the transformation of the Movimento Sociale Italiano into Alleanza Nazionale. On the contrary, as far as reconstructions of neofascism, *stragismo* and the Strategy of Tension are concerned, the ingroup encompasses both Alleanza Nazionale and the organisations which continue to subscribe to fascist ideals. Differences of opinion do exist, but they cut across the divide between the neo- and the postfascist right, as will become even clearer in the next sections.

## First-generation neofascist activists: fiercely independent or 'collaborationist'?

Connected to the first issue is the thorny question of the independence versus subordination (to other forces) of neofascist activists. Judicial investigations and trials, as we saw in Part I, have established, on the basis of considerable evidence, that there existed close links between the Ordine Nuovo cells in the Triveneto, the Nuclei for the Defence of the State, and some corps of the *Carabinieri* as well as Italian and overseas intelligence structures. The prevailing interpretation argues that certain neofascist organisations subordinated their anti-American stance to the pressing need of fighting a greater enemy, that is, communism, and specifically the Italian Communist Party. It is well documented that the American precursor of the CIA, the Office of Strategic Services (OSS), started to recruit Italian fascist elements as early as 1944, precisely with the aim of securing the collaboration of proven, and indeed in many cases bitterly ferocious, anti-communist elements who would be prepared to engage in combat actions should the need arise. According to various sources, including ex-member of Ordine Nuovo Vincenzo Vinciguerra, ex-OSS officer Peter Tompkins (1995; 2005), and an official American history of counterintelligence (Rafalko 1998), Prince Junio Valerio Borghese, the Commander of the X MAS for the Republic of Salò, was one of the fascists who agreed to collaborate with the Americans and for this reason was saved from reprisal by the partisans. On the basis of the testimony of Carlo Digilio, Vinciguerra and others, as we saw, it was alleged that many members of Ordine Nuovo were in the pay of American intelligence structures. Among these were

Carlo Digilio himself, Delfo Zorzi and Marcello Soffiati. Further substantial evidence, already examined in Part I, points to close links between Ordine Nuovo and the Italian military intelligence structures, as well as between Avanguardia Nazionale and the Office of Classified Affairs within the Ministry of the Interior. Finally, many accredited interpretations of the Strategy of Tension, as we saw in Part I, attribute considerable importance to the conference that took place on 3-5 May 1965, at the Hotel Parco dei Principi in Rome, organised by the Istituto Alberto Pollio, a private institute close to the Ministry of Defence. The main topic discussed at this conference was 'Revolutionary Warfare', that is to say, the use of unorthodox and irregular means in order to fight the communist threat. The meeting is often considered both the starting point of and the theorising platform for, the Strategy of Tension.

The reconstructions of the Strategy of Tension put forward by representatives of Alleanza Nazionale on the *Commissione stragi* by and large dismissed these allegations as demonstrably untrue. During the hearing in the Commission of Judge Salvini, Fragalà made it clear that in his view the prosecuting magistrate had made a serious mistake when he had come to the conclusion that Ordine Nuovo was 'the armed right-hand man of the CIA and the Americans'. Anyone who had studied the documents produced by this group would know that its political ideology was openly anti-American, since American imperialism and the CIA were considered 'the enemies and political adversaries of Ordine Nuovo on the same level as the Soviet Union and the KGB' (Commissione parlamentare d'inchiesta sul terrorismo in Italia e sulle cause della mancata individuazione dei responsabili delle stragi, *Elenco Audizioni, Aggiornamento al 17 gennaio 2001*, 12th Session, hearing of Guido Salvini, 20 March 1997). When Salvini replied that it was possible to make a tactical choice and justify it in the name of fighting 'an absolute evil', while remaining loyal to an overarching ideology, Fragalà insisted that Ordine Nuovo had 'first and foremost been anti-American, much less so and only secondarily anti-Communist. If this is your idea, I respect it, but it contrasts with History'.

Even more vehemently, Gian Paolo Pelizzaro, journalist and coauthor of some of the reports submitted by Alleanza Nazionale to the *Commissione stragi*, rejected any possible connivance between the intelligence services and neofascist organisations. Asked about the role played by the Italian secret services in the Strategy of Tension, he replied by defending the figure of Federico Umberto D'Amato, the Head of the Office of Classified Affairs of the Ministry of the Interior. D'Amato, he said, was 'the greatest servant this state has had … he was turned into a monster which he was not … the offices headed by this prefect are offices which brought prestige to Italian intelligence because they were able to prevent much worse things than those that happened' (interview with the author, 5 October 2005). He went on to say that if D'Amato had had contacts with Avanguardia Nazionale leader, Stefano Delle Chiaie, it was because it was part of his duty but there was no evidence to prove that he had given orders to plant the bombs as this was 'historically false.' Of the same tenor was Pelizzaro's defence of the figure of Guido Giannettini, the SID informer and collaborator who had contacts with the neofascists and helped important witnesses escape abroad at the time of the first trial for the Piazza Fontana massacre: 'Giannettini worked for the SID [the military intelligence], he was an incredible man, what he managed to report – he utilised Freda and Ventura and others as sources ... he wrote extraordinary things and used to give the SID extremely important analyses ... Giannettini must be viewed with respect' (interview with the author, 5 October 2005). As far as the (in)famous conference at the Istituto Pollio was concerned, Pelizzaro was quite contemptuous of prevailing interpretations:

> To elevate that conference – which incidentally was a conference not an unlawful assembly – to take that conference which was significant in political terms and then to turn it into something almost elusive ... It was a public meeting, with the armed forces, intelligence services, politicians [who believed] that there were two options: either to insulate the military world and preserve it from any political interference or to contrast the by then well-rooted political interference by the left with a cultural counter-offensive by the right. If we go and read the public contributions [to the conference] I challenge anyone legitimately to establish any link, however remote, between that public event and an act of *strage*.

It is possible to see from the above that Pelizzaro's reconstruction is seemingly more concerned with defending the reputation and honour of the Italian state and intelligence structures than those of the neofascists. One senses from his analysis that he reserves his admiration for the work of these state structures, even while he 'condones' and justifies the actions of the neofascists. In effect, Pelizzaro's reconstruction adopts a statist and nationalist viewpoint, rather than originating from a neo- or postfascist perspective. It is also quite openly pro-American. As well as the Italian state, he also defended NATO and the CIA, stating that the real and serious risk Italy ran during the Cold War was that it might end up leaving NATO: if this had happened, the country would have found itself in the same 'purgatory' as the nonaligned countries. As for the CIA, contrary to prevailing myths, it 'did its best to prevent the worst': 'is there any evidence that the CIA was implicated in acts of terrorism? If there is, it should be brought out. Where is the evidence?'

Going back to the issue of the independence or subordination of the neofascists, it is clear that both Fragalà and Pelizzaro argue in favour of the former, but with different preoccupations. Fragalà, as representative of Alleanza Nazionale, seems concerned primarily to safeguard the 'honour' and 'purity' of Ordine Nuovo against the charge that it stooped to strike a tactical deal with 'the enemy', putting aside its ideological creed. Pelizzaro, a right-leaning independent journalist, seems more concerned to safeguard the honour and reputation of the Italian state and its intelligence structures. As we shall see in the next chapter, Fragalà's viewpoint, for understandable reasons, is the one shared by the vast majority of neofascist activists in their memoirs.

On the side of the 'subordination' thesis we find other representatives of the right, including the neofascist right. Asked to elucidate his interpretation of Piazza Fontana, Rauti stated telegraphically: 'The secret services. The Strategy of

Tension' (Brambilla, 1995: 34). Even more significantly, Rauti candidly admitted that his group, Ordine Nuovo, had collaborated with the state in the name of a common enemy, thus implicitly giving the lie to the reconstruction Fragalà was to assert before the Parliamentary Commission on the Massacres a few years later. The exchange between Brambilla and Rauti is illuminating, as can be seen below:

Brambilla:   Do you believe that at a certain moment the extreme right, in order to fight communism, came to an agreement, collaborated with the Republican and anti-fascist state?

Rauti:       Yes. It collaborated more or less under the counter, and at some moments especially under the counter.

Brambilla:   What do you mean by 'under the counter'?

Rauti:       The secret services. The links with the military.

Brambilla:   Were there such links?

Rauti:       There were. The idea of the coup, for example, at one point circulated among the extreme right. As a shortcut to achieve power. Faced with a communist threat …

Brambilla:   In which years?

Rauti:       Well, in the 1960s. I myself was involved in links with the military.

Brambilla:   Let us say: you deluded yourselves that part of the anti-fascist state (the army, the *Carabinieri*, the secret services) would help you back into power?

Rauti:       No, that part of the state would resist extremely harshly the coming to power of the communists, and that we would find ourselves on the side of this part. But we did not delude ourselves. This is a fact.

Brambilla:   You made this reasoning: rather than the communists, better

Rauti:       better a takeover on the part of the military.

Brambilla:   A reasoning you regret, I believe. More than once you have said that your anti-communism was a mistake.

Rauti:       Yes it is true. I always had the suspicion that the communist threat was an invention; that the Soviet Union would never invade the West … The fact of growing up with the conviction that there existed a communist threat prevented us from being ourselves, in the fullness of our programmes.

Brambilla:   Are you saying that someone played you off against the communists? That the clear-cut opposition between you and them was 'willed', a set piece devised artificially?

Rauti:       I am saying that over the years certain questions have grown within me.

(Brambilla 1995: 31–33)

Rauti was just as explicit in an interview he gave to Nicola Rao for his book *Neofascisti* (1999):

We lived in a nation with limited sovereignty and with the communist threat on its borders. And we thought that a reaction on the part of the armed forces could promote more healthy, less democratic (in the negative meaning of this word) ideals. But also, I repeat, we were terrified by the communist threat. And so we lost sight of the fact that, in any case, in a Western nation, therefore within the American orbit of influence, any military coup would have to take place not against but only with the *placet* of the USA. (Rao 1999: 99)

A similar interpretation was put forward by Giorgio Pisanò. When asked who planted the bombs, he replied, 'The Ministry of the Interior. The Office of Classified Affairs within the Ministry of the Interior' (Brambilla 1995: 34). He went on to state that: 'These people had studied a strategy: we mobilise some madmen from the right and some from the left, we make them plant a few bombs here and there, a bit of red and a bit of black, we feed the press, and we demonstrate that if we do not strengthen the centre, the "opposed extremisms" will prevail' (ibid., 1995: 53). Pisanò seemed to agree with Rauti that the neofascist activists had been unaware of playing 'into the hands of the anti-fascists', yet he also believed that they had consciously collaborated with the secret services. In other words, they may have fallen into a trap as far as Piazza Fontana is concerned, but they fell into it with their eyes open in terms of their collaboration with the secret services. These two interpretations are not far removed from the one that emerged in the recent judicial trials, and they are quite antithetical to the reconstructions put forward by Fragalà, Pelizzaro and others during the hearings of the Parliamentary Commission on the Massacres and in the final reports submitted in 2001. The different factors accounting for these two diverging reconstructions are explored below.

An alternative interpretation was put forward by Adalberto Baldoni. In an interview with the author (7 October 2005), Baldoni sidestepped the issue of the likely involvement of, and possible motivations behind, the neofascist activists suspected and/or convicted of *stragismo*, placing the responsibility for it entirely at the door of political strategists. In his view the theory of the Italian secret services masterminding the Strategy of Tension was a ridiculous one, since military and intelligence structures carried out the politicians' orders. He did not rule out the possible involvement of external bodies, given that Italy occupied a strategic position in the Cold War and had a very strong Communist Party, which obviously would have greatly concerned both NATO and the USA. In his words:

The Strategy of Tension must be viewed from this angle. Who took advantage from it? As for the perpetrators on the ground, it did not really matter if they were social dropouts and/or right-wing extremists who hated the system. Who gave them the explosives, the logistics, the money, and protected them if not the secret services? Who managed the secret services? Are we saying that Musumeci, Santovito etc. [Heads of Italian intelligence services] were not linked to the Defence Minister and the Prime Minister? And they say, ah the services were all deviated – but deviated from what? The Prime Minister did not know anything? What about Cossiga and others? The *stragi* were carried out to stabilise the system, I am not the only one to say this. (Interview with the author, 7 October 2005)

As for the convicted neofascists, such as Vinciguerra, 'they were mavericks, it had nothing to do with it, even if a few culprits were found among extreme-right activists, I challenge anybody to explain what were their motivations.' In short, Baldoni placed the blame at the door of the secret services and DC politicians but he also dismissed the issue of the material culprits as largely irrelevant.

It is easy to understand why the issue of a possible collaboration of the extreme right with state structures in the name of anti-communism during the period of the Cold War has proven to be such an intractable topic for the right. To start with, as we saw, this reconstruction puts the ideological purity of the extreme right into question. It is true that this ought not to be an insurmountable obstacle, since it would indicate that Italian neofascism was prepared to sacrifice its ideological principles in the name of the greater interest of the fatherland. Indeed, this argument should appeal to Alleanza Nazionale much more than to unredeemed neofascists such as Pino Rauti, yet the latter was prepared to give ground as far as his own group was concerned, whereas the former strenuously denied any such allegations with reference to the same group.

Second, and more importantly, in the eyes of many these allegations lead straight to the conclusion that the neofascists had collaborated with state structures in the guise of subordinate allies and, even worse, in the guise of perpetrators of particularly ignoble deeds. As Marcello De Angelis pointed out:

> The preferred scheme was that after the Second World War, in order to face the communist danger, Italian sectors within the armed forces and among the industrialists, which in turn were controlled by the CIA, recruited some veterans of the Social Republic who were viscerally anti-communist and trained them as sappers and guerrillas and they in turn became the recruiters and trainers of new generations and so forth. (Interview with the author, 6 October 2006).

De Angelis did not deny that there could have been collaboration at some level, but he was keen to frame and justify it in the context of a climate of fear and witch-hunting in relation to fascist veterans after the Second World War:

> Obviously for the people who came from the experience of the Social Republic the memory of the purges and systematic executions was still alive and vivid, with the *foibe* in the region of Venezia-Giulia and the massacres, the mass killings in the Emilia triangle; for this reason many thought that upon achieving power these [the communists] would go around from house to house to round up entire families and do to them what was done in the majority of communist parties – this was a deeply felt problem among the extreme right.

Another ex-leader of Terza Posizione, Giuseppe Dimitri, who, like De Angelis, is today a member of Alleanza Nazionale, also strongly reaffirmed the autonomy and independence of all neofascist organisations, arguing that the fate of various neofascists would have been very different had they been closely linked to other forces:

The neofascist groups were the victims, precisely those which suffered the most from state repression. I saw this with my own eyes, I lived these experiences, I saw the way in which Delle Chiaie and many people close to Borghese used to live. These were people who lived a life of sacrifices. With the experience of life I have acquired, I believe today that if these people had been directed by other forces they would have been able to enjoy a much easier existence, not least from a political point of view. (Interview with the author, 11 October 2005)

Third, what particularly infuriates many representatives of the right is the widespread assumption that all the neofascist groups collaborated with state structures, regardless of the political context and the timing of the collaboration. As Dimitri stated:

Once we start applying this mechanism, we end up applying it everywhere. My own generation is not exempted. This is why in the end it becomes possible to say that the Bologna massacre was carried out by Ciavardini and Fioravanti when I am certain this was not the case. I am certain not just from a personal point of view, because I know what they were up to, what kind of people they were, but also taking into consideration issues of strategy and tactic. (Interview with the author, 11 October 2005)

Fourth, what is also refuted is the 'demonisation' of the neofascists in contrast to a prevailing idealised vision of the political violence perpetrated by the extreme left. Once again, it was De Angelis who articulated these feelings most clearly, as is evident both from the above and from his own assessment of the need for a 'shared memory':

There is a problem of shared memory because we cannot allow that our children will be taught, as we were taught and it is still being taught, the reading that on the right we had the massacres and the most cowardly and sinister type of terrorism, whereas on the left they carried out an armed struggle for other motives, both social and political. Hence as far as we are concerned we continue this fight for the truth about what happened from the 1960s onwards, not just the massacres but also terrorism, because tons of books have been written on the connivance between real or presumed extreme-right elements and representatives of the secret services etc. etc., and there are at least as many [cases] on the extreme left but these are still untold or if they come out they do not become exemplary ... if on one side there were the links with the CIA so it is proved that on the other side there were links with the KGB, the Stasi and various Arab socialist countries; in the same way as on the right there were people who were given weapons or at least information by the police and the *Carabinieri* this was true also for the left.

The prevailing attitude of denial can also be accounted for by the fact that what is perceived by the right as false negative stereotyping of Italian neofascism appears to emphasise traits which are the exact opposite of the ones the neofascist right has always attributed to itself. Among these are 'honour', 'bravery' and 'truthfulness', whereas participation in *stragismo* implies 'dishonour', 'cowardice' and 'deceit'. The problem is that it is perfectly possible to argue that some neofascist groups, especially the first-generation ones, had links to state structures and were implicated in *stragismo*, while the later ones had a different dynamic (as we shall now see) and operated against the state rather than on its side. Yet this (more balanced) interpretation is generally studiously avoided or indeed openly rejected by the right, for two main reasons.

First, it would severely puncture the positive self-representation of neofascism as a homogeneous ingroup which was collectively victimised both by its enemy and by the state. Second, as Dimitri's and De Angelis's reconstructions reveal, it would cast a shadow over all the neofascist groups, including those of the second generation, such as the NAR led by Valerio Fioravanti, thus providing ammunition to those who believe that 'once *stragisti*, always *stragisti*' and indeed that 'once in the service of other forces, always ready to be manipulated'. In this context, the strategy adopted by many representatives of the right is to proceed in reverse order. They thus start by focusing on the second generation of neofascists, portraying them as both idealistic and fiercely independent of any state structures or foreign agencies. This representation is then projected backwards onto the first generation of neofascist groups, who are (or must be) exonerated of any 'false' accusations of collaborationism. It is a vicious circle, and one which seems impossible for the right to break down (despite Rauti's own admissions).

At any rate, even the second generation of neofascists, albeit much less problematic than the first one in terms of lending itself to positive self-representation, raises some controversial issues for the right. It is with considerable difficulty that a unitary reassessment of the past is achieved concerning the beliefs, motivations and actions of the groups operating in the second half of the 1970s. It is the reconstructions of the activities of these groups that will be analysed in the next section.

## Second-generation neofascist activists: defenceless victims or reckless hotheads?

In all the reconstructions of their own past put forward by the right, there appears to have been a clear-cut break between the first and second generations of neofascist activists. While it is (begrudgingly) granted that the former may in a few cases have been collaborating with the armed forces, the *Carabinieri* and/or intelligence structures, the latter are unanimously exonerated from any similar charges. All accounts depict a harsh political climate in the first half of the 1970s, in which it was increasingly impossible for neofascists, not only those belonging to 'fringe' organisations, but also all those who were members of the MSI, to carry out even the most peaceful and blameless activities, such as affixing posters in the streets or even simply meeting in the party sections. They were constantly being harassed and attacked by the left and, after the formation of terrorist groups such as the Red Brigades and Prima Linea, increasingly selected as the designated targets of deliberate killings. All reconstructions recall a slogan of the extreme left which stated that, 'To kill a fascist is not a crime', and refer to specific examples of ignoble assassinations of innocent people for political reasons: an arson attack against the house of MSI member Mario Mattei, carried out at Primavalle, near Rome, on 16 April 1973, in which two of his sons, aged twenty-two and ten, lost their lives; the murder of a Greek student, Mikis Mantakas, shot dead in Rome on 28 February 1975; and a massacre at Acca Larentia, near Rome, on 7 January 1978, when two young members of the MSI were shot dead by extreme-left terrorists, and another, later on the same day, was killed by a *Carabiniere*.

This last episode is generally considered emblematic, as it marked the dividing line between a period in which the extreme right was purely and simply a victim of the extreme left, and a period in which the neofascists decided that it was time for them to take up arms and to respond to the killings with more killings. Furthermore, the episode marked a new phase in so far as from then on the extreme right considered the police and the *Carabinieri* – indeed, the Italian state – as their enemies rather than their (potential) allies. It is for this reason that the possibility that the second generation of neofascist activists also had some links to state bodies is totally dismissed in any reconstruction put forward by the right (as we saw in Part I, other reconstructions, by contrast, cast some doubts over this presumed autonomy). The new phase saw the formation of new organisations, Costruiamo l'Azione, Terza Posizione and the Nuclei Armati Rivoluzionari, which either contained within themselves a paramilitary core, such as the first two groups, or were entirely dedicated to the armed struggle, like the NAR.

The prevailing 'narrative of victimhood' is quite powerful, but it also presents a very idealised and one-sided picture of the political violence of the late 1960s and 1970s, even if we leave aside the issue of *stragismo*. It is true, as the journalist Luca Telese has recently documented in a book which reconstructs the murders of twenty-one young neofascists, entitled *Cuori neri* ('Black Hearts'), published in 2006, that the 1970s witnessed an impressive series of violent attacks by extreme-left groups upon presumed or real extreme-right activists and sympathisers, which at times constituted a preordained strategy aimed at physically eliminating the 'enemy'. Nevertheless, there were also numerous acts of aggression and violence perpetrated by the extreme right against the extreme left. According to Piero Ignazi, a political scientist and expert on the Movimento Sociale Italiano, 'between 1969 and 1973, 95% of 'minor' episodes of violence (beatings, aggressions, damages) can be attributed to extreme-right activists and more than half of the attacks for which there was claiming of responsibility were carried out by extreme-right groups' (1994: 38). Similarly, della Porta and Rossi (1984) had concluded that in the period 1969–75 the vast majority of violent events were to be attributed to the extreme right. Indeed, as della Porta and Tarrow (1986: 623) pointed out, acts of violence perpetrated by the extreme left between 1966 and 1973 tended to occur during 'large groups events', whereas the extreme right was more involved 'when violence [was] directed at people.' It was only in the second half of the 1970s that the violence perpetrated by extreme-left organisations became dominant as well as more targeted. Summing up the evidence, Weinberg and Eubank (1988: 531) stated that, 'Not only was right-wing violence frequent, it was also particularly virulent. Almost three quarters of those individuals killed or seriously injured by the terrorist groups were the victims of neo-Fascist attacks, not those of the revolutionary organisations.' By contrast, Marcello De Angelis was adamant that 'during the 1970s in ninety-eight per cent of all cases the radical right played the role of victims' (interview with the author, 6 October 2005).

However, while there is a general consensus on the right over the victim status of the second generation of neofascists during the phase which preceded Acca Larentia, as well as over the 'spontaneity' and 'autonomy' of their activities, there are differences of opinion concerning the justifiability of their actions and the extent to which they can still be considered as victims during the second phase, in which they became perpetrators of violence. On the one hand, we find the reconstructions of those, like Marcello De Angelis, who were directly involved in the events of those years and, in the light of their own experience, justify the decision to obtain and to use arms. On the other hand, we have the reconstructions of those who condemned the turn to violence at the time and/or are severely critical in retrospect. In this second camp we should also place those representatives of the right who hold nationalist and 'statist' values and beliefs, and to whom a rebellion against state forces on the part of extreme-right organisations is simply anathema.

Let us consider the views of Marcello De Angelis, today's Editor of *Area* and a Senator for Alleanza Nazionale. He was one of the leaders of Terza Posizione, the group founded by Gabriele Adinolfi, Giuseppe Dimitri and Roberto Fiore, and for this reason was charged with participation in an armed band. After several years on the run, he returned to Italy, where he spent a period in jail before being released in 1992. His youngest brother, Nanni De Angelis, was also an activist, as he was a member of the NAR, led by Valerio Fioravanti; captured by the police on 4 October 1980, he was found dead in his cell the next day. His death is considered suspicious by many on the right, who reject the verdict of suicide and believe he was killed by the police (Semprini 2003; Telese 2006: 650–714).

In De Angelis's reconstruction, the arson attack at Primavalle and the killing of Mantakas were the first major episodes of violence against the extreme right that were to lead many young activists towards taking up arms, not least in the face of a perceived passivity on the part of the MSI, a total denial of involvement on the part of the left, and no serious attempts to discover the culprits on the part of the police. With reference to Mantakas, he stated that:

> the entire left mobilised in order to ... maintain that in reality it was not extreme-left activists who had carried out the shooting but it was those on the right who had shot at each other ... the culprits were without doubt the fascists because they are capable of doing this and more, so much so they carried out the *stragi*, and if they were guilty for Piazza Fontana they are clearly capable of killing one of their own. (Interview with the author, 6 October 2006)

After that episode, according to De Angelis, many young members of the MSI left the party in protest, after pleading in vain to be given permission to carry weapons in order to defend themselves. In their view, by taking up arms they would be able to prevent more deaths. As De Angelis remarked, their position was 'debatable', yet it was clearly justifiable.

Another ex-leader of Terza Posizione, Giuseppe Dimitri, presented a less clear-cut reconstruction of the political violence of the 1970s. While maintaining that there was a widespread climate of violence in the 1970s and that any radical political movement could not operate without being armed, he also conceded that within Terza Posizione there was a military core, and that the group was involved in armed robberies: 'We had to go and find the weapons somewhere, you did not find them lying around. That means we had to organise ourselves, carry out robberies in gunsmiths or in banks' (interview with the author, 11 October 2005). Asked explicitly whether he believed that the aggressors were always on one side and the victims on the other, he replied that this was not the case, since,

> We deliberately decided to carry out military actions which would allow us to be politically active in the [Rome] neighbourhoods … This we did and from that time onwards we were able to engage in politics in these neighbourhoods. I know this because I studied these sociological dynamics, I can guarantee you that they still work successfully today. Hence we carried out various successful military actions which wounded a great number of our enemies but lastly allowed us to engage in politics without any problems, in the sense that our activists were no longer attacked'. (Interview with the author, 11 October 2005)

While Dimitri came across as more impartial than De Angelis in his assessment of the political violence of the 1970s, it is also the case that he remained neutral in terms of the choice of taking up arms, concurring with De Angelis that the recourse to violence was inevitable for anyone who wanted to engage in radical politics.

Less sympathetic is Adalberto Baldoni (interview with the author, 7 October 2005). While he subscribed to the view that the extreme right were being constantly attacked by the left, he still blamed the decision to take up arms as one that played right into the hands of those forces which had an interest in exacerbating the conflict in the country. First, in his view, the fact that the extreme right were numerically small should have prevented them from exposing themselves to terrible reprisals. Unlike De Angelis, who appeared to suggest that they had been heroic in engaging in a struggle against much more powerful enemies, Baldoni believed that they had been irresponsible. Second, they had been naïve, just like the extreme left: they 'too fell into the trap of those who masterminded this creeping civil war.' Third, their actions, far from 'defending' extreme-right activists, had caused many more deaths among them, including innocent members of the MSI. Fourth, many of the new organisations, such as Terza Posizione, produced no original ideas of their own other than inciting hatred through their writings, which in turn generated and justified violence. In short, the armed struggle on the part of the right was 'a folly'.

Even more drastic are those, such as Pelizzaro, who adopt a nationalist and statist perspective. In contrast to his leniency towards Freda and the other neofascists implicated in the *stragi*, he reserved harsh words for the later generation of neo-fascist activists, totally rejecting their self-proclaimed status of victims. It is worth reporting his words in full:

> I know many of these people, they complain of being victims. Why victims? If you behaved better and kept your place and accepted the democratic logic – that first one side then the other goes [in government] – without starting to burn the country, perhaps you would have avoided all your troubles. They all say: I am a victim, I have been skinned alive. Yes, the state one day got sick of you, deeply sick of you and caught all of you from whichever side and threw you in jail and punished you also for what you had not done; but it was a reaction and all human reactions are imperfect, it was a reaction to a bottom-up uprising which risked destabilising this country. (Interview with the author, 5 October 2005)

The apparent contradiction, in Pelizzaro's reconstruction, between this stern indictment of the neofascist activists operating in the second half of the 1970s, and the staunch defence of the early generation of neofascists implicated in *stragismo*, is somewhat puzzling. It is probably best understood in the context of his overall assessment of the exigencies dictated by the Cold War and above all the need to contain communism in Italy. As we saw in a previous section, Pelizzaro strenuously defended the role played by Italy's intelligence structures during the Cold War and at one point he hinted at a possible role of Franco Freda as crucial informer to Giannettini. From his perspective, this would contribute to placing Freda in a positive light, because he was useful to the state, while the second-generation neofascist activists were simply a nuisance to and an enemy of the state; thus he considers them personally responsible for aggravating a situation of emergency.

There are many more reconstructions of the second phase of neofascist activism, but the ones summarised above encapsulate the more common ones. However, it is important to set apart from the above the reconstructions put forward by individual protagonists of Italian neofascism through their personal memoirs, since these tend to follow a different logic and should be examined through different lenses. This is especially the case with those protagonists who were directly responsible for acts of violence, which led to their imprisonment for a number of years. In their cases, much more so than for the ones whose views we have recorded thus far, personal and lived experience, and self-identity, as well as issues of credibility and truthfulness, both come into play and are at stake. For this reason, we have chosen to examine them in the next chapter.

## Conclusion

Reading and listening to the historical reconstructions produced by the neo- and postfascist right, it would be impossible to underestimate the strong sense of bitterness, grievance, self-victimisation and demonisation of 'the other' which pervades such narratives. The narrators present their 'ingroup' systematically as a collective victim and constantly shift the blame away from members of the group and their past actions. As Marcello De Angelis told the author: 'We were victims of the political situation, of the political unrepresentativeness of our community – a community exposed to fierce reprisals.' The reconstructions examined in this chapter thus establish an implied equivalence between neofascism and oppressed and persecuted groups and between neofascist violence and defensive struggles to ensure the physical survival of the group. These representations do not take into account the exploitative and oppressive nature of the fascist/neofascist ideology and construct as oppressed and persecuted a group whose ghettoisation was as much constructed from within as imposed from the outside, and which operated within a democratic framework, as opposed to an authoritarian regime. While there can be no moral justification for representing the collective experience of the 'ingroup' in terms of persecution, conveniently forgetting that the referent ideology and the regimes founded on it were discriminatory and oppressive, there is nevertheless no doubting the widespread resentment among both the neo- and the postfascist right at real or presumed injuries suffered by its members in the recent past.

Even after the transformation of the Movimento Sociale Italiano into Alleanza Nazionale, the new party appears to continue to rely upon 'negative identity', that is, requiring 'a threatening "other", in order to make sense of its own identity' (Liechty and Clegg 2001: 119). Rather than replacing the old oppositional identities with more pluralist ones, the party – or at any rate, a significant section of the party – still endows neofascist groups with positive values such as honour, integrity, truthfulness and bravery, whereas the extreme left is charged with negative values, such as deceit, cynicism and cowardice. Thus one of the most popular images among the right is that of representing the violent conflict of the 1970s as a fight between two uneven sides, of which one (the left) found strength in numbers and rarely risked their lives, whereas the other, the right, despite being heavily outnumbered, heroically stood its ground. Another recurrent narrative concerns the left's systematic propensity to tell lies, which is referred to disparagingly as the 'so-called revolutionary truth'. In this context, new groups have now joined the category of the 'other' in the eyes of the party, including magistrates and 'repented' witnesses. The latter are not explicitly defined as 'traitors', nevertheless the contempt and hatred they seem to inspire in many commentators close to Alleanza Nazionale can only be explained in this light.

This situation, in which 'the new attitudes are not necessarily integrated with one's pre-existing value structure and belief system' (Kelman 2004: 118–19), largely explains the current 'politics of nonreconciliation' prevalent among the postfascist as well as the neofascist right, with reference to the violent conflict that took place from the late 1960s onwards. But what can in turn explain the persistence of the old set of beliefs among Alleanza Nazionale? At the level of the party members and middle ranks, especially those subscribing to the Destra Sociale faction, this attitude can be attributed to a large extent to personal life experiences. There are many who, even when they reluctantly accept that 'on the opposite side' people may have totally different memories of the political conflict, also remain fully convinced that their own experienced reality of 'victims' can be factually verified and indeed constitutes the 'objective truth'. Once again, it was Marcello De Angelis who best explained this specific mindset:

> Personally I went to an assembly at my old school, Mameli, with a very dear friend of mine from the left with whom I have remained very close friends; I realised when we talked of our daily experiences that on his side there was a completely different view ... we lived the same lives, same age, same culture, identical, but in two different situations ... however, I could write down all those dates [of the various acts of aggression] and verify with the trials [that the culprits were predominantly from the left]. (Interview with the author, 6 October 2005)

As we saw, scholars like Piero Ignazi and della Porta present a markedly different picture with regards to the perpetrators of political violence in the late 1960s and early 1970s. Furthermore, at a collective level, the prevailing attitude can be accounted for by the difficulty of negotiating a new, nonvictimising identity for a party which for so long depended upon an adversarial set of beliefs to ensure existential cohesion and purpose. Finally, as the preceding analysis showed, the difficulty of overcoming old sets of beliefs can also be explained by a strongly felt grievance that many acts of violence carried out in the 1970s against neofascists are still unresolved and no culprits have been brought to justice. This encourages an attitude of: 'We have our own dead to mourn, why should we mourn our enemy's dead?' This same attitude, as we shall see in the next chapter, is replicated in the self-narratives of neofascist protagonists of the political violence of that period.

This chapter has indeed highlighted, among other issues, the question of the existence of victims among the extreme right, which is not the same as the extreme right as victim. In his interview with the author, Marcello De Angelis appeared to imply that for him the bottom line for reconciliation was a reconstruction which acknowledged the role of victims of many young neofascists of the second generation. In his own words,

> the same problem we have with the *stragi* we also have with the Primavalle arson attack, the murder of Mantakas and the massacre at Acca Larentia, as well as the murder of nearly thirty other people; for two or three of these we know the culprits but for the more serious episodes like Primavalle or Acca Larentia the police did not do anything. Hence one thing is an amnesty; another is simply putting a tombstone over the dead and not giving a damn. (Interview with the author, 6 October 2005)

Claiming that there were innocent victims among the right whose sufferings and injustices deserve to be properly acknowledged can be seen as a step in the right direction. However, what is glaringly missing is the other side of this acknowledgment; that is to say, that there were also culprits on the same side, including those found guilty of *stragismo*, and that any claim of victim status for the extreme right as an ingroup is unfounded.

In short, there has not been a discernible process of self-transformation among the postfascist right, or indeed the emergence of a more balanced self-identity. Similar conclusions were reached by the journalist Luca Telese in his book *Cuori neri* (2006). According to Telese, 'despite everything, the many divisions within the contemporary right have not undermined the sense of belonging to a community which is still united by a shared history, a common myth. The right is fragmented in a thousand paths and in innumerable individual histories, in fierce disputes and irresolvable personalisms, yet it maintains a sense of belonging to a common world' (ibid.: xvi). In this context, the neofascist victims of extreme-left violence, 'weigh today upon the identity of the right more than the memories of fascism: if it is true that Gianfranco Fini's trip to Israel systematised the tormented chapter of Salò, it is also true that the dead of the 1970s remain a non-resolved chapter, so much so that the party, today, continues to divide itself (at times schizophrenically) between a radical cult of the "black boys" and the more pragmatic cult of government' (ibid.).

However, the uncompromising attitude shown by the representatives of Alleanza Nazionale on the *Commissione stragi* cannot solely be attributed to the sentiments outlined above, as it was predominantly linked to issues of party strategy. To acknowledge neofascism's role in *stragismo* at a time when the party was seeking, and indeed had already largely acquired, democratic legitimacy, was probably considered too risky. It was easier to deny and 'erase' one's own 'skeletons in the cupboard', especially since the party's longstanding enemy, the Communist Party, had in their eyes escaped too lightly from its past subservience to the Soviet Union and its failed denunciations of Stalin's crimes. Alleanza Nazionale's alliance with Forza Italia further explains its positioning, since neither party had any interest in reopening the issue of the involvement of state structures (or indeed American structures) in *stragismo* and the Strategy of Tension. In this context, neofascism would have been exposed to the public as the only villain in the plot, which would have been another powerful incentive to construct an alternative truth to the one established by the Courts.

The combination of widespread sentiments of bitterness and resentment among Alleanza Nazionale members and middle ranks, and party political strategic calculations, have therefore led to the prevalence of what I have called the politics of nonreconciliation on the part of the postfascist right, since any process of reconciliation implies revisiting and renegotiating the past. Whether it also means that such a process should not be attempted or would be redundant in the Italian case is a moot point which will be addressed in the final Conclusion to this book.

# CHAPTER 6
# The Self-narratives of Extreme-right Protagonists of the Political Conflict

## Introduction

As far as the protagonists of right-wing violence are concerned, the sources tend to be scarce, particularly when compared to those available in relation to ex-members of extreme-left paramilitary organisations. They are also of a different nature compared to the reconstructions put forward by representatives and sympathisers of Alleanza Nazionale and discussed in the previous chapter. First, many of these sources take the form of political memoirs, biographies and autobiographies written by individuals who were convicted or suspected perpetrators of political violence, including acts of *stragismo*. They also consist of interviews granted to journalists and to the author. Second, their memoirs, being of a personal nature, provide first-hand, potentially very valid, accounts of the terrible events related to their political militancy, but also run the risk of being simply vehicles for self-serving and self-justificatory renditions, designed primarily to create a degree of credibility for the narrators and an aura of 'romantic' heroism for the (extreme-right) protagonists of their stories. Third, as has been argued in the case of political memoirs in Northern Ireland, 'the primary purpose of such publications can be to continue the conflict by other means ... whereby the protagonist seeks to use memoir as a proxy weapon. For those authors/subjects who have played an "active" role in the conflict, and belong or have belonged to paramilitary organisations, this can serve as a means of conducting the battle by force of argument, rather than by the argument of force' (Hopkins 2001: 75). Finally, there is an aspect that appears to be specific to the Italian situation and the phenomenon of unidentified and unclaimed 'terrorism' in the shape of *stragismo*. Given that no paramilitary organisation (unlike in Northern Ireland) has ever admitted responsibility for this type of terrorism, and that there is a general consensus across the entire political spectrum that a *strage* constituted an abject, cowardly and morally inadmissible act, the memoirs of the protagonists of right-wing violence are especially preoccupied with refuting any charge of *stragismo*. This is true even in the case of individuals who have been convicted and sentenced through the Courts.

In light of the above, the self-narratives of both first- and second-generation neofascist leaders are examined in this chapter through recourse to the literature on narrative psychology and narrative analysis. The chapter examines in detail the stories of three neofascists, each of whom can be considered emblematic of a group, a strategy and even a generation. Stefano Delle Chiaie, born in 1936, founder and leader of Avanguardia Nazionale (AN) in 1959, is emblematic of the first-generation neofascists, suspected of plotting coups d'état and carrying out acts of *stragismo* in connivance with the secret services, the armed forces and the Americans. Gabriele Adinolfi, born in 1954, founder and leader of Terza Posizione (TP) in 1979, is emblematic of the second-generation neofascists, who were influenced by the students' movement and the youth rebellion of 1968 and devised a new, 'Third Way' strategy with a view to synthesising the ideologies of the extreme left and the extreme right and embracing anti-capitalist revolutionary movements. While officially refuting the armed struggle, Terza Posizione contained a paramilitary inner core within its ranks and carried out various violent actions, including robberies, beatings and arson attacks. Giuseppe Valerio Fioravanti, born in 1958, founder and leader of the Nuclei Armati Rivoluzionari (NAR) in 1979, is emblematic of the last generation of neofascists, who, when still in their teens, openly took up arms against the state, the police forces, the extreme left, and above all the MSI, in a spiral of violence which was as self-destructive as it was destructive. Born almost as a splinter group of TP, the NAR soon turned against this group, killing one of its members and plotting the murder of its leaders. Fioravanti was also found guilty of the worst act of *stragismo*, the 1980 bombing attack at Bologna station, a crime he has always vehemently denied. The main biographical material for these neofascists consists of interviews granted to the author in October 2005, complemented by other memoirs, writings and/or interviews.

## Narrating the self

Ever since the so-called 'narrative turn' in the social sciences, the concept of narrative has become increasingly prominent in various disciplines, including psychology, sociology and history. Narrative research is considered especially important when the object of analysis is personal experience and personal identity. Autobiographies, memoirs, personal and life histories, even interviews, constitute 'texts of lives, literary artifacts that generally seek to recount in some fashion what these lives were like' (Freeman 1993: 7). In 'narrating the self', people make sense of their lived experience, construct and convey meanings, and also construct their own individual as well as group identities. Thus narrative approaches to research are often informed by social constructionism, according to which neither 'the real world' nor 'the self' exist independently of linguistic and sociocultural representations. Taken to its most extreme implications, this leads to the concept of a 'saturated self', where the self ultimately 'vanishes fully into a state of relatedness. One ceases to believe in a self independent of the relations in which he or she is embedded' (Gergen 1991: 17). Among the main casualties of this postmodern condition are sincerity and truth, given that language does not refer to inner feelings or to the world 'out there' but is used to negotiate relationships:

> If one is multiply populated, harboring myriad voices from culture and history, there is no expression that stands as the true. And for the postmodern, words do not 'reflect' or 'picture' states of mind. Words are not mirrors or pictures but integral parts of ongoing interchange. They construct the individual as this or that within continuos patterns of relationships. One may profess 'I am sincere', but such an expression is not so much a reflection of a mental state as a state of relatedness. (Gergen 1991: 38)

Many scholars from different disciplines have shown concern over the loss and disintegration of both the social world and the inner self, and have striven to salvage both from radical versions of social constructionism, while recognising the central role played by language and narrative in personal lives and identities. Within a recent strand of psychology, known appropriately as 'narrative psychology', Crossley and Freeman, among others, postulated the need for an alternative approach. According to Crossley (2003: 289), what was needed was 'a different kind of psychology – one which retained the ability of appreciating the linguistic and discursive structuring of "self" and "experience", but one which also maintained a sense of the essentially personal, coherent and "real" nature of individual subjectivity'. Specifically, Crossley is convinced that lived experience matters: 'we do not totally create the materials we are to form. To a certain degree, we are stuck with what we have in the way of characters, capacities and circumstance' (Crossley 2000: 53). She distinguishes between 'historical truth' ('what has actually happened in the past') and 'narrative truth' ('a story about what has happened'), and argues that even a narrative approach to psychology must remain committed to the historical truth in the stories people tell of their lives and experiences. As she put it: 'There is a difference between acknowledging that a variety of frameworks can fit the same set of facts rendering them differently significant, and denying the existence of those facts' (ibid.: 62).

As for Freeman, he explicitly rejects what he calls 'the skeptical challenge' (1993:10), and sees his task primarily as 'to maintain and embrace this primacy of word *without losing world in the process*' (ibid.: 16) (his emphasis). Freeman argues forcefully that 'to deny the possibility of knowledge, whether of world or of self, is ... to engage in a profound act of bad faith, the consequence of which can only be a deafening silence.' If this is the case, the notion of 'truth' can be salvaged, even though this does not mean that people will be truthful:

> On some level, of course, we can virtually ignore the question of knowledge and truth, and create stories of ourselves that all but leap over the text of our existence; we can simply ignore who and what we have been, and fashion that picture of ourselves that we would most like to own. Functionally speaking, this may sometimes work quite

well for us – as long, that is, as the various 'facts' we have skipped over do not rear their ugly heads and punish us for all we have forgotten. But functionality and knowledge are by no means equivalent. Defenses, for instance, are often highly functional; they may allow us to take comfort in dangerous and threatening situations. But as a general rule they don't help us too much in knowing ourselves – at least not until they are exposed as such. (Freeman 1993: 147)

From this point of view, looking back upon, rethinking and retelling one's own past can be put to the service of truth: 'Narratives ... rather than being the mere fictions they are sometimes assumed to be, might instead be in the service of attaining exactly those forms of truth that are unavailable in the flux of the immediate' (Freeman 1993: 224). Freeman cites the example of Primo Levi, whose postwar reflection on his experiences in a German concentration camp (*Se questo è un uomo*; 'If This Is a Man') contributed first to making him apprehend the full horror of what had really happened and consequently to his suicide. During his captivity, Levi had mainly been preoccupied with surviving on a daily basis and this had, to an extent, made him blind to the human degradation of both torturers and prisoners that constituted the reality of life in the camp (Freeman 2003).

Both Crossley and Freeman attribute great importance to the ethical dimension of self-narratives. Crossley, drawing on the work of Taylor (1989), argues that issues of morality are closely linked to our sense of self and identity. Our lives are given meaning through a vision of 'the good', which often links us to other people in a 'defining community' (Crossley 2003: 298). Freeman and Brockmeier (2001: 97) introduced the concept of narrative integrity, which they defined as 'the conceptual space where autobiographical identity and the meaning of the good life meet.' According to them, one always accounts for one's own life 'in line with an overarching cultural system of ethical and moral values' (ibid.: 83). However, whereas in the past we tended to mould and narrate our lives in accordance with ideal models of 'the good life' – 'as embodied in the historical figures of the citizen of the Greek *polis*, the paterfamilias, the committed monk, the courageous warrior, and so on' – nowadays what constitutes 'the good' is virtually 'model-free' and much more open to a multiplicity of voices and visions (ibid.: 89). This is clearly connected to the 'end of grand narratives', but also to personal and historical contexts marked by change and transformation, when traditional assumptions are questioned and past events are reconsidered in a new light, both from the perspective of, and providing meanings for, the present. In terms of the ethical dimension of self-narratives, Freeman and Brockmeier argued that, in those reconstructions of the past where there is a 'master narrative' at play, there tends to be 'a high degree of conviction and certainty about the meaning of the past', but also greater constraints on the moral lessons that can be drawn from these memoirs, precisely because there is little room left for (self-) doubt. Hence 'what we might call the moral space of self-interpretation, and thus the space of auto-biographical memory itself, remains very much circumscribed' (ibid.: 85–86). This is partly because such narratives tend to be prescriptive, presenting one's own life as an example of a moral code in action.

However, Bamberg (2006) questioned Freeman's emphasis upon self-reflection, claiming that it constituted only one of the ways in which we ought to analyse narratives. According to him: 'Narrative analysis is less interested in a narrator who is self-reflecting or searching who s/he (really) is. Rather, we are interested in narrators who are engaging in the activity of narrating, that is, the activity of giving an account; for instance, when we engage in making past actions accountable from a particular (moral) perspective for particular situated purposes' (Bamberg 2006: 5). As well as the 'what' and the 'how' of a narrative, it is important therefore to pay attention to the audience, and to the ways in which 'speakers position themselves vis-à-vis the world out there and the social world here and now' (ibid.: 6). This means that we have to analyse self-narratives at the interface between narrator, content and audience: 'In working from these two levels of positioning (one with respect to the content of what the story was designed to be about, the other with respect to the coordination of the interaction between speaker and audience), we are better situated to make assumptions about the ideological positions (or master narratives) within which narrators are positioning a sense of self' (ibid.: 6).

On the issue of ideological positions, many scholars believe that any analysis of narratives has to take into account not only the individual perspective, but also the perspective of the group(s) to which the individual may feel s/he belongs. In particular, according to Bruner (2001: 35), who draws on the works of Taylor (1989) and Tajfel (1978), 'defining the Self and its allies also defines who are in the out-group.' Hence the contraposition which, as we saw in the previous chapter, marks groups' narratives, especially the attribution of positive traits to one's own group and negative ones to outgroups, is also recurrent in personal self-narratives which are framed by a strong master narrative and group affiliation. 'When members are strongly identified with a group, members' autobiographies may be expressed with the same narrative form that the group story has' (Feldman 2001: 143). These narratives tend to adopt a specific genre, that of a 'quest story', in which a hero is on a spiritual mission and has to overcome a series of obstacles and enemies, as well as undergoing many geographical and/or metaphorical travels. Typically, 'a superior hero is opposed by a much stronger, but morally inferior, antagonist with whom he has a climactic battle in the end' (ibid.: 133).

In short, when ideology and group identification are at play, the 'moral space' of the narrative becomes restricted. When 'narratives of various forms are used to reshape the past to fit certain ideological ends' (May 2004: 3), the truth is not at stake. When, in addition to this, the narrators adopt a prescriptive positioning and are primarily concerned with convincing the audience of their, and their group's, version of 'the good', their narratives are not about distancing themselves from the past and reflecting upon it in order to understand the historical truth. Similarly, the ways in which praise and blame are assigned in personal memoirs is greatly dependent upon one's adoption of a group and/or ideological perspective. Where the narrators are primarily concerned with showing themselves and their group in a positive, heroic, even triumphalist, light, and constantly shift the blame for past actions upon others, we cannot rely on their stories to achieve a more impartial reappraisal of the past.

Matters are complicated in the case of narratives dealing with (past) violence. In this case, too, it is possible to distinguish between legitimating narratives, aimed at justifying recourse to violent deeds with reference to myths, values, ideology and group identification, and critical/reflective narratives, which open up space for acknowledegment of wrongdoing on the part of the narrator and his/her group. Legitimating narratives of violence, and especially of ideologically and politically inspired violence, are constructed on the basis of recognisable patterns. First, crucially, 'violence is deemed acceptable only when it can be narratively constructed as necessary, inevitable, or as a last resort undertaken by people with pure or innocent motivations. … The premise of an "evil other" itself dedicated to unswerving violence is therefore a precondition for the hero's use of violence' (Smith, quoted in Cromer and Wagner-Pacifici 2001). Second, the narrator tends to rely on specific myths, often revolving around the adoption of the historical model of the warrior or soldier, with its accompanying virtues – honour, loyalty, dedication and martyrdom. Third, justification is also predicated on the degree of (real or presumed) oppression and persecution experienced by the narrator and/or the collective group in whose name the violence is/was committed. This often leads to representing the narrator/protagonist as a victim, which is important in terms of positioning one's own story vis-à-vis the audience, since 'we feel sorry and we sympathise for victims, while we are repulsed by villains' (Franzosi 1998: 535). Such myths reduce (or are presented as reducing) 'available options for individual behavior in occasions of crisis', which in turn 'is all too likely to engender a climate of violence', as the individual is forced to obey 'the dictates of honour and loyalty' (Paine 2001: 187). Finally, narratives of political violence generally present a specific 'dynamics of utopian transformation, which is encouraged and supported by a group of fellow believers, whose mutually reinforcing convictions protect them from horror or remorse' (Gomel 2003: xl). Individual emotions and sufferings are all but erased from representation, which follows its own rigid script: 'while the terrorist times his strike to coincide with the prime time news, his own self-representation substitutes dedication, sacrifice, or despair for the atrocity that is so plainly visible on the screen' (ibid.: xli).

By contrast, critical and reflective narratives told by protagonists of (past) violence will show at least some of the following: an awareness of and sensitivity to the plight and sufferings of others as victims, as opposed to the self-as-victim; the substitution of a master narrative and a rigid role model with a new capacity to recognise a plurality of selves and one's own capacity for evil, as well as for good; the ability to apportion praise and blame to self and others in a relatively impartial manner, perhaps accompanied by an expression of regret for past deeds; an explicit rejection of an adversarial genre based on the construction of *us* versus *them* (my friends versus their friends, my dead versus their dead, my victims versus their victims), and of the 'quest story', with its corollary of heroism and triumphalism. These would be replaced with alternative genres, which can include a 'conversion' story or, less dramatically, a story centred upon the 'rewriting of the self', and focusing on adapting, revising, even revolutionising the narrator's conception of the moral good.

It goes without saying that a linguistic analysis is an integral component of any narrative analysis, and attention must therefore be paid to the linguistic, syntactical and structural properties of a story. This kind of approach (Labov and Waletzky 1967; Labov 1972 and 2001) examines the linguistic construction of a narrative and focuses upon the sequence of 'temporally ordered clauses' (Labov 1972: 361), and the functional elements which characterise any 'fully formed narrative': Abstract, Orientation, Complicating Action, Evaluation, Resolution (ibid.: 363–70). Of these, the 'Complicating Action' represents the core of the narrative and the 'Evaluation' gives meaning and interpretation to the narrated events. The choice of language is a crucial part of the narrative and, together with the formal building blocks of the story, its temporal clauses, provides important clues as to possible omissions, untruths and misrepresentations. Structural and linguistic discrepancies in the story help the listener/reader detect a narrator's transformation of the original sequence of events (usually carried out, consciously or unconsciously, to present the narrator/character in a positive light and to shift blame away from oneself) and even reconstruct the correct, untransformed, sequence (Labov 2001: 2). A linguistic analysis therefore provides a valuable tool for identifying the extent to which the story is 'truthful', that is to say, it conforms to the lived experience, or is partially fabricated in order to make both the narration and the events to which it refers compatible with the ideal model and master narrative adhered to by the narrator. In the former case, the narrative would create 'moral space' for a critical evaluation of past events; in the latter, it would prevent any such opening.

Let us now turn to the self-narratives of three individual protagonists of political radicalism and violence in 1960s and 1970s Italy and uncover their structures, meanings, myth-making and representations of the personal and historical past, with a view to assessing the nature and purpose of these stories, their positioning vis-à-vis the audience, and the contribution they can offer, if any, to a process of truth telling and reconciliation.

## Stefano Delle Chiaie

Known as the 'black pimpernel' for his ability to escape arrest and live in clandestinity, Stefano Delle Chiaie was the founder and leader of the extreme-right group Avanguardia Nazionale, which he created in 1959 in frustration at Pino Rauti's inability to transform his Centro Studi Ordine Nuovo, set up in 1956 as a cultural centre, into a fully fledged political organisation. His narrative material consists of an interview with a journalist, dating from 1986, a book written in collaboration with his longstanding friend and comrade Adriano Tilgher (1994), two transcribed hearings with the Parliamentary Commission of Inquiry into the *stragi* and the reasons for the failed identification of those responsible, held on 16 and 22 July 1997, and an interview with the author, held on 14 October 2005.

As someone who was investigated, charged and brought to trial for the 1969 Milan massacre, but was subsequently acquitted, Delle Chiaie's story is predominantly concerned with distinguishing between 'legitimate' and 'illegitimate' political violence, and in locating the self-as-character and the group of which he was leader squarely within the context of legitimate political violence, inspired by pure and noble revolutionary ideals and uncontaminated by dubious connivances or underhand deals.

Violence, in his view, can be fully justified: 'Which country in the world has not used it at some stage in her history? In Latin America as in Europe, all independentist movements have been its product' (quoted in Pisano 2004: 95). As far as political violence in the Italian case is concerned, Delle Chiaie locates its origins in the Second World War, when the fascists felt betrayed and excluded by the nation, yet stoically kept up their faith:

> We came from a side which had lost the war and hence we felt excluded and indeed so we were, even from the point of view of societal norms and daily life – and we believed that those who had allied with the other side had betrayed our country, hence this fact for us was very significant and provoked a clash. There were deaths from both sides, each of us bore witness to the dead on our side and to our own death. They were years of deep passion, deep faith, hence how can you think that in this context there was even a shadow of a 'second state', whoever thought of a second state? We thought only of achieving a beautiful death, this was our decadent romanticism. (Interview with the author, 14 October 2005)

After the war, the neofascists were on the defensive, but were not prepared to give up their political militancy, at the cost of engaging in (unequal) fighting: 'There were fights almost every day and I can assure you that we never shirked away from fighting but it is not true that we were deliberately looking for a fight, through the clashes we sought political space [which] was often restricted by the opponents, hence, if we wanted to conquer it, we had to fight.' Things, however, turned nasty after Piazza Fontana: 'The hatred and the fighting went beyond the boundaries of physical clashes [in the streets] only after the Piazza Fontana massacre, which in my opinion was point zero. Before then there had been more or less violent street clashes but in my view there had been no cruelty, no venom, there was a [peaceful] confrontation' (interview with the author).

Given this preamble, Delle Chiaie totally rejected, during his interview, any accusation of involvement with the bombing massacres and the Strategy of Tension, both at an individual and at a collective level. In his view, true neofascists would never have taken part in such abject attacks as massacres of innocent victims, for obvious reasons. First, because the underhand nature of such attacks was not part of their culture: 'Do not forget that our culture included the concept, today little understood, of the courage of honesty ... Evola would never have forgiven someone who committed a massacre, even though some ignorant judges later tried to take Evola's books [to the Courts] in order to prove that that type of behaviour could be justified on the basis of his texts.' Second, because they would have had nothing to gain from such a strategy, and in fact any serious analysis of the 'facts' would show very clearly that the Communist Party, which allegedly was the intended victim of the massacres, actually benefited from them, in electoral and political terms. Third, because the neofascists, being isolated and excluded, formed an ideal scapegoat: 'Who should the blame fall upon? Upon those who had no protectors: in 1969 it fell upon us and after that it continued to fall on us since that was our fate, if it can be done once it can be done twice, three or even four times. ... This was the political logic, the culprits had to be the neofascists.' Fourth, because once the theorem of the 'dual state' was constructed, it was easy to apply it indiscriminately: 'if I carry out a historical analysis I do this on the basis of the facts, it is upon these that I put forward various alternative hypotheses, I do not start from the preconceived idea that there existed a "second state" in which there were the fascists and then I explain each fact on this basis.' Lastly, because of the innate 'truthfulness' of his own side, especially when compared to the inveterate tendency to lie on the part of his opponents:

> Since we are not Marxist-Leninists we cannot lie. It is difficult to construct a false story; this is why I always argue with my comrades – at least those with whom I still associate – that we should not despair. For one reason only, that is, that as long as the facts can be established, history will prove us right, because we never altered anything, we never falsified anything. Apart from anything else, we are unable to falsify reality because the concept of 'revolutionary truth' is not part of our culture.

The one subversive event which he admits he fully supported, even though he continues to deny having personally taken part in it, is the 1970 attempted coup d'état organised by Prince Junio Valerio Borghese. Borghese was his leader and is clearly still his hero, a man whose superior qualities and incorruptible nature as a true fascist are nonnegotiable and cannot be put in any doubt. Delle Chiaie invariably referred to him as *Il Comandante* ('The Commander'), and was primarily concerned in defending the pure revolutionary character of his actions and especially of his attempted coup from any possible accusations of connivance with state apparatuses or indeed the Americans. Asked whether it was true that Borghese had collaborated with, or indeed had been recruited by the Americans after the war, Delle Chiaie was fiercely dismissive:

> Recruited, what are you saying? Nobody could have recruited the Commander, not even God himself ... It was said that the Commander had contacts with Miceli, nobody knows whether it was true. But this was when Miceli was not yet Head of the Secret Services because Miceli became Head in 1970 ... when he became Head the Commander gave orders not to have any more contacts with him ... To show you that the idea of a parallel state was far from us, we had this intention, to get to a zero hour when we could set up – set up, not reinstate – a different order in our country; in order to do this there obviously would have been [the participation of] military forces, there

would have been attempts to contact political forces, or at least political components, which differed from ours, but there was neither Andreotti nor anybody else behind us, this is a lie.

It is clear that in Delle Chiaie's reconstruction of the past there is still a master narrative at play, based on an adversarial genre in which the neofascists play the part of the good guys, unswerving in their beliefs and true to themselves, even while persecuted through deceitful and degrading means by much more powerful and cunning opponents. There is not much space left open for a moral reappraisal of his past actions, and indeed these are proudly reaffirmed as testimony to his honourable, humane and forgiving nature, as when he recalled an episode which occurred while he was on the run in Bolivia:

> They told me that there was a person who was being tortured in a cellar of the Ministry of the Interior because torture was common in Latin America in those days, but not just on one side this is another lie, so much so that when I left I had many comrades tortured by the democrats who had arrived in the same Ministry … it is not a question of being good or bad, it is a question of style, of a way of being, I used to subscribe to the values of the errant knight not to the values of those who tortured people in cellars – so I went down these backstairs, there were two I knew … and I had them freed … I had sufficient credibility to be able to do this, I can say that the prisons were emptied.

The myth of the 'errant knight' and the adoption of the quest story merge in his narrative to present the image of a hero who has triumphed against all odds, refusing to be browbeaten by constant criminalisation on the part of the 'system':

> No, I do not consider myself at all a victim, I consider myself an offended person. I fought against the system and the system used all its base and mean methods to destroy me but I feel offended, not a victim, so much so that I have not followed others in asking for a sum of money from the state, I would never do this … I have thanked those who forced me to leave because I lived seventeen intense years. I will tell you an episode, I tell it because it is emblematic in the life of a man – when I left Italy I first went to a bar, our usual bar, and I asked Bernardino the barman to make me a coffee which he did … Nineteen years later I arrived in Piazza Rusconi [and went into the same bar] Bernardino a coffee I said, he started to cry, and I said 'Bernardino, why do you cry? You have spent nineteen years attached to a coffee machine so you should be crying for yourself, not for me, as I was saved from a coffee machine for nineteen years.' I have no hard feelings; I have lived more, fascinating experiences, I am only sorry to see my country reduced to this.

The linguistic devices adopted by Delle Chiaie are very effective in conveying the image of someone who has been unjustly persecuted by powerful enemies, together with his fellow comrades. In particular, he repeatedly makes use of terms which emphasise the exclusion, marginalisation, repression and violence allegedly exercised against himself and the other neofascists:

We were *excluded* from the political context … *for years I did not defend myself because I believed it was totally useless.* (Commissione parlamentare d'inchiesta sul terrorismo in Italia e sulle cause della mancata individuazione dei responsabili delle stragi, *Elenco Audizioni, Aggiornamento al 17 gennaio 2001*, 25th Session, hearing of Stefano Delle Chiaie, 16 July 1997)

Many of us were the *emarginated* of this society and democracy … they wanted to *destroy* us. (ibid.)

You take away *stragismo* and the relations with the Secret Services, for the rest I have been a radical opponent of the regime. I accept responsibility for all the actions which could serve to overthrow the regime of the state but do not accuse me of *stragismo* or of links with the Secret Services … I played a role against the system and thought it legitimate that the system had persecuted and punished me. It was not legitimate, however, *to destroy the honour of a man*, because this was equivalent to saying that my life has been for nothing … I have to be condemned for something else … which is the opposite of what I have been and am. (Ibid.)

The theme of the 'fabricated monster', that is to say, the image of himself as a 'criminal monster', artificially created by the state and falsely disseminated through the media, has been a constant of Delle Chiaie's self-narrative since his 1986 interview with Isabel Pisano (2004). The book written in collaboration with his fellow comrade Adriano Tilgher (1994), was significantly entitled *Un meccanismo diabolico* ('A Diabolical Mechanism'), and constituted his attempt to counteract the dominant image of a monster with that of a wronged victim. In the preface to the book, the authors compared themselves to voiceless citizens who were victims of the crushing mechanism of power: 'This … document intends to be the protest of someone without voice … who was designated by those in power as *stragista*, monster, criminal.' The same concept was reaffirmed in 1997, when Delle Chiaie testified to the *Commissione stragi* (25th Session, 16 July 1997): 'Fantasy, plus more fantasy, plus archival news create the monster. I arrived at the Bologna and Catanzaro trials and everybody looked at me thinking "this is the monster" … That is how my image was created and applied.' Finally, it was repeated even more forcefully in his interview with the author:

> It offended and continues to offend me that I am constantly being involved in a satanic structure set up by the Secret Services; it is something that drives me up the wall. Once I watched the programme *Blu notte* and I wanted to hit the screen because this is the impotence of truth when faced by codified falsehood – it is something terrible; I do not wish it on anyone. I lived, I saw the events as they took place, we know how they went but they all repeat and codify [a lie], they even add nonexistent details.

It is clear from the above that Delle Chiaie shares the view that the perpetrators of the massacres were indeed monsters and he said so without mincing his words: 'I am saying that we certainly were not involved, in any case I do not justify the culprits because I have always maintained and still maintain that whoever did it, whether the hand was black or red, were criminals.' For this reason it is vitally important to him that any suspicions regarding his role and that of his comrades be dispelled and all charges refuted. The only time during his interview with the author that Delle Chiaie conceded that neofascist elements may have played some kind of (marginal) role in the massacres is when he referred to the political vacuum which occurred in the extreme right after the demise of both Avanguardia Nazionale and Ordine Nuovo and the dispersion of their activists. At that point, leaderless, disoriented and fragmented elements may have fallen into a trap and been utilised for other aims: 'It was easy to use [activists] for one's own ends, as long as someone arrived and said "let us have a revolution", but it was never the activist who contacted the man of the services, rather it was the man from the services who disguised himself as an agitator, it could also be someone from a different political sector.'

Asked explicitly about the role of the various neofascist groups, including those operating in the Veneto region, Delle Chiaie repeatedly stated that he could only speak on behalf of his own group, Avanguardia Nazionale, but then his wording became somewhat cryptic: 'In the case of Ordine Nuovo I do not believe the story of the CIA, one has to know the ON activists, if someone in ON had got to know that someone else had an agreement with the CIA he would have cut his head off. Having said this, I do not deny that there may have been an infiltrator, you can read what a man like D'Ambrosio thought about Digilio ...'

This part of Delle Chiaie's reconstruction, as put forward during his interview with the author, is very revealing of his entire mindset and of the political nature of his testimony. He was clearly concerned with exonerating the two main neofascist groups from any involvement in *stragismo*, but he was also careful to acknowledge (especially in the light of juridical evidence) that there may have been a few individual perpetrators on the extreme right. However, he was quick to clarify (a) that these individuals were almost certainly infiltrators from state institutions and (b) that they coincided with the 'repented witnesses' in the trials for the massacres (hence his mention of Carlo Digilio, the main witness for the prosecution in the Piazza Fontana trial). In other words, these people were not really members of the radical right at all, but spies bent on defaming and/or manipulating the extreme-right groups. This was also true of the presumed 'repented witnesses' in the trials, whose sole purpose, it was implied, was to discredit and falsely accuse the right.

In contrast to his damning judgement of the 'repented' neofascists, Delle Chiaie justified the behaviour of the second-generation groups, including their taking up of the armed struggle:

> At the trial I said one thing ... that I felt co-responsible for the armed struggle because we had been the first to raise the revolutionary flags but then we had been unable to translate them into a political strategy, a political action, for that generational fracture I spoke about earlier, so that the new generations found themselves alone; on the other hand I have never agreed with the armed struggle as a form of political identity.

Is Delle Chiaie's narrative true or false? It clearly mixes both true and false statements, because its political and ideological nature does not lend itself to a self-reflective search for the truth. The narrative is put to the service of constructing a steadfastly positive, indeed pure, image of the self-as-character and the first-generation neofascists, who are presented as misunderstood heroes in the midst of nasty villains and are also portrayed as victims of the sinister plots of others. In this way his story continues to rely on ideology and self-serving myths to block out deliberately any moral reassessment of past deeds. His aim is political, his targeted audience are militant neofascists, and his constructed identity is that of a revolutionary activist, part hero and part martyr.

## Gabriele Adinolfi

Gabriele Adinolfi's story shares some elements with Delle Chiaie's self-narrative, in that he presents himself as true to his (fascist) ideals in the face of all adversity, and as determined to continue his militancy. Self-victimisation also plays an important part in his narrative, as in Delle Chiaie's, but the nature of the villains is different in these two cases. While for Delle Chiaie the villain is 'the system', for Adinolfi, in line with all other representatives of the second generation of neofascists, it is the extreme left and the MSI. In addition, in contrast to the previous protagonist, he severely downplays agency and locates political violence in the context of an inevitable and inescapable 'civil war', which allegedly raged throughout Italy in the 1970s and conditioned the actions of all extreme-right activists.

Adinolfi's reconstruction is extremely interesting precisely because, as a second-generation activist, he is able to distance himself from the more murky and ambiguous activities of the early neofascists. Despite this, he chooses to extend his legitimating narrative to include the first-generation neofascists, absolving their past actions from blame or at least strongly mitigating their responsibilities. In this way, his story clearly locates the self within the same dominant master narrative which we analysed in the previous chapter, and, similarly to De Angelis's reconstruction, reappraises the past so as to construct a seamless, pure and oppressed ingroup, papering over the (many) cracks. Such a reappraisal is ideologically inspired and politically motivated. Adinolfi's narrative material consists of two self-authored books and an interview with the author, carried out in Rome on 5 October 2005.

Let us consider first of all Adinolfi's portrayal of the self and of the group he founded, Terza Posizione. His narrative relies deliberately on group identification, so much so that his two books appeared with titles which emphasise the primacy of a political community and its identity over the stories and perspectives of individuals: *Noi Terza Posizione* ('Us Terza Posizione'), co-written with another ex-leader of the group, Roberto Fiore, and published in 2000, and *Il domani che ci appartenne. Passato, presente e futuro in camicia nera* ('The Tomorrow Which Belonged to Us. Past, Present and Future in a Black Shirt'), published in 2005.

The story is told using the impersonal form or the first person plural; only sporadically it is told by a narrating 'I'. The self-as-character tends to be referred to through the use of the third person singular. In his interview with the author, however, he adopted a more explicitly autobiographical perspective, referring to the self-as-character as to himself and using the first person singular. Adinolfi's is a linear 'quest story' in which the self-as-character, as we saw above, represents 'a superior hero' and a 'warrior' battling against 'a much stronger, but morally inferior, antagonist' (Feldman 2001: 133). The same individual 'quest story' is applied to all members of Terza Posizione and is located within a triumphalist group story, at least as far as TP itself is concerned.

Referring to himself, Adinolfi stated that:

> In 1968 I was fourteen and was fascinated by the students' revolt; however, I was horrified by Marxist language and by the Soviet solution, hence I tried to find an innovative position, revolutionary yet anti-Marxist. This was how I came to join what we can call fascism and neofascism even though they are not the same thing let us call it the radical right. I started from the fact that I wanted a generational change, I wanted something innovative, youthful, I wanted a chance to be free from hypocrisy and to be able to decide one's own destiny and I saw that on the left there was a huge deceit as they talked of revolution but practised a form of international servility ... hence I elaborated this position, that is to say, I wanted to show myself and the others that I was more revolutionary than they were'. (Interview with the author, 5 October 2005)

This passage encapsulates the existentialist, rather more than ideological, nature of his turn to the extreme right, which indeed Adinolfi openly affirmed when asked to specify what he and his group meant by 'revolution': 'our idea of a Revolution had three dimensions: first, it was an inner existential question as well as a cultural one, being able to live within ourselves and, if possible, in free, or rather "freed" areas, alternative life styles to mercantilism or utilitarianism. Then to affirm what we called "counter-power" ... and finally the ability to influence the cultural sphere so as to overturn the ready-made patterns of thought imposed by Marxism and Christian Democracy' (interview with the author). Asked whether his turn to the extreme right was inspired by the experience of the Italian Social Republic, he replied: 'For me it became important later because when I started I was fourteen, I hardly knew of its existence; we were open books, we had to construct ourselves. Historically speaking, I discovered fascism much later.'

The group founded by Adinolfi, Terza Posizione, was inspired by a political ideology which owes much to Julius Evola and Franco Freda (Ferraresi 1988; Rao 1999), yet his reconstruction of this group and of the violent clashes of the 1970s again betrays the 'spontaneist' turn of Italian neofascism. While contending that the ideological link with fascist doctrine was very strong, he emphasised the mythological links, 'including the runic symbols and the idea of the warrior', and portrayed the struggles between left and right as 'heroic' and indeed 'titanic', a judgement he extends to the extreme left: 'We were both titanic; however for us titanism was meant to be an heroic dream whereas for the other side it was an iconoclastic dream' (interview with the author). Despite this acknowledgement of the 'worth' of his opponents, he made it perfectly clear that the real heroes were all on one side. His own group, in particular, was exemplary:

> In the years of lead, of civil war, of daily clashes, years in which what mattered was to survive or to eliminate the enemy, Terza Posizione succeeded in being politically active and renewing ideas and programmes without abandoning its origins and orientation.
>
> All this takes second place to the shootings, the dead, incarcerations, exiles, all that which is sensational. Yet it has its importance and leaves a trace.
>
> The story of the radical right [...] is not solely a sequence of events as crime news, it is something more which stands the violence of time, like a seed which blooms when the snow melts. (Adinolfi 2005: 92)

In terms of assigning praise and blame, Adinolfi places the responsibility for starting the civil war squarely upon the extreme left:

> The problem is also to understand when and where the civil war originated ... when the student movement split into the extreme right and the extreme left and got lost in internal fights instead of trying to change society, there were the ex-partisans who were teaching that to kill a fascist is not a crime and then there were groups like Avanguardia operaia [Workers' Vanguard] which first theorised and then practised the elimination of fascists. On a TV programme the other day they said that on the extreme left the armed groups were started in self-defence. However, the first person to be beaten with a bar in Italy, Spanò, who ended up in a wheelchair, was beaten up by the [left] student movement, the first person to be killed by a bottle full of sand was Ermanno Vinturini in Genoa, the first person to be shot dead was Mikis Mantakas in Rome, I believe that even the first person to be knifed was Falvella in Salerno. In other words the escalation [of violence] has always taken place from left to right, contrary to what is commonly told ... if on the right we had buffooneries à la Almirante, on the left the situation turned really nasty, therefore the taste for civil war was developed by the extreme left ... I mean to say that the left developed a strategy of hatred, this is important ... on the left there was a culture of hatred, because if we look at what happened in Italy in 1919–21, [the left] used to kill in a heinous way, they dismembered alive those whom they took prisoners during the civil war. As far as I know in Emilia-Romagna nobody was ever lynched or had their eyes clawed out [by the fascists]. (Interview with the author)

When he talked about the physical violence perpetrated by his group, TP, justification was provided with reference to the myth of the warrior and the need for self-defence:

> The physical struggle for us had value as a test of strength, but also the problem is that we need to contextualise it and at the time there were something like 5,000 attacks and 600–700 deaths, at least five violent events per day, and it was not possible even to affix posters without a physical clash ... in Italy between 1973 and 1982 at least we lived in a condition of real civil war hence it was not possible to reject a fight, it meant giving up going out into the streets.

However, when asked whether on both sides there was a prevailing logic of preparing for a fight, his narrative becomes more ambiguous and the linguistic terms adopted more fuzzy, as can be seen in the passage below:

> No, we never did that, we went to conquer the streets which is different, as we studied how the left were behaving. The left in Rome were strong only between 1947 and 1950 and later between 1973 and 1976, but for the rest it was a relatively easy place for us, unlike other cities like Milan. Between 1973 and 1976 we studied the manner in which the left had conquered the various neighbourhoods so that when we decided to act we knew how they behaved and how we would behave, so we went physically to conquer the neighbourhoods but we already had some nuclei there. It was not the case that where there was a left stronghold we went there to give out leaflets looking for a fight, we never did that. We opened up and consolidated the areas where we had a nucleus; as soon as we decided to position ourselves we made sure we gained physical supremacy.

The latter sentence clearly indicates that the Rome neofascists often deliberately initiated a violent fight in order to secure 'control' of a neighbourhood, yet the narrative introduces a rather convoluted distinction between neighbourhoods where the neofascists could rely on an existing group of supporters ('nucleus') and areas where they had none. The narrator implies that going on the attack in the former areas constituted a legitimate form of violence, whereas attacking the areas where the left was predominant would have been unjustified. The rationale is (deliberately?) left vague, perhaps to leave open the interpretation that the neofascist violence was carried out in some neighbourhoods only in order to defend the nuclei from hostile attacks. As we saw in the previous chapter, another ex-leader of Terza Posizione, Giuseppe Dimitri, offered a much more explicit explanation of the strategy adopted by Terza Posizione with regards to the use of violence in Rome neighbourhoods. He also talked openly of 'military actions' and of 'several enemies wounded' in the course of such actions.

Having thus clarified who were the aggressors and who were the victims, Adinolfi then proceeded, during his interview with the author, magnanimously to 'absolve' all participants in the Italian civil war of the 1970s:

> It is as if you asked a Red Indian or a Palestinian or a Spanish fighter for the Republic or the national side whether it is right or wrong to fight – but he does not have a choice, either he deserts or he fights, there is no third solution … We need to understand the period in which we lived … at the time, I repeat, there were five attacks per day. It is like saying why do people fight a civil war? It is not that people fight because they decide to do it, a civil war happens … we cannot attribute to the individual persons a responsibility for having lived in that period, when one lives in a certain period one becomes involved in the issues prevalent at the time … now if we talk of a young man studying engineering this person will not become involved but if there are political passions …

Adinolfi also makes it clear that he 'absolves' and 'justifies' those militants who left TP to join the NAR and embrace the armed struggle, not least for what appears

to be an acknowledgement on his part that TP bears certain 'ethical and historical responsibilities' for their choice. Nevertheless, the main responsibility is attributed to 'the system', which carried out a 'rash repression' against young neofascist
militants in a 'climate of witch-hunting': 'it was the effects of two particularly violent repressive waves which led young people who had been militant in TP ... to
opt for the NAR' (Adinolfi and Fiore 2000: 65).

Adinolfi's primary narrative device therefore consists of portraying Terza
Posizione as an island of true revolutionary beliefs and restrained behaviour which
for these reasons became the target of violent attacks on the part of both extreme-
left armed groups and the repressive apparatus of the state. He does this by completely erasing TP's role as a paramilitary organisation – or at least as a group with
a paramilitary inner core – something which was explicitly acknowledged by
other leaders, including Marcello De Angelis and Giuseppe Dimitri. The other
device his story uses is to shrink the moral space available to the narrator at the
time of his actions, by locating political violence in the context of a 'civil war'
which all those who were active in politics had no option but to join. In the after-
math of this war, each side should be left free to lament the loss of their own dead,
be they their trusted fellow 'fighters' or simply their dearest friends. In short, only
some 'victims' gain a voice, and these are the ones who fought on the same side
as the narrator, before they were killed either by the police or by extreme-left militants. Indeed, the narrator is able to empathise with those who fought on the
'opposite side' to a greater degree than with the innocent victims of Italy's 'civil
war', whose existence he never even acknowledged. As the entire narrative is centred around a 'clash of titans', the fate of mere bystanders and/or innocent casualties of this heroic struggle clearly fades into insignificance.

Today, Adinolfi continues to be involved in radical-right politics, albeit primarily at the cultural level, and is one of the editors of the monthly journal Orion.
He is especially concerned with the need to reestablish the credibility of Italian
neofascism as a whole, and not simply of the group he founded. To this end Adinolfi, too, is keen to put forward his own interpretation of the Strategy of Tension, minimising the involvement of the extreme right while blaming both
extreme-left and 'centrist' groups (such as the MAR, led by Carlo Fumagalli).
Referring to stragismo, he stated that the attackers who are known culprits
belonged to all political sides, but especially to the extreme left. He cited Giangiacomo Feltrinelli, the anarchist group '22 Marzo', and Gianfranco Bertoli,
responsible for the 1973 bomb attack at the Milan Questura, whom (in interview) he insisted on defining as an anarchist and an ex-member of the PCI, while
in his book he oscillated between this definition and a more nuanced portrayal as
'a strange anarchist ex-agent of the secret services' (Adinolfi 2005: 64). On the
extreme right, he cited only Nico Azzi ('a rather isolated case') and Vincenzo Vinciguerra (not a 'typical' stragista) (ibid.: 64). Consequently, as he put it, 'how
come that only the extreme right is considered guilty whereas the left totally dis-
appears from historical knowledge?' (interview with the author).

As for attempted coups d'état, 'why speak of "fascist" coups when all those who have been investigated for authoritarian attempts (Di Lorenzo, Pacciardi, Fumagalli, Sogno) had been partisan leaders: the only exception, in a case which was, to say the least, picturesque, being Commander Borghese?' (Adinolfi 2005: 58). Furthermore, every political movement had practised a 'coup strategy' in the postwar period; but while the communists, from 1946 onwards, had been practising a silent and effective coup, consisting of infiltrating the judiciary and controlling the teaching profession, the extreme right had relied on amateurish means. In this context, 'if the difference between the neofascists and the PCI lies in the quality of the coup and in its impact, it follows that what is deplorable in neofascism is not so much the putschist trend in itself but rather the forms in which it was put into practice' (ibid.: 58–59).

In conclusion, in reappraising the political events of the 1960s and 1970s and his own role in these events, Adinolfi plays down the divisions between his own and the older generation of neofascists. While remaining critical of Italian neofascism, 'oscillating between an embarassing subordination to the DC and the Anglo-Americans and an unconditional form of radicalism', he, like so many others, is primarily concerned to overturn the predominant interpretation of the Strategy of Tension, amounting to nothing more than an 'acritical dogma', according to which:

> to prevent the progress of Italian society thanks to the growth of communism … Americans, secret services and nasty neofascist plotters allegedly carried out attacks and massacres, in the hope of determining a coup d'état which would have failed only thanks to the extraordinary 'democratic conscience' of the country … This dogma, willed by the PCI and welcomed by all the other protagonists of this tragicomedy, repeated acritically by media, intellectuals, commentators and even some ignorant, not to say grovelling, black protagonists of the years of lead, was transformed into a historical truth. (Adinolfi 2005: 63)

The analysis of Adinolfi's narrative once again confirms the closing of ranks between first- and second-generation neofascists, as well as between neofascists and postfascists, in relation to the role played by the radical right in the Italian First Republic. Shared myths of the 'heroic' behaviour of the ingroup, confronted by treacherous and deceitful adversaries, common stories of wars, conspiracies and betrayals, and constructed identities of stoic revolutionary activists and/or martyrs, help to cement an overarching unitary reconstruction which appears designed to replace genuine memory with 'conventionalised stories not unlike the mythicised ones enshrined in the cinema' (Freeman 2003: 13).

## Giuseppe Valerio Fioravanti

Ex-leader of the Nuclei Armati Rivoluzionari (NAR), Giuseppe Valerio Fioravanti was responsible for eight murders of policemen, extreme-left militants, right-wing militants considered traitors, and judges (Bianconi 1992). Together with his partner, Francesca Mambro, who later became his wife, he was also charged and found guilty of the bomb attack at Bologna station in August 1980, in which eighty-five people lost their lives. Both Fioravanti and Mambro have always strenuously denied any involvement in this massacre, and they have gained considerable credibility in support of their innocence among all political sectors, as well as among legal experts, journalists and scholars of terrorism. Investigations into this massacre were reopened in 2005 but have so far failed to produce substantive new evidence. Both have granted interviews and have talked freely about their violent past. In his interview with the author, carried out on 6 October 2005 in Rome (in which he was joined by Francesca Mambro at the end), Fioravanti stated that he and his wife hardly ever refused to give interviews, because for them it was

> A constant price to pay ... If a person comes and politely asks me the reasons for the evil things I did, if s/he asks me civilly, I have a duty to reply. If someone wants to study upon myself the mechanisms through which violence is created, then I must take part in this mechanism. Because of my nature and personality I will tell those who address me aggressively to fuck off, but a thousand times polite, intelligent, decent people have come and said: 'Fioravanti, I would like to understand how someone can go as far as killing.' Well, this is a debt I have to pay. If I can tell the mechanism through which good people, who come from good families, who do not have personal problems, in the end go crazy and do certain things, I believe that this is something I have to tell. It is not something that pleases me; I would rather forget.

This quotation alone makes it clear that Fioravanti's reconstruction of the past is very different from the ones that have been analysed thus far. First, while he was evidently concerned during the interview with presenting himself in a positive light, as we shall see later, he fully acknowledged his responsibility and expressed regret for past evil acts. Second, he deliberately presented the self-as-character as an individualist, totally in discordance with master narratives or ideal models of 'the good life', or even with the perspective of political and ideological group identification. In this he only partially succeeded, yet he made a real effort to apportion blame in a relatively impartial manner. Third, in relation to the violent events of the 1970s, his story was (again deliberately) unheroic, bent on ridiculing, as opposed to salvaging, the 'civil war' and its ideals, especially that of martyrdom for a revolutionary cause. Interestingly, the heroic motive, and to an extent even the myth of the martyr, resurfaced when Fioravanti talked about himself in the present. Fourth, his use of language and style reflected his choice of content – there was a distinct underplay of rhetorical and/or dramatic devices, quite unlike Delle Chiaie's and Adinolfi's narratives, and a much greater use of ordinary, everyday vocabulary. This is not to say that his story was also devoid of myths. Rather, the prevailing myths were anti-heroic: democracy, tolerance, diversity and dialogue. Finally, underpinning his entire narrative was a rejection of all violence as illegitimate, including and indeed singling out violence inspired by supposedly noble and superior ideals. The framework adopted for his narrative can be gauged from the following quotation:

> When you look at interviews by members of the Red Brigades, they limit themselves to saying that the revolution failed because the necessary historical conditions were absent, this is why I take it on myself to say that the revolution failed because we were not better persons than others, because we used to lecture the others but were just like the others, because we, in our sitting in judgment over others and becoming their executioners, condemned to death people who had done very serious things and forgave instead those on our side who had done even more serious things. Hence we are as corrupt as the people we were fighting, we did not succeed in being better than them … I believe I have to keep repeating this, but it is also a form of punishment to me.

As stated above, the explicit rejection of an adversarial genre based on the construction of *us* versus *them* succeeded only partially, as the tendency to apportion greater blame to the other side occasionally reemerged:

> The left … have a kind of mental obsession in persisting to explain that they are the goodies and that if evil triumphed it was because some bad people somehow managed, through a series of nasty, mean, and deceitful actions, to prevent them from coming to power. Hence there is still this part of the left which feel they are morally much superior to everybody else … I believe that the PCI had this really serious failing, it incited historians, intellectuals, magistrates and journalists to give chase to the CIA, the fascists, the bad Christian Democrats, it carried out this great work of denunciation of all the mistakes made by the other parties but it never spoke of its own mistakes, of its compromises, what it did with Russia, the KGB, so that in Italy … we have only half of the story being told.
>
> Ninety-nine per cent of the readings put forward by the left argue that the armed struggle or at any rate the use of weapons by the left started after the Piazza Fontana massacre. And to me frankly this theory that Marxism before '68, before '63 condemned violence … I never read it anywhere. We need to know the use of violence wherever and whatever and I suspect they do not want to tell the story as it was. Now who exactly started first, the fascists to kill the communists or the communists to kill the fascists … what is certain is that there was a conflict and I do not believe it was created artificially, I think it was in the blood of the people, then we can still argue whether the strategy adopted by the secret services and by the DC made things worse or better … In my view this conflict had autonomous and personal origins in the rage felt by the fascists for losing the war and by the communists for failing to take over power after the war. These were the two big forces and the two big hatreds that parents transmitted to their children.

Fioravanti's re-appraisal of the collective violence of the 1970s resembles Adinolfi's and echoes the reconstruction put forward by Baldoni and De Angelis, in that he blames primarily a concerted strategy of attacks and aggression on the part of the extreme left, as well as the attitude adopted by the MSI, which left its young activists unprotected and defenceless:

It was a very dangerous period for those who were active in politics, both on the left and on the right. There was a lot of violence. I remember that when we went out at night my mother would wait for us until two or three in the morning and she used to tell us of the many explosions she had heard. It was not infrequent to open a paper and find news of ten bombs which had exploded in one day. Where I lived we had five attacks, at Francesca's house there were two, they put a bomb on the windowsill in the mezzanine room where she slept, aged eighteen and with two younger brothers ... Then there was this episode which she witnessed in person of a captain of the *Carabinieri* who killed one of ours. He did it in front of all the leaders of the MSI. And the whole MSI pretended not to have seen. And the reactions [of the party] in the papers the next day were extremely harsh, but when Francesca said 'We need to report what we saw, we need to go to the police', nobody wanted to go with her, because for the party to lose the votes of the police forces was too serious ... And so for me, for her, for all the others, this triggered a final revolt against the MSI which had sold us out ... So, during the following three days, there were about three hundred of us, we had been responsible for patrolling the party, and we were in the streets shooting at the police and the *Carabinieri* ... but in reality our target were not the *Carabinieri*, our aim was to kill our treacherous father, in a mythological sense, to kill the MSI which had sold us out ... It is true that the characteristic of the NAR, even from a criminal statistics point of view, was that of a group which in percentage terms shot at members of the police forces more often than all the other groups of the extreme left. But what is really serious, from an ethical point of view, is that in reality our hatred was not directed at the police, our wish was to get the MSI into trouble once and for all. And also to break that mechanism that we had seen also with the radical groups, according to which the big groups use the small ones to acquire more power for themselves and later abandon them when the time is right. This is what was happening with Terza Posizione, we had seen it happen with Avanguardia Nazionale, we had seen it happen with Ordine Nuovo, and we saw it happen within the MSI ... Hence this was our big revolt, which was not really against the state. It was reported by the papers as a revolt against the state, it was interpreted as a revolt against the state.

Blaming the left, the MSI, or indeed the police, however, is tempered by his narrative apportioning part of the blame to the extreme right. More importantly, Fioravanti's story shows a clear distinction being made between 'then' and 'now' – the motives and feelings, both personal and collective, which he attributes to the self-as-character acting in the past are reevaluated very differently by the narrator in his self-reflection thirty years later. It is this questioning of past assumptions which separates Fioravanti's narrative from those examined in the previous sections:

The problem with our story is that it is the story of losers – we totally lost, and unfortunately some people have difficulty in recognising that for a good part our defeat was not due to the wickedness of our adversary but to the fact that our ideas were wrong ... and so many today prefer to take refuge in a conspiracy theory – it was a conspiracy that defeated us. I believe instead that it was our stupidity that defeated us ... Hence I am not surprised – I often meet ex-Red Brigades members as well – that the stories of many of us are still full of these conspiracy theories, it is a kind of existentialist justification.

We invented a war to fight, we invented it on an abstract level. A war that did not exist because objectively we can say everything about Italy except that it was not a country with a decent level of democracy. It was not a perfect democracy, but what I mean is, we were not in Chile, we were not in Argentina. We made it up that this country was sick.

Rage plus exaltation plus the fact that there were many of us, it was not such a heroic thing because in the end the group makes you feel protected, there was this getting each other worked up and this kind of awareness.

All the fucking things we did were the result of our total stupidity.

Asked whether the neofascists had played a role in the bombing massacres, Fioravanti replied by endorsing Judge Salvini's reconstruction, which in his view was both highly plausible and less rigidly codified than others, since it rejected the stereotypical view of the neofascists being mere executors of the orders of other organisations, whether the CIA or the P2:

Salvini's reading was extremely innovative – he said that there had been collusions etc., but the main reason for the collaboration between the extreme right and the police and armed forces was due to childhood friends who followed different paths so that one, say, became a captain of the *Carabinieri*, the other a civilian and when the civilian ran into trouble his friend who was a captain helped him out. This happened a thousand times, there was low- and medium-level collaboration between corporals, warrant officers, lieutenants, captains, majors and colonels, this is how he explained things, as a series of transversal relations ... In this way I made peace with the old generations [of neofascists] after hating them for so long, after causing the death of some of them and seriously discussing murdering Delle Chiaie or Signorelli; we [the NAR] wanted to kill these people, but twenty years later I can tell you that, partly for personal experience because the same type of charge [of acting by proxy for other groups] was put forward against me, but also in part for Salvini's excellent investigation, I made peace with them, because Salvini, who was a man of the left, explained to me that in those years this is the way people engaged in politics. I mean to say that Salvini made me understand that objectively in the 1960s it was not an obscenity for a man of the right to collaborate with the *Carabinieri* because at that time both the *Carabinieri* and the men of the right were naïve, were simple ... I am practically convinced that Delle Chiaie and Signorelli collaborated with the *Carabinieri* but since Salvini's reading this does not appear to me as scandalous as when I was eighteen. When I was eighteen I thought that whoever collaborated with the *Carabinieri* was a spy, then I read Salvini and I understood that in the 1960s this was the way to do politics. If I had been twenty in the 1960s and '70s and they had told me that there was Gladio, that there was this thing with the paratroopers and the Americans against the Russians I would probably have taken part ... when I was twenty I was angry, my predecessors were less angry and so I am practically convinced that the old extreme right collaborated with certain sectors but I no longer believe that it is such a dirty and inexplicable thing as it had seemed when I was twenty.

Fioravanti's own reading of Salvini's conclusions is somewhat rosy, since Salvini had actually come to the conclusion that it was not just a question of 'childhood friends' helping each other, but also of highly organised transversal structures. Fioravanti's romanticised reading of the activities of the older generations of neofascists also clashes with the grim, indeed gruesome, reality of the kind of actions they (allegedly) had undertaken. However, Fioravanti's reconstruction is probably best understood as a bridge offered to the older neofascists to help them cross the wide gulf that separates them from an acknowledgement of their past actions:

> I am really sorry that people cannot find the courage to talk about this because I believe that the public would understand. This is what I said when I was in jail in Ascoli Piceno, when I proposed that we should write a white paper in which the old generation would tell of their existential and political compromises and I can tell you that I had almost convinced two or three of them because I said to them: look, in my view you did certain things and if you do not tell them then they will be a matter for blackmail against you forever, after fifty years they will still accuse us of certain things, but if you confess them, for a time people will hate you but later it will be forgotten … I had almost convinced a few people, but then those who were more extremist than I was told them not to collaborate with the state, or admit or confess anything. I would like Cossiga to tell his things, I would like the old fascists to tell their own things, I would like the idea that after thirty or thirty-five years we talked about the massacres.

Fioravanti put forward the view that a verdict of acquittal in the Piazza Fontana trial might even facilitate a confession:

> I believe that in ninety per cent of cases the group responsible for Piazza Fontana has been identified correctly [by the judiciary] and even for the massacre at Brescia they got very close to the truth, but the problem is that they tried to 'force' the trials, as they did not have the evidence … in the end these people were acquitted hence they can no longer be tried. Hence these people today could confess if it were not for the fact that they have assumed the role of victims.

Asked how it was possible to confess to a massacre, to being labelled a monster, Fioravanti replied:

> It is possible for at least ninety per cent of the truth; we have Achille Lollo and the others [from the extreme left] who burnt a boy alive in his house [the Primavalle arson attack] and there was a scandal for a week but then on the eighth day it stopped there. I believe they would do a great service [to the country], obviously we would need these crimes to become statute-barred; in any case, my personal opinion is that it is not indispensable to know who were the two or three people who materially carried out that act. All in all we do not need to have ten more people to hate; what is really poisoning our country, has already poisoned it and has prevented its democratic growth is this enduring climate of all against all. Well, then, why not protect as a state secret the real identity of the two people who deposited the parcel [with the bomb]? Let us protect them, let us ask them for a confession in exchange for their identity becoming a state secret, but let us also try and reconstruct the climate of connivances; we need to dissipate this chain of cross grievances which even today generates diffidence, hatred towards the others – in this context are the five or six material perpetrators really of concern? They are probably even dead.

Fioravanti's narrative regarding the massacres and their perpetrators offers a new perspective on the relationship between representations and 'reality'. Rather than attributing the damning label of 'monsters' to the perpetrators of the massacres, while simultaneously portraying the neofascists as innocent victims of the sinister plots of others, as in Delle Chiaie's, Adinolfi's, and many others' accounts, he chose to 'normalise' and 'rehumanise' the authors of the massacres, by historicising their actions, and in so doing he also accepted the likelihood of the culprits being neofascists. This is obviously a very daring, difficult and upsetting reading of political reality for both left and right, for the victims of the massacres and all those who continue to believe in retributive justice, as well as in the unforgivable and inhuman nature of those crimes. It may therefore be a morally unacceptable way of constructing a more consensual narrative about the political conflict in Italy during the Cold War, even though it may be the only one that can allow the truth to emerge. In any case, Fioravanti's view is an isolated one among both neo- and postfascists, and there are also many who believe that he himself has not told the whole story regarding his past actions and connivances. While potentially attractive, it is therefore extremely doubtful that his proposal can be used to dent the current uncompromising attitude of nonreconciliation on the part of the right.

Despite what has been said above, it is interesting to observe that Fioravanti's narrative follows a similar pattern to those of Delle Chiaie and Adinolfi, albeit in a less obvious manner, in the sense that his story, too, ultimately presents the self-as-character as both a hero and a victim. However, unlike the other two stories, Fioravanti's is marked by a temporal dimension, as we saw; that is to say, he distinguishes between the self-as-character acting in the past, whom he portrays retrospectively as a villain, and the self-as-character acting in the present, whom he represents as a hero as well as a (willing) sacrificial victim. Indeed, even the self-as-character acting in the past is attributed an ethical quality, thus partly mitigating the overall negative portrayal.

The story of the self-as-character as hero starts with the Bologna station trial and the subsequent (unfair) sentence which established that he and his wife had perpetrated the massacre:

> Cossiga, during the course of the years, apologised to the fascists: 'I am sorry that I said that the massacre was without doubt a fascist crime, in my view it was not fascist'; he released a few statements in which he showed affection for me and Francesca, he gave some interviews in which he said that he was certain we were innocent, he made a series of declarations to the press, but he never gave us anything concrete to go on. So we took the bull by the horns, as they say, we went to see him and I said: 'President, we thank you for your declarations of affection but could you help us to find a piece of paper to reopen this trial'; and we said to him: 'We think the Libyan trail is the correct one, and we believe that you and those who came after you kept it secret for two reasons. First because if it is true that the Americans tried to kill Gaddafi [at Ustica] you are obliged to cover Gaddafi for his reprisal because if you say that Gaddafi carried out the reprisal you must also denounce the Americans. Because if you accuse Gaddafi, he will say "Yes, but I did it for this reason." Hence you, to protect your NATO ally,

are also compelled to protect Gaddafi. Hence these two things go together, I realise you tried not to hurt us, that is to say, you channelled the investigations against us but so as not to hurt us, you did not have us murdered, you quickly invented a neofascist trail, you did it badly and without conviction, hence from this I must deduce that your wish was not to hurt us but to protect other situations ... And then I say: 'This concerns you, as it was probably you who gave the order to channel the investigations towards us ... Hence I perfectly understand the need not to jeopardise our alliance with the United States, I fully undertsand the need not to create a petrol crisis in Italy, in short I understand that we were used to this end and I accept this but now so many years have gone by, can we not revisit this thing?' And he said: 'No. I do not believe in the Libyan trail, in my view the trail is not Libyan, I believe it is Palestinian, and I believe [the Bologna station massacre] was an accident that happened while the Palestinians were transporting [explosives].' Francesca and I left Cossiga in a very sad state ... Later we tried again, we sent a journalist friend to interview him, and he repeated more than once the hypothesis of an accidental explosion on the part of Palestinian terrorists ... Cossiga seems to be saying: 'What was done during that Summer was done in good faith, we did it to protect Italy from new attacks' ... In my view, on 2, 3, 4 August 1980 they did not know who had perpetrated the Bologna massacre. They did not know whether it had been the Palestinians by mistake, or the Libyans or the Mossad. They did not know but decided that whoever it had been [it was better not to find out] so the investigations were conducted for the good of the country. Now [Francesca and I] are seriously contemplating the hypothesis that they do not really know who did it, they chose not to find out because it was better to let things go as they did.

And so, without delegitimating the judiciary, with the suspicion that the judiciary had been called upon to do something useful for the country, we told ourselves that something strange had happened. We had been sentenced but they had also let us out. So there is a kind part of this country which as good as told us: 'I used you, I wronged you terribly, but I made amends for this.' In truth it would have been very easy for the secret services to have us killed in jail. So we told ourselves many times: 'They do not have a grudge against us, they do not hate us, nobody hates us out there. They had to use us and later in their own way they left us alone.' And we reflected upon this. When all is said and done, this country, this Christian Democracy, yes they did carry out some nasty acts, they probably ordered that some evidence against us be fabricated. Some judges put an end to the trial because it was necessary for public opinion, for something. However in the end it was the same judges, not the ones in Bologna, the ones in Rome, who let us out. So we have the heroic version, which is the one I do not share: they let us out because they know that their [Bologna] colleagues played a dirty trick on us. And there is the more normal version, which is that we all know the trial was badly conducted, but there is no point in reopening old wounds, and it is as if they were telling us ... 'Do not make a racket. You are doing well, you have work, you have a daughter. Do not make a racket.' So there is this message, which was of forgiveness somehow. The paradox is that we were, in theory we ought to be, the worst criminals in Italy, worse than Toto Riina, for the number of deaths caused, yet nobody believes it. The state does not believe it. When we go to the police, the DIGOS, they treat us really well. They know [the truth]. At a human level, individually, they know.

We have this difficult balance; on the one hand they have forgiven us and so we must be grateful for the fact that, since we are guilty of other wrongs, this country has treated us well. It has treated us well on account of the ten murders we really did commit and it has added eighty-five more for its own convenience. We are very angry for those eighty-five but are at fault for the other ten. And we have always told ourselves: let us bear those eighty-five as part of the punishment for the mess we really made. We were just a grain of sand in the mechanism of this country. We made such a mess, we were such assholes that as part of our punishment we must accept this role of scapegoats. And then calmly, without hysterics, without cries of conspiracy, we constantly work hard in our attempt to solve this situation, without playing the victims, without saying 'I want a monument.' I am not a hero of this country, I am a person who has made his mistakes. I am determined that some of these mistakes be cancelled from my criminal record, and so I always ask for this in a polite way, but also with determination, and we try and do this by respecting the rules, that is, through having a dialogue, appealing to the public. Not by looking for friends ready to shout 'they are innocent', or with a hunger strike. Nothing of the kind. Only through reasoning. Every now and then Cossiga offers us a little grain of truth. Our journalist friends are good, then there are those on the left who have friends on the left. And so there is this constant gathering of information, this sharing of information, and we hope that one day a shared reading will emerge. The other day we met Sergio Segio, who was head of Prima Linea. Morucci has come to see us several times. Often the members of the Red Brigades say to us: 'Let us make a speech together, let us organise a meeting at the university. Let us make a TV documentary on those years. We need to reexplain those years, we need to reexplain those years, we must reexplain those years.' I agree with this, but I would like to be certain that the reason for which the others want to reexplain those years is the same as mine. It seems to me almost as if they want to revalue those years and I am not sure I want to revalue them. I am not very interested in revaluing my mistakes. It is something else I would like to understand, but at this stage we are no longer protagonists, we are only witnesses, we should attack certain fundamentals of the falsified scripts of the history of this country.

In short, Fioravanti sets himself up as a kind of anti-heroic hero, in that in his representation he has taken upon himself the burden of coming to terms with the official label of 'monster', in the conviction that he and his wife were made the scapegoats of the Bologna massacre in order to shield the country from further attacks. In an indirect way, therefore, they too helped to protect their country and to spare the lives of more innocent victims. In his narrative, the formal judicial verdict is recognised as false by a majority of public opinion, or at least by the better informed public, who believe in their innocence and are sympathetic. Indeed, their role as sacrificial scapegoats has gained them the forgiveness of many of the relatives of their 'real' victims, as well as the hatred of the relatives of the victims of the Bologna massacre:

Bolognesi [President of the Association of the Victims of the Bologna Massacre] hates us and that is that. I accept this. The paradox is that he hates us and we had nothing to do with it. Then there are the relatives of those we really murdered and they have a right to hate us. The paradox is that they, too, offended by the virulence of Bolognesi, on three occasions the relatives of our real victims called us and said, 'What they are doing to you is really excessive.' So we have the paradox that because of this false charge they forgave us for our real crimes.

Finally, Fioravanti also sets himself up as a hero retrospectively for his past actions. In his narrative, his old self becomes a hero because, by causing the death of a number of neofascists, he and his group, the NAR, were directly responsible for exposing and hence putting an end to the indoctrination and violence carried out by the radical right:

> We are proud of this, because we destroyed their little games. You have to think that since the NAR there have been no extreme-right parties. We destroyed them at their roots. We eliminated the last few legacies, the last compromises, the last ambiguities, by shooting at a few people, burying a few others. We did a bad cleansing job [*laughs*] in which a few innocent people were caught up in, but in the end it worked. I lay claim to this, not for hating those people, but because at last we broke the vicious circle of creating new martyrs. Our mechanism, the mechanism of the Red Brigades, is similar to that of the Muslim kamikazes: You take a young guy; you convince him that the world is bad and corrupt and you push him to rebel. This is what was being done; generations of rebels were constructed in Italy, both on the extreme left and the extreme right. The older people see a young boy and mould him until he becomes a robber, a murderer, a terrorist. We intervened to break this mechanism ... I have nothing against existential despair, against robbers, dealers, drug abusers. I have a lot against bad teachers, against those who construct generations of angry and desperate young people ... We carried out this task and we always considered it part of the price we have to pay. We are convinced this is one of the reasons why various right-leaning intellectuals have asked for an official pardon on our behalf, saying that we at last broke the spiral [of violence] on the extreme right. And it is true. We broke it not by explaining that the world is beautiful. Every one of us can be shocked by the bad things they see. What must be broken is the mechanism by which others profit from the rage of the young.

At the end of the interview, however, Fioravanti's narrative became once again unheroic, conjuring up the image of the ex-terrorists, on the left as on the right, as middle-aged people who have achieved nothing and are condemned to conduct extremely ordinary lives, having dreamt of being leaders of masses:

> I believe that the strategy carried out by Violante [of the DS, ex-Communist Party] – Violante decreed that many extreme-left terrorists be freed – I believe it was a genial decision, because the end of terrorism came when the terrorists were freed. Because they put an end to the myth of the communist who suffers for the proletariat ... How can you make a myth out of an idiot who works for the Radical Party in a room with no windows [Fioravanti himself] or of Barbara Balzarani [ex-Red Brigades] who works with Caritas. What kind of a myth is this? If they left us in jail there was such a risk, but as we are now we are not a myth ... Indeed, you can still read on the wall below the writings 'Fioravanti friend of the queers, Fioravanti friend of the communists.' And at the beginning it seemed such an insult that I worked with gays and Radicals. But we willingly worked to self-destruct this myth, in fact one of the things that created a lot of tension with those in Terza Posizione, so much so that they sent little boys to paint swastikas down below, was when we declared that we would join Gay Pride demonstrations. And there was this huge scandal: ah, fascists at Gay Pride. What's the problem? Do we really want to go back to the fascists [saying] gay people should be killed,

the Jews should be killed? No. Enough, then. … There are still some people, some poor devils, who blow on the fire, but they are not getting anywhere, they have no hope whatsoever.

In conclusion, Fioravanti's narrative stands out from the others for its temporal dimension, with an explicit recognition of 'then' and 'now' and a self-reflective reappraisal of the past from the perspective of the present; for its deliberate rejection of an ideological community of reference, since the community he is addressing is that of the nation (as indicated by his constant use of the expression 'our country'); and for his declarations of regret for past wrongdoing, coupled with terms indicating forgiveness and a new beginning. Yet his narrative does not follow the pattern of a personal conversion, in which the narrator rejects and condemns the self-as-character acting in the past and sees him/herself as a reborn creature. Rather, the narrator reaffirms the moral validity of some aspects of his past actions, and represents the self-as-character in the present as a hero and a (willing) sacrificial victim. While he is penitent, he is also proud. In short, his narrative shares some of the elements of the stories of the other neofascists, and it does not mark a complete distancing from longstanding myths and representations. Precisely because of this, however, it offers much food for thought in terms of the possibility of constructing a new narrative of the past which, in salvaging some of the myths of the neofascists, allows them to acknowledge their wrongdoing and accept blame for past actions. It is also the case, however, that Fioravanti's controversial reputation among both neo- and postfascists, as well as his individualist stance, make it highly improbable that he can play a positive role in ushering in a phase of political reconciliation.

## Conclusion

If we go back to the notion of the two levels of positioning of a story, 'the one with respect to the content of what the story was designed to be about, the other with respect to the coordination of the interaction between speaker and audience', it seems clear that the first two stories were told for the benefit of a specific audience, as was acknowledged by a proposed report presented to Parliament by Senator Giovanni Pellegrino, Chair of the Commission on the Massacres, in 1996. With reference to one of the neofascists who collaborated with the magistrates, the report stated that: 'his interlocutor was not the magistrate, nor was his aim that of obtaining the benefits granted by law; his interlocutor was the revolutionary right and his aim that of accrediting himself as a revolutionary combatant who fought against the state with means which he considered valid because they differed from *stragismo* and who now called the others to a process of clarification in order to uncover the mechanisms and reasons for a defeat' (Commissione parlamentare d'inchiesta sul terrorismo in Italia e sulle cause della mancata individuazione dei responsabili delle stragi, *Il terrorismo, le stragi e il contesto storico-*

*politico*, 1996, http://clarence.dada.net/contents/societa/memoria/stragi/9.htm:1; Various Authors 1998). In short, these stories are addressed to the radical right and, I would add, they intend to prop up political militancy. Delle Chiaie's and Adinolfi's self-narratives fall into this category.

It is also interesting that these two protagonists retrospectively justify and 'absolve' each other's generation, thus directly contributing to the construction of a uniform identity and a seamless, blameless ingroup, in direct contrast to their prevailing opinions during their period of political activism. Indeed, this constitutes virtually the only aspect of the past they are prepared to revisit and reevaluate. In this way, their personal narratives of victimhood become vivid testimonies of the collective persecution of a whole 'community', and can be used to reinforce the group narratives examined in the previous chapter.

While neofascist violence is legitimised in these two narratives, *stragismo* is categorically condemned and attributed to inhuman 'monsters'. This is due both to its indiscriminate choice of targets (innocent civilians as opposed to representatives of 'the enemy') and to its inherent duplicity, since it was meant to place the blame upon others, as opposed to being used to openly assert one's own aims and ideals. Whoever admitted to such an act would be exposed to universal condemnation, not least on the part of the neofascists themselves. As Delle Chiaie stated during his interview in 2005, 'whether the hand was red or black they are criminals.' However, by definition the neofascists cannot possibly have been *stragisti*, since the traits of all neofascists are presented as invariably and uniformly positive. For obvious reasons, therefore, Delle Chiaie's and Adinolfi's self-narratives are a far cry from 'conversion stories', the typical narrative form which has been adopted by many on the extreme left in order both to account for their past actions and to mark the birth of a new 'self' in place of the monster that s/he once was. As I will argue elsewhere, in the case of many ex-terrorists from the extreme left, the conversion story 'is used to separate a previous "self as monster" operating in the public sphere, from a new "self-as-penitent" who has retreated to the private sphere. It therefore also officially marks the end of political activism' (Cento Bull forthcoming). By contrast, in many extreme-right narratives, 'the monster is exorcised not through a personal conversion but as the creation of other people's inventions and lies ... This type of narrative uses myths as barriers for new interpretations and in order to reassert the validity of a value system. While it closes off new personal experiences, it aims to re-open a space for political activism' (ibid.).

In short, the positioning of the self-narratives of past protagonists of a violent conflict vis-à-vis their audiences depends on two interrelated factors: the community of reference, and the narrator's own positioning in relation to social reality. If the narratives are to open up new reflections and new perspectives on the past, two conditions need to be present. First, the community of reference needs to be radically different from the one prevalent during the years of political militancy, and to encompass a plurality of groups, including former enemies (as in the case of a 'common nation'). Second, the narrator needs to consider the period of political activism as self-contained and finished, not as something that continues in the present. Neither of these conditions apply to the testimonies of Delle Chiaie or Adinolfi.

Fioravanti raised another important issue in his interview, arguing that the juridical situation in Italy also acts as a deterrent preventing any acknowledgement of involvement in acts of massacres on the part of the likely (neofascist) culprits. Article 2 of the Law of 18 February 1987, which officially established the category of *dissociati* from terrorism and allowed them to apply for a reduction of their sentence, explicitly excluded those responsible for acts of *stragismo*, thus creating an obvious disincentive to admit to any such crimes. In the case of Delle Chiaie, Adinolfi and many others, however, this factor seems largely irrelevant compared to their aim to safeguard the 'purity' of fascist ideology and to continue to engage in political activism in its name. Delle Chiaie is a free man and cannot be put on trial for a second time for the Piazza Fontana bombing, while Adinolfi has been fully cleared of any charge of involvement in the murky events related to *stragismo*. Maggi, Zorzi and the others recently acquitted for the Piazza Fontana bombing have similarly shown no signs of changing their stories or providing new openings for the truth in light of their formal status as free citizens. The few neofascists who have repented and offered new evidence to the investigating magistrates have been rubbished by both the neo- and the postfascist right, as we saw, which is an added incentive for all past protagonists not to depart from dominant narratives and myths. It is true that Delle Chiaie has often hinted that he would be prepared to reveal more on the Borghese attempted coup on condition that the protagonists would no longer be judicially prosecuted. Almost certainly, however, he does not mean by this that he would be willing to revisit his adopted narrative framework in relation to the coup, but simply that he would add a few details concerning the modality of and the participants to that specific event.

This leaves us with an eccentric voice, the voice of a protagonist who just as adamantly rejects any accusation of involvement in a massacre (despite and beyond his official guilty sentence), yet also acknowledges past wrongdoing. With reference to Freeman's ethical perspective, Fioravanti's narrative does provide a self-critical reappraisal of the past. It also fulfils the two conditions identified above, since his referent community is the Italian nation and his current perception of himself is of a 'witness' and a 'private citizen', no longer a protagonist. However, the 'moral space' this opens up for truth telling is limited by an evident preoccupation with presenting the self-as-character in a positive light and with playing down his capacity for evil in comparison to his virtues. Nevertheless, in the context of our analysis it is perhaps less relevant whether Fioravanti's story is true or false with regards to the Bologna station massacre. What it does offer in the service of truth is a chance for an alternative reading, in which all 'monsters' are rehumanised and put in a condition of being able, however partially and incompletely, to speak up and add a few crucial pieces to the puzzle of *stragismo*, for the sake of a (common) nation. Fioravanti's standpoint is predicated on the renunciation of a radical ideology, yet it allows the retention of certain myths, such as heroism, bravery, even victimhood and martyrdom, side by side with quite ignoble, as well as simply ordinary and distinctly unheroic, individual and collective traits. Fiora-vanti himself endeavours to put into practice his own suggestion in his portrayal of the self-as-character, who is presented alternatively as a villain, a hero, and a middle-aged, ordinary, and totally unimportant person; someone his fellow citizens should hate and yet also understand (even possibly thank!); a subscriber in his youth to a bad ideology (which however was no worse than others), and today a mature supporter of a liberal and tolerant form of relativism. His rather complacent, occasionally flippant, and often romanticised representation can be at best irritating and at worst deeply disturbing; nevertheless it goes several steps forward when compared to Delle Chiaie's and Adinolfi's crystallised narratives. As yet, though, it remains an isolated case on the extreme right.

# Conclusion to Part II

As the previous chapters have shown, the dominant narratives and self-narratives of the neo- and postfascist right in relation to *stragismo* and the Strategy of Tension are in total contrast to the judicial findings and mainstream interpretations. The main differences concern the targets and goals of this Strategy, the role played in it by neofascism on the one hand, and communism on the other, and, lastly, the nature of the judiciary and of the 'repented witnesses' for the prosecution.

With regard to the aims and targets of the Strategy of Tension, all neo- and postfascist narratives examined in these chapters argue that the Communist Party was never the intended victim, since *stragismo* aimed at promoting an overarching anti-fascist alliance which included the Communist Party and excluded the extreme right, through its criminalisation and persecution. In this sense it is true that *stragismo* aimed at stabilising, rather than destabilising, 'the system', but the system itself included the communist left. Alternatively, a subordinate interpretation claims that it was the extreme left, led by Giangiacomo Feltrinelli, which masterminded the Strategy of Tension, as a means of accelerating the revolutionary process by galvanising a guerrilla-based resistance movement against what would be perceived as an attempted coup by the right. In either case the neofascists were the designated scapegoats for massacres which had been conceived and carried out by other forces; indeed they were the only pure and uncontaminated political group.

As to the roles played by the extreme right and the extreme left, they are fairly clear cut, since, in the reconstructions of the right, the latter were the villains, and the former were the victims. However, this simple truth about *stragismo* was deliberately obfuscated by the enemies of the neofascists, who for a long time succeeded in driving a wedge between different generations of activists, purposely disseminating fabricated information, generating suspicions among members of the community, and falsely blaming many of them for infamous acts. It is only nowadays, in retrospect, that both neo- and postfascists are able to see through this conspiracy and to acknowledge their common status of victims. Virtually all the narratives analysed in Part II contribute to this positive reassessment of Italian neofascism throughout the First Republic, beyond the political, ideological and strategic divisions and bitter fighting which characterised the various groups and their leaders in the 1960s and 1970s, and to a large extent continue to characterise them in the present.

Lastly, the judicial investigations and trials are dismissed as irrelevant, since the Italian judiciary, in the eyes of the right, have long been infiltrated by the communists. Indeed, both Accame and Adinolfi, as we saw, argued that this was a deliberate, Gramsci-inspired strategy on the part of the communists after the Second World War, aimed at achieving hegemony. According to Adinolfi, it was a much more genial (and cunning) strategy than the rather crude and generally naïve putchist attempts of the extreme right. As for the 'repented witnesses' for the prosecution, they are simply not credible, because their collaboration was actively solicited by partisan judges and because they consist of sick, deviant, and/or criminal subjects, possibly even of infiltrators and spies, whose 'confessions' should be considered an integral part of the wider conspiracy against neofascism.

These reconstructions have effectively turned charges of *stragismo* on their head, reversing the roles of villains and victims, and constructing neofascism as a virtuous, persecuted, battered community, whose members have been heroes and martyrs, surrounded by corrupt and evil enemies. In this way a 'common history' of the ingroup is forcefully reasserted, perpetuating its distinctiveness, collective identity and continuity over time. This is perhaps what is most puzzling about the current reconstructions of *stragismo* by both the neo- and the postfascist right, that is to say, the fact that they paint a picture of sameness and continuity for an ingroup which has politically separated into two, with Alleanza Nazionale now claiming discontinuity in respect to fascist ideals and a fascist past, and the smaller groups to its right reasserting their faith in fascism.

It is easier to understand the positioning of individual protagonists of Italian neofascism, such as Delle Chiaie and Adinolfi, who are obviously eager to paint themselves in the light of persecuted and misunderstood heroes, particularly since they both continue to subscribe to fascist ideas and to be engaged in political activism, albeit at a cultural rather than party political level. It is just as easy to understand the wish of current neofascist groups to preserve the legacy of the fascist tradition, including the ideology and political activities of Italian neofascism during the period of the First Republic. The only exception are those groups which, while still subscribing to fascist ideals, see neofascism as responsible for betraying those ideals and allying with the former enemies of the fascist regime, the Anglo-Americans, as well as for conniving with the armed forces and intelligence services of the much-hated Italian Republic. These groups, which include the Italian Association of the ex-Combatants for the Social Republic, are inspired primarily by the figure of Vincenzo Vinciguerra and by his reconstructions of the Strategy of Tension and *stragismo*, which were analysed in Part I. It is for these reasons that, in a recent work (Cento Bull 2005), I painted a fragmented picture of the Italian extreme right, one in which the legacy of the past plays a crucial divisive role, preventing the reconstruction of a community of belonging. However, at the time I had (wrongly) assumed that Alleanza Nazionale would stand apart from the reconstructions put forward by the neofascist right, both as regards the Delle Chiaie variety (neofascism as victim and scapegoat of the

Strategy of Tension) and the Vinciguerra variety (neofascism as complicit in this Strategy and as traitor of the true fascist creed).

As we saw in Chapter 5, the dominant narrative adopted by the middle ranks (and even some leaders) of Alleanza Nazionale, as well as by right-leaning intellectuals close to the party, is extremely close to the reconstructions put forward by those neofascist groups which subscribe to a victimhood scenario. Indeed, in terms of conceptual frames, images and narratives in relation to the role of neofascism in the political violence of the 1960s and 1970s, there seems to be a seamless continuity between the bulk of the radical right and Alleanza Nazionale, especially some of its factions, such as Destra Sociale and the youth organisation, Azione Giovani. The importance of these factions in transmitting a specific collective identity should not be underestimated. As revealed in a survey of Alleanza Nazionale activists conducted in the second half of the 1990s (Catellani et al. 2005: 213–14), most tended to stress 'their belonging not so much to the AN party itself, but to a subgroup inside the party ... The consequent development of a strong subparty identity, was the only way for them to overcome the heterogeneity of the new party and not lose their roots.' This may explain why, in the context of my own study, it has been possible to detect almost a greater propensity to acknowledge past (mis)deeds on the part of those, like Pino Rauti, who still consider themselves fascist, than those who have publicly renounced fascist ideas and ideology.

The picture that emerged in Chapter 5 was one in which the moderate leaders of the party have only partially been able to reframe the traditional narrative about the ingroup and the enemy, despite the often instrumental role political leaders play in this respect (Rouhana and Bar-Tal 1998). According to Bargal and Sivan (2004: 133–35), who base their analysis on Lewin's work (1947), the process towards reconciliation between former enemies requires various steps, starting with the 'unfreezing' of the status quo, which in turn generates opportunities for, and driving forces towards, change. At every step, however, opposition groups put up both 'passive' and 'active' resistance to change. As Bargal and Sivan (2004: 137) explain, 'active opposition is often adopted by groups that have opposed any dialogue with the former enemy at the outset'. By contrast, 'passive opposition involves denial of the new reality created by the reconciliation, and may be manifested by neglecting to reframe one's views and test old stereotypes in light of the changing relations with the former enemy' (ibid.: 137).

On the basis of the findings discussed in Chapter 5, one can talk of the existence of substantial 'passive opposition' within Alleanza Nazionale to any reframing of traditional views or overcoming of old stereotypes. This widespread attitude of passive resistance greatly strengthens the 'active opposition' expressed by those who left the party to form alternative organisations, such as Pino Rauti, who opted to break away from the MSI after the 1995 Fiuggi Congress and formed the Movimento Sociale-Fiamma Tricolore (MS-FT). Such findings confirm the recent reassessment of the nature of Alleanza Nazionale by Piero Ignazi (2003: 7), according to whom 'a cleavage between leadership and party cadres cuts across the party', even though the resistance put up by part of the middle ranks 'remains underground, underrepresented'. According to Ignazi, the mainly passive resistance to change demonstrated by the cadres does not affect the behaviour and strategy of the leaders; nevertheless, 'it still weighs on the wing of the leadership, somewhat restraining its freedom of manoeuvre' (ibid.: 7). The already mentioned study by Catellani et al. (2005) strikes a somewhat more positive note. While acknowledging that activists of both the neo- and postfascist right shared similar values and ideologies, as well as strong narratives of victimhood, and that 'a difficulty in dealing with the party's "black history" existed' (2005: 219), they also found that within Alleanza Nazionale, as opposed to the groups to its right, frequent reference was made to the issue of reconciliation, represented as 'the healing of an open wound in the political life of the country' (ibid.: 219).

One has the impression that the paradox of a more intractable, nonnegotiable defence of Italian neofascism on the part of the postfascist Alleanza Nazionale, compared to the radical groups to its right, represents almost a quid pro quo in exchange for the acquiescence of many cadres to the transformation of the MSI and the official renunciation of fascist ideals and goals. As was discussed in Chapter 5, another important reason was that Alleanza Nazionale's need to consolidate its newly acquired democratic legitimacy among the wider public and the electorate was not conducive to acknowledging the judicial truth about *stragismo*, especially since becoming a partner in government. This is not to say that the transformation of the MSI into Alleanza Nazionale was only cosmetic; rather, that it applies mainly to the present and the future, but only on condition that the past remains 'frozen' in a mythical and ahistorical dominant narrative, which the party continues to share with its previous comrades. This is a highly risky strategy, since the construction of a 'common past' always works towards the creation of a community of belonging in the present. As Wagner remarked,

> The conjuration of 'common history' ... is an operation that is always performed in the respective present – as a specific representation of the past with a view to the creation of commonalities. Such an operation may well 'work' in the sense that an idea of proximity and belonging is created between people in the present. Yet it is not the past in the form of 'common history' that produces this effect, but the present interaction between those who propose to see the past as something shared, and those who let themselves be convinced to accept such representations for their own orientation in the social world. (Wagner 2002: 51)

With specific reference to the French extreme right, Flood (2005: 222) also argued that 'the transmission of collective memory structures the identity of the group by reiterating shared interpretations of the group's own past in relation to that of the nation as a whole.' He concluded that the extreme right's constant reaffirmation of their heroic past behaviour and values constituted an important practice for the preservation of the ingroup: 'The practice of counter-memory is thus essential to the maintenance of the subculture' (ibid.: 235).

Seen in this light, Alleanza Nazionale's current position is clearly untenable, as well as extremely precarious, since it is constantly at risk of becoming reversible. It was not surprising that one of the people I spoke to, who on this occasion shall remain anonymous, candidly stated that, 'Today I support a different political project which pursues a democratic path. While then [in the 1970s] I could not envisage a political project which relied on popular consensus in order to gain office, in order to change things, today by contrast I understand that this is the only foreseeable formula in the current historical phase. I am not saying this applies universally, but it does apply to this historical phase.'

The party needs to complete its transformation by constructing a different narrative for Italian neofascism, one which takes into account the outcomes of judicial investigations and trials and includes the reconstructions put forward by those ex-neofascists who have become witnesses for the prosecution. In this respect, the self-narrative of Fioravanti, examined in Chapter 6, can provide a valuable blueprint for a critical revisitation of longstanding myths and a reconstruction of Italy's violent past which, at the very least, sees the role played by the neofascists as a dual role of villains and victims, and acknowledges the legitimacy of the judicial process. This does not exclude questioning the outcome of individual trials in the light of new evidence, as in the case of the Bologna massacre. It does, however, include accepting the outcome of other, less welcome, retrials, such as the one on the Piazza Fontana massacre which ended in 2005 with substantial new evidence against neofascist groups, primarily Ordine Nuovo and Avanguardia Nazionale. New evidence can work both ways. It cannot be heralded as vindication of the truth in one case but dismissed as fabricated falsehood in another. Indeed this kind of reasoning is typical of 'fundamentalist' groups, which convince themselves of being the only repository of 'the truth' and view other versions of events as conspiracies.

A reframing of the narrative constructed and popularised by Alleanza Nazionale would make it possible for (some of) the culprits to admit to their own misdeeds and to agree to be part of a process of truth telling. This reframing may actually require the party to rethink the systematic attribution of the label of satanic monsters to the authors of the massacres, which is currently the one theme all political actors, as well as the victims, appear to share. The perpetrators are seen as constituting a particular species of monster, since they are unspeakable, unlike the 'monsters' the repented left terrorists have been able to recognise in their past selves and to leave behind with their acts of 'conversion'. While it is morally fully understandable that for the culprits of the bombing massacres special opprobrium is reserved, it is also the case that the truth can only emerge if what is currently unspeakable is at last revealed. This can only happen as part of a wider narrative which, while condemning past deeds, is also able to account for the historical and political context within which certain acts became possible even to contemplate. Such a narrative can only originate from a source able to empathise with the mindset and goals of the old ingroup, yet also ready to look critically at its past actions. As Fioravanti suggested, truth telling may even require that the identity of the perpetrators – those responsible for depositing the bombs in public places – is protected in exchange for an explanation of the context, strategy and connivances behind *stragismo*. Whichever form it may ultimately take, a new narrative conducive to truth telling can only emerge if the postfascist right detaches itself from the radical groups and ceases to construct all neofascists as blameless victims.

Whether the party can perform this operation of its own accord or indeed unilaterally is a moot point. It is for this reason, as well as for others which will be discussed in the final chapter, that a process of national reconciliation, in which different political actors are made to revisit the past and to face up to each other's reconstructions, for the sake of the relatives of the victims of the massacres and all the citizens, should be seen as desirable and ought to be attempted.

# CHAPTER 7
# Conclusion

The preceding chapters raised various questions as regards a possible process of national reconciliation, with reference to the violent conflict that took place from the late 1960s onwards. Does Italy need such a process? Is truth telling a necessary part of this process? Can a self-critical reassessment of the past by the different parties to the conflict contribute to less conflictual political relations? The literature on postconflict reconciliation is fairly unanimous on the need for truth telling and for more balanced and self-critical reconstructions of the past in order to achieve long-lasting peace and stability. However, there are dissenting voices on this issue. Mendeloff, for example, forcefully argues that 'lies, distortions, or amnesia in the service of tolerant, non-self-glorifying, nonvictimizing national identities are preferable to truths that can fuel victimization myths, scapegoating, and intolerance' (2004: 372). In his view, Spain represents a good example of a country which managed to achieve a remarkable transition to democracy and reconciliation without the pursuit of justice or a process of truth telling (ibid.: 367).

In the light of the analysis of the Italian case, particularly the reconstructions of the past put forward by the political right, we can make the following observations. First, as Mendeloff himself acknowledged in the quotation above, the crucial issue for successful reconciliation concerns the construction of non-self-glorifying and nonvictimising identities, rather than truth telling per se. It may well be that in some countries this result is best achieved through benign lies and distortions, however immoral and Machiavellian such means may appear to some. In the Italian case, however, it is precisely the use of lies and amnesia that is preventing the emergence of tolerant identities and is fuelling 'victimisation myths'. Indeed, this situation points to the relevance of what the literature on postconflict reconciliation refers to as 'acknowledging the truth', as opposed to simply 'telling the truth'.

According to Mendeloff (2004: 367), 'even this formulation remains problematic', yet the Italian case shows how crucial the distinction really is. In Italy, successive judicial investigations and trials have uncovered at least a partial truth in relation to *stragismo* and the Strategy of Tension, yet in a sense it is as if this truth simply does not exist, given that it is either dismissed and ridiculed by the right, as being the product of a partisan and left-leaning judiciary, or altogether ignored in their own reconstructions. While the right may have a point in arguing that the communist threat, the role of the KGB, the existence of paramilitary organisations on the extreme left as well as, for a period after the end of the war, within the Communist Party, ought to be incorporated in any historical reconstructions of the Italian First Republic, their chosen strategy is to lie about the judicial findings or to erase *stragismo*, as opposed to adding a new layer to the truth already unearthed by the trials.

In this context, the judicial truth is of no use for long-lasting reconciliation. It is also of little use to the victims of the massacres, both because very few people have been convicted as culprits, and because the findings are often dismissed as largely irrelevant. Indeed, the attitudes towards the victims of the massacres prevalent among the right are paralleled by those prevalent among many political representatives of the First Republic, among them ex-President Francesco Cossiga, who consider that a few hundred victims constitute a relatively small price to pay for a country which was under the impact of the wider Cold War conflict. There is little doubt that the victims feel aggrieved, demoralised and even abandoned by the state (Various Authors 2005; Fasanella and Grippo 2006). Acknowledging the truth outside of the judiciary circuit through a process of national reconciliation, on the other hand, can bring the victims restorative justice, as opposed to retributive justice. By this term, the emphasis is placed upon the 'acknowledgment of the abuses [as] part of a process of restoration of the "human and civic dignity" of the victims' (Dyzenhaus 2000: 473). In addition, according to Dyzenhaus (ibid.: 473), the restorative process gives a central role to the victims and to their stories, whereas in retributive justice 'victims figure only as sources of information while their former oppressors take centre stage' (ibid.).

An important issue concerns the intensity and extent of the past violence, as it may be argued that in the Italian case political violence was relatively contained and did not produce a high number of victims, thus militating against the need to carry out some form of restorative justice. However, according to Hayner (2001: 22), 'the actual number of victims does not seem to determine how heavy the past will weigh on the future, nor the intensity of interest in accountability. In some countries, a very small number of victims of government abuse has resulted in serious political repercussions and a strong emotional response from the public.' Among these countries, Hayner cites the example of Uruguay, where widespread protests took place in the second half of the 1990s to demand full disclosure of the truth regarding an estimated 135–190 people who had disappeared two decades earlier. She concluded that 'even with such relatively small numbers of victims, the pressure for full truth and justice can be as great as in those countries where hundreds of thousands were killed' (ibid.).

Another important issue concerns the presumed need for a 'shared memory' of the past, of the kind Giovanni Pellegrino attempted to achieve in his role as Chair of the Parliamentary Commission of Inquiry on the Failed Identification of the Authors of Terrorist Massacres. The concept proved extremely controversial and was rejected by many historians, who were concerned that the intended outcome would be to blur the distinction between fascism and anti-fascism, erasing the moral superiority of the latter. Indeed, the risk is acknowledged in the literature on reconciliation. Kelman (2004: 123), for instance, wrote of the need 'to avoid the simple relativistic stance that each side has its own truth and that their conflicting narratives are therefore equally valid.' Nevertheless, 'the different narratives of different groups reflect different historical *experiences*.' Kelman, therefore, suggested an alternative way to confront history: 'Reconciliation does not require writing a joint consensual history but it does require admitting the other's truth into one's own narrative' (ibid.: 123).

A similar argument was put forward by Shenhav (2006), with reference to Israeli and Palestinian national narratives:

> Possible changes in national political narratives do not necessarily evolve from thematic changes in the narratives themselves, but rather from the emergence of new positions regarding the representational ability of political narratives. Given the dynamic nature of these positions (as opposed to the stagnant nature of thematic elements in national political narratives) it is plausible that in this aspect we will find the initial signs of social changes that will eventually lead to the construction of new political narratives. (Shenav 2006: 259)

In other words, what needs to change is the basic view that a particular national (or in our case ideological) narrative represents a fixed and immutable truth or reality, together with the emergence of 'a shared view that no narrative can claim to represent the truth exclusively' (ibid.: 259). To an extent, this is what some historical as well as personal reconstructions of the past have started to do in Italy, for example with the book written jointly by Baldoni and Provvisionato (2003), already discussed in Chapter 5. However, even in the case of this work, as we saw, the authors ended up presenting their separate narratives *alongside* each other, only occasionally making space for the other's truth in their own reconstruction.

A final consideration arising from the Italian case is that too often the advantages or disadvantages of a national reconciliation process are assessed in terms of the possible recurrence of the armed conflict. While it is understandable that considerations of this kind are given prominence in the debate, this is not the only type of conflict that needs to be taken into account. Since the collapse of the First Republic, Italy has shown extremely high levels of political conflict, albeit not at the level of physical violence. Verbal violence and abuse, however, have been both widespread and persisting, reaching an alarming peak in the run-up to the 2006 political elections. The analysis carried out in Part II, with reference to the right, clearly showed that belittling, dehumanising and demonising the adversary continue to take absolute precedence over tolerance and self-transformation, indicating the resilience of political 'sectarianism'. This situation also points to the limits of institutional arrangements designed to promote democratic procedures, ensure the inclusion of all actors in the political system/game, and provide appropriate mechanisms for a peaceful alternation of parties in government (Kriesber, 2004: 89). Institutional arrangements are obviously crucial in promoting a normalisation of political relations, and the Italian case has clearly demonstrated that, since the fall of the Berlin Wall in 1989 and of the First Republic in the early 1990s, previously 'extreme' parties and arch-enemies like the MSI and the PCI have been able to join governing coalitions and to gain a new legitimacy. In this context, as we saw, the leaders of the postfascist and postcommunist parties were able to speak of 'reconciliation' and to make some positive public gestures towards each other. However, the new institutions could not prevent the political conflict from escalating into mutual demonisation and de-legitimation of the adversary. Hence the Italian case appears to validate the increasing attention and importance attributed in the literature to the 'constructionist' approach, which emphasises the role of narratives and discourse, and in particular the need to overcome partial truths and stereotypical sets of beliefs, in the reconciliation process.

In this light, Mendeloff's argument that 'amnesia' may bring peace and consolidation more successfully than truth telling is problematic, as it may result, as in Italy, in bitterly conflictual political relations, albeit short of physical violence. In Spain, one of the examples given by Mendeloff, amnesia may simply have brought the country medium-term 'normalisation', since requests for truth telling and truth acknowledging with regards to the civil war have recently been gathering momentum as a result of a bottom-up popular movement (Blakeley 2005). Indeed, as Blakeley argued, even achieving full democratic transition is not in itself a guarantee for successful 'amnesia':

> Transitional justice generally surfaces as an issue during democratic transition. It is less common for this issue of past human rights abuses to be raised when democratic transition has been completed and democracy is fully consolidated. The subject of this article, however, is Spain, where the human rights abuses committed during the 1936–39 civil war, and the long Francoist dictatorship that followed, have only recently come to the fore, a full quarter of a century after the transition to democracy. The article argues that the current struggle to recover the bodies of the disappeared, and their historical memory, represents a significant case which not only provides new insights into the particular democratization process in Spain but also provides more general lessons for other countries grappling with similar problems. (Blakeley 2005: 44)

It is true that a comparable mass mobilisation is lacking in Italy at present, nevertheless the issue may simply resurface in a not too distant future, and in a manner which may not be easily controlled from above.

To conclude, it is only at the level of violent conflict that Italy may be deemed to have achieved a long-lasting peace. By any other criteria – tolerance, nonvictimisation, rehumanising and nondemonising the adversary, self-transformation and a more balanced self-identity – national reconciliation remains a distant target. With reference to *stragismo*, retributive justice has uncovered at least part of the truth but there has been no proper *public acknowledgement* of this truth, to the detriment of the victims of the massacres. In this context, there is merit in the idea that retributive justice has run its course, and that some kind of process of national reconciliation, which takes on board at least some of the phases identified as necessary by the experts and highlighted in the literature, can help overcome the present dangerous impasse.

The obvious question is, who can initiate such a process at a time when there is no longer any perceived urgency for change, since the country has achieved a political normalisation of sorts, the *Commissione stragi* has folded, the trials have reached an impasse, and the culprits have no incentive for trading the truth for leniency in the criminal courts, since most of those suspected of *stragismo* have been acquitted? The answer can only be that the initiative has to come from older politicians and 'statesmen', who can see the longer-term benefits to the democratic process of disclosing the 'political truth', as Manlio Milani, President of the Association of the Relatives of the Victims for the Brescia Massacre, poignantly defined it. Milani himself was convinced that responsibility for the next step forward rested with the politicians: 'If at the political level they could understand that the public good relies upon disclosing the truth on these things, we probably would make a qualitative leap forward even at societal level [preventing any recurring violence].' According to him, two of the people who ought to speak up are Cossiga himself and Gianfranco Fini, the latter for the sake of both democracy and his own party, because 'you do not gain credit by denying your history, since you will always be open to blackmail.' Together with these, Milani also advocated that the parties of the left should be able to reexamine their own past, with a view to acknowledging their own responsibilities. This means bringing to light any links between sections of the Communist Party and the more radical groups to its left, as well as the role of the KGB, the Stasi and other Eastern intelligence services, including their support for extreme-left terrorist organisations and their possible involvement with the Moro affair. It also means revisiting the origins of extreme-left terrorism, questioning especially the widespread view that it emerged solely as a response to the Piazza Fontana bombing and to neofascist violence, which mirrors in reverse the neo- and postfascists' own reconstructions of events.

In view of recent developments, one could add to Milani's list the current President of the Republic, Giorgio Napolitano, who has taken pains, since his election in August 2006, to express regret for the support pledged by his old party, the Communist Party, to the Soviet Union when it invaded Hungary in 1956. Napolitano's own apparent readiness to reexamine previously intractable issues may provide an opening for a wider process of truth telling and reassessment of awkward and unpalatable past deeds and events. At any rate, despite the failure of Pellegrino's attempt to transform the *Commissione stragi* into a surrogate commission of truth and reconciliation, and the difficulty in finding new champions for such a delicate process, this study has confirmed the validity of a workable alternative so as to engage the former political adversaries in a meaningful effort aimed at complementing the criminal justice findings. In the absence of such a process, it is a moot point whether the Italian situation can naturally evolve towards 'normalisation' and collective amnesia, in the interests of the public good but at the expense of truth and justice, or whether it may further deteriorate, therefore failing to secure institutional and political stability, having first sacrificed both truth and justice for its sake.

# Bibliography

Accame, G. 1996. *La Destra Sociale*. Rome.

Accame, G. 2000. *Una storia della Repubblica*. Milan.

Adinolfi, G. 2005. *Quel domani che ci appartenne. Passato, presente e futuro in camicia nera*. Cusano Milanino.

Adinolfi, G. and R. Fiore. 2000. *Noi Terza Posizione*, Rome.

Alemanno, G. 2002. *Intervista sulla destra sociale*. Venice.

Ambrogetti, A. 1999. *La democrazia incompiuta. Attori e questioni della politica in Italia, 1943–1978*. Rome.

Anderson, A. (with G. Ruggiero). 2003. *I percorsi della destra*. Naples.

Andrews, G. 2005. *Not a Normal Country: Italy After Berlusconi*. London.

Arcuri, C. 2004. *Colpo di stato*. Milan.

Baldoni, A. 1996. *Il crollo dei miti*. Rome.

Baldoni, A. and S. Provvisionato. 2003. *A che punto è la notte?*. Milan.

Bamberg, M. 2006. 'Stories: Big or Small? – Why Do We Care?', *Narrative Inquiry*, 16(1): 139–47.

Bar-Tal, D. 2000a. 'From Intractable Conflict through Conflict Resolution to Reconciliation: Psychological Analysis', *Political Psychology* 21: 351–65.

Bar-Tal, D. 2000b. *Shared Beliefs in a Society: Social Psychological Analysis*. Thousand Oaks, CA.

Bar-Tal, D. and G.H. Bennink. 2004. 'The nature of reconciliation as an outcome and as a process'. in Y. Bar-Siman-Tov (ed.), *From Conflict Resolution to Reconciliation*. Oxford, 11–38.

Bargal, D. and E. Sivan. 2004. 'Leadership and Reconciliation', in Y. Bar-Siman-Tov (ed.), *From Conflict Resolution to Reconciliation*. Oxford, 125–48.

Battini, M. and P. Pezzino. 1997. *Guerra ai civili. Occupazione tedesca e politica del massacro (Toscana, 1944)*. Venice.

Bellini, F. and G. Bellini. 2005. *Il segreto della Repubblica. La verità politica sulla strage di Piazza Fontana*, edited by P. Cucchiarelli. Milan.

Benvenuti, P. 2004. *La rivoluzione della destra moderna*. Rome.

Bermani, C. 2005. *Il nemico interno. Guerra civile e lotta di classe in Italia (1943–1976)*. Rome.

Bernardi, E. 2006. *La riforma agraria in Italia e gli Stati Uniti. Guerra fredda, Piano Marshall e interventi per il Mezzogiorno negli anni del centrismo degasperiano*. Bologna.

Bianconi, G. 1992. *A mano armata. Vita violenta di Giusva Fioravanti*. Milan.

Biorcio, R. 1997. *La Padania promessa. La storia, le idee e la logica d'azione della Lega Nord*. Milan.

Blakeley, G. 2005. 'Digging up Spain's Past: Consequences of Truth and Reconciliation', *Democratization* 12(1): 44–59.

Bocca, G. 2005. *L'Italia l'è malada*. Milan.

Borris, E.R. 2002 'Reconciliation in Post Conflict Peacebuilding: Lessons Learned from South Africa?', in J. Davies and E. Kaufman (eds), *Second Track/Citizens' Diplomacy: Concepts and Techniques for Conflict Transformation*. Lanham, MD and Oxford, 161–81.

Boschi, M. 2005. *La violenza politica in Europa, 1969–1989.* Yema editore.

Bosworth, R.J.B. 1998. *The Italian Dictatorship: Problems and Perspectives in the Interpretation of Mussolini and Fascism.* London.

Brambilla, M. 1995. *Interrogatorio alle Destre.* Milan.

Bruner, J. 2001. 'Self-making and World-making', in J. Brockmeier and D. Carbaugh (eds), *Narrative and Identity. Studies in Autobiography, Self and Culture.* Amsterdam and Philadelphia, 25–37.

Campi, 2004. *Il nero e il grigio. Fascismo, destra e dintorni.* Rome.

Cartocci, R. 1991. 'Localismo e protesta politica', *Rivista italiana di scienza politica* 21(3): 551–81.

Cartocci, R. 1994. *Fra Lega e Chiesa.* Bologna.

Catellani, P., P. Milesi and A. Crescentini. 2005. 'One Root, Different Branches. Identity, Injustice and Schism', in B. Klandermans and N. Mayer (eds), *Extreme Right Activists in Europe. Through the Magnifying Glass*, London and New York, 204–23.

Cento Bull, A. 1992. 'The Lega Lombarda. A New Political Subculture for Lombardy's Industrial Districts' *The Italianist* 12: 179–83.

Cento Bull, A. 1993. 'The Politics of Industrial Districts in Lombardy. Replacing Christian Democracy with the Northern League' *The Italianist* 13: 209–29.

Cento Bull, A. 2005. 'Casting a Long Shadow: The Legacy of *stragismo* for the Italian Extreme Right', *The Italianist* 25(2): 260–79.

Cento Bull, A. forthcoming. 'Political violence, *stragismo* and 'civil war': an analysis of the self-narratives of neofascist protagonists', in P. Antonello and A. O'Leary, A. (eds), *Imagining Terrorism: The Rhetoric and Representation of Political Violence in Italy, 1969-2006*, Oxford.

Cernigoi, C. 1997. *Operazione foibe a Trieste.* Udine.

Chiarini, R. 1990. ' "Sacro egoismo" e "missione civilizzatrice". La politica estera del Msi dalla fondazione alla metà degli anni Cinquanta', *Storia contemporanea* 21(3): 541–60.

Chiarini, R. 2005. *25 aprile. La competizione politica sulla memoria.* Venice.

Chiarini, R. and Maraffi, M. (eds). 2001. *La destra allo specchio. La cultura politica di Alleanza nazionale.* Venice.

Colombo, F. and A. Padellaro. 2002. *Il libro nero della democrazia. Vivere sotto il governo Berlusconi.* Milan.

Cooke, P. 2006. ' "A riconquistare la rossa primavera": The Neo-Resistance of the 1970s', in A. Cento Bull and A. Giorgio (eds), *Speaking Out and Silencing. Culture, Society and Politics in Italy in the 1970s.* London, 172–84.

Cornwell, R. 1983. *God's Banker: An Account of the Life and Death of Roberto Calvi.* London.

Cromer, G. and R. Wagner-Pacifici. 2001. 'Introduction to the Special Issue on Narratives of Violence', *Qualitative Sociology* 24(2): 163–68.

Crossley, M.L. 2000. *Introducing Narrative Psychology: Self, Trauma and the Construction of Meaning.* Milton Keynes.

Crossley, M.L. 2003. 'Formulating Narrative Psychology: The Limitations of Contemporary Social Constructionism', *Narrative Inquiry* 13(2): 287–300.

Cucchiarelli, P. and A. Giannuli. 1997. *Lo Stato Parallelo: L'Italia oscura nei documenti e nelle relazioni della Commissione Stragi.* Rome.

Curi, U. 1997. 'La Lega e l'eversione', *Micromega* 4(97): 41–53.

D'Agnelli, A.R. 2003. *Conoscenza storica e giudizio politico. Il ruolo degli storici nelle Commissioni parlamentari d'inchiesta sul terrorismo.* Paper presented at the Conference 'Cantieri di storia', Sissco, Lecce, 25–27 September 2003, available at: http://www.sissco.it/attivita/ sem-set-2003/relazioni/dagnelli.rtf

De Felice, R. 1995. *Rosso e Nero* [interview edited by P. Chessa]. Milan.

De Palo, G. and A. Giannuli (eds). 1989. *La strage di stato: vent'anni dopo*. Rome.

Delle Chiaie, S. and A. Tilgher. 1994. *Un meccanismo diabolico. Stragi Servizi segreti Magistrati*. Rome.

Di Nolfo, E. 1998. *I vincoli internazionali di una democrazia incompiuta*, in A. Giovagnoli (ed.), *Interpretazioni della Repubblica*. Bologna, 117–39.

Diamanti, I. 1993. *La Lega. Geografia, storia e sociologia di un nuovo soggetto politico*. Rome.

Diamanti, I. 1996. *Il male del Nord. Lega, localismo, secessione*. Rome.

Di Nucci, L. and E. Galli della Loggia. 2004. *Due nazioni - Legittimazione e delegittimazione nella storia dell'Italia contemporanea*. Bologna.

Donno, G. 2001. *La Gladio Rossa del PCI (1945–967)*. Messina.

Dyzenhaus, D. 2000. 'Survey Article: Justifying the Truth and Reconciliation Commission', *The Journal of Political Philosophy* 8(4): 470–96.

Evola, J. 1934. *Rivolta contro il mondo moderno*. Milan.(*Revolt against the Modern World: Politics, Religion, and Social Order in the Kali Yuga*, Rochester, VT, 1995).

Evola, J. 1953. *Gli uomini e le rovine*. Rome. (*Men among the Ruins: Post-War Reflections of a Radical Traditionalist*, Rochester, VT, 2002).

Evola, J. 1961. *Cavalcare la tigre*. Milan. (*Ride the Tiger: A Survival Manual for the Aristocrats of the Soul*, Rochester, VT, 2003)

Evola, J. 2001. *I testi di 'Ordine Nuovo'*, ed. R. del Ponte. Padua.

Fasanella, G. and C. Sestieri with G. Pellegrino. 2000. *Segreto di Stato: La verità da Gladio al caso Moro*. Turin.

Fasanella, G. and G. Pellegrino. 2005. *La guerra civile. Da Salo' a Berlusioni*. Milan.

Fasanella, G. and A. Grippo. 2006. *I silenzi degli innocenti*. Milan.

Feldman, C.F. 2001. 'Narratives of National Identity as Group Narratives: Patterns of Interpretive Cognition', in J. Brockmeier and D. Carbaugh (eds), *Narrative and Identity. Studies in Autobiography, Self and Culture*. Amsterdam and Philadelphia, 129–44.

Ferraresi, F. 1988. 'The Radical Right in Postwar Italy', *Politics and Society* 16(1): 71–119.

Ferraresi, F. 1996. *Threats to Democracy: The Radical Right in Italy after the War*. Princeton.

Flamigni, S. 2005. *Trame atlantiche. Storia della loggia massonica segreta P2*. Milan.

Flood, C. 2005. 'The Politics of Counter-Memory on the French Extreme Right', *Journal of European Studies* 35(2): 221–36.

Fo, D. 1997. *Morte accidentale di un anarchico*, edited with introduction, notes and vocabulary by J. Lorch. Manchester.

Focardi, F. 2005a. *La guerra della memoria. La Resistenza nel dibattito politico italiano dal 1945 a oggi*. Bari.

Focardi, F. 2005b. 'La questione dei processi ai criminali di guerra tedeschi in Italia: fra punizione frenata, insabbiamento di Stato, giustizia tardiva (1943-2005)', *Storicamente* 1, http://www.storicamente.org/sommario_archivio1.htm

Franzosi, R. 1998. 'Narrative Analysis - Why (and How) Sociologists Should Be Interested in Narrative', in J. Hagan (ed.), *The Annual Review of Sociology*, 24: 517–54.

Freda, F. 1969. *La disintegrazione del sistema*. Padua.

Freeman, M. 1993. *Re-writing the Self: History, Memory, Narrative*. London and New York.

Freeman, M. 2003. 'Myth, Memory, and the Moral Space of Autobiographical Narrative'. Paper delivered at the Second Tampere Conference on 'Narrative, Ideology and Myth', Tampere.

Freeman, M. and J. Brockmeier. 2001. 'Narrative Integrity: Autobiographical Identity and the Meaning of the "Good Life"', in J. Brockmeier and D. Carbaugh (eds), *Narrative and Identity. Studies in Autobiography, Self and Culture.* Amsterdam and Philadelphia, 75–99.

Gagliani, D. 1999. *Brigate nere: Mussolini e la militarizzazione del Partito fascista repubblicano.* Turin.

Galli della Loggia, E. 1996. *La morte della patria. La crisi dell'idea di nazione tra Resistenza, antifascismo e Repubblica.* Bari.

Ganapini, L. 1999. *La Repubblica delle camicie nere.* Milan.

Ganser, D. 2005. *NATO's Secret Armies: Operation GLADIO and Terrorism in Western Europe.* London.

Gergen, K. 1991. *The Saturated Self. Dilemmas of Identity in Contemporary Life.* New York.

Germinario, F. 1999. *L'altra memoria. L'Estrema destra, Salò e la Resistenza.* Turin.

Germinario, F. 2001. *Estranei alla democrazia: negazionismo e antisemitismo nella destra radicale italiana.* Pisa.

Germinario, F. 2005. *Da Salò al governo. Immaginario e cultura politica della destra italiana.* Turin.

Gianfranceschi, F. 2004. *Il bestiario della Sinistra.* Rome.

Giannuli, A. 1997. *Relazione di perizia.* Bari. Unpublished copy of the report courtesy of the author.

Giannuli, A. and N. Schiavulli. 1991. *Storie di intrighi e di processi: dalla strage Di Piazza Fontana al Caso Sofri.* Rome.

Gibson, J.L. 2004. 'Truth, Reconciliation and the Creation of a Human Rights Culture in South Africa', *Law and Society Review* 38(1): 5–40.

Gibson, J.L. 2005. 'The Truth About Truth and Reconciliation in South Africa', *International Political Science Review/Revue internationale de science politique* 26(4): 341–61.

Ginsborg, P. 2003. *Berlusconi. Ambizioni patrimoniali in una democrazia mediatica.* Turin.

Ginsborg, P. 2005. *Silvio Berlusconi: Television, Power and Patrimony.* London.

Giustolisi, F. 2004. *L'armadio della vergogna.* Rome.

Gomel, E. 2003. *Bloodscripts. Writing the Violent Subject.* Columbus.

Griffin, R. 1996. 'The Post-fascism of the Alleanza Nazionale: A Case Study in Ideological Morphology', *Journal of Political Ideologies* 1(2): 123–46.

Griffin, R. 2000. 'Between Metapolitics and *apoliteía*: the New Right's Strategy for Conserving the Fascist Vision in the "Interregnum" ', *Modern and Contemporary France* 8(2): 35–53.

Guarino, M. 2006. *Gli anni del disonore. Dal 1965 il potere occulto di Licio Gelli e della loggia P2 tra affari, scandali e stragi.* Bari.

Hayner, P.B. 2001. *Unspeakable Truths: Confronting State Terror and Atrocity.* NY.

Hopkins, S. 2001. 'History with a Divided and Complicated Heart? The Uses of Political Memoir, Biography and Autobiography in Contemporary Northern Ireland', *Ethnopolitics* 1(2): 74–81.

Ignazi, P. 1989. 'La cultura politica del Movimento sociale italiano', *Rivista italiana di scienza politica* 19(3): 431–65.

Ignazi, P. 1994. *Postfascisti? Dal Movimento sociale italiano ad Alleanza nazionale.* Bologna.

Ignazi, P. 2003. 'Italy: The Beacon That Faded and the Populist Surge', in P. Ignazi (ed.), *Extreme Right Parties in Western Europe.* Oxford, 35–61.

Ignazi, P. 2005. 'The Extreme Right: Legitimation and Evolution on the Italian Right Wing: Social and Ideological Repositioning of Alleanza Nazionale and the Lega Nord', *South European Society and Politics* 10(2): 333–49.

Ignazi, P. 2006. 'Italy in the 1970s between Self-Expression and Organicism', in A. Cento Bull and A. Giorgio (eds), *Speaking Out and Silencing. Culture, Society and Politics in Italy in the 1970s*. London, 10–29.

*Il Resto del Siclo*. 2005. 'I "misteri" di Piazza Fontana. Intervista al giudice Guido Salvini', no. 16, http://www.vho.org/aaargh/ital/attua/rs0504.pdf

Ilari, V. 2001. *Guerra civile*. Rome.

Intelligence and Security Committee. 2000. *The Mitrokhin Inquiry Report*, available at: http://www.archive.official-documents.co.uk/document/cm47/4764/4764.htm

James, W. and L. van de Vijver (eds). 2000. *After the TRC: Reflections on Truth and Reconciliation in South Africa*. Cape Town.

Kelman, H.C. 2004. 'Reconciliation as Identity Change: A Social-psychological Perspective', in Y. Bar-Siman-Tov (ed.), *From Conflict Resolution to Reconciliation*. Oxford, 111–24.

Klinkhammer, L. 1993. *L'occupazione tedesca in Italia (1943–1945)*. Turin.

Kriesberg, L. 1998. *Constructive Conflicts: From Escalation to Settlement*. New York.

Kriesberg, L. 2004. 'Comparing Reconciliation Actions within and between Countries', in Y. Bar-Siman-Tov (ed.), *From Conflict Resolution to Reconciliation*. Oxford, 81–110.

Labov, W. 1972. *Language in the Inner City*. Philadelphia.

Labov, W. 2001. 'Uncovering the Event Structure of Narrative'. Paper given at the Georgetown Round Table in March 2001, available at: http://www.ling.upenn.edu/~wlabov/uesn.pdf

Labov, W. and J. Waletzky. 1967. 'Narrative Analysis: Oral Versions of Personal Experience', in J. Helm (ed.), *Essays on the Verbal and Visual Arts*. Seattle, WA, 12–44.

Lane, D. 2005. *L'ombra del potere*, trans. Fabio Galimberti. Rome-Bari.

Lanza, L. 2005. 'Quella verità da non dimenticare (intervista a Guido Salvini)', in L. Lanza, *Bombe e segreti. Piazza Fontana: una strage senza colpevoli*. Milan, 137–76.

Lewin, K. 1947. 'Frontiers in Group Dynamics: Concept, Method and Reality in Social Science; Social Equilibria and Social Change', *Human Relations* 1: 5–41.

Liechty, J. and C. Clegg. 2001. *Moving Beyond Sectarianism. Religion, Conflict, and Reconciliation in Northern Ireland*. Dublin.

Llewellyn, J.J. and R. Howse. 1999. *Restorative Justice - A Conceptual Framework*. Paper for the Law Commission of Canada. Available at: www.lcc.gc.ca/research_project/99_justice_1-en.asp

Long, W.J. and P. Brecke. 2003. *War and Reconciliation: Reason and Emotion in Conflict Resolution*. Cambridge, MA.

Luzzatto, L. 2004. *La crisi dell'antifascismo*. Turin.

Mammone, A. 2006. 'A Daily Revision of the Past: Fascism, Anti-Fascism, and Memory in Contemporary Italy', *Modern Italy* 11(2): 211–26.

Mantica, A. and V. Fragalà. 2001a. 'Il contesto delle stragi. Una cronologia 1968–75' in Commissione parlamentare d'inchiesta sul terrorismo in Italia e sulle cause della mancata individuazione dei responsabili delle stragi, XIII legislatura (2001), *Elaborati presentati dai commissari*. Rome, Vol. I, Tome III, 1–330.

Mantica, A. and V. Fragalà. 2001b. 'La dimensione sovranazionale del fenomeno eversivo in Italia', in Commissione parlamentare d'inchiesta sul terrorismo in Italia e sulle cause della mancata individuazione dei responsabili delle stragi, XIII legislatura (2001), *Elaborati presentati dai commissari*. Rome, Vol. I, Tome V, Second Part, 1–246.

Mantica, A. and V. Fragalà. 2001c. 'Il parziale ritrovamento dei reperti di Robbiano di Mediglia e la "Controinchiesta" Br su piazza Fontana', in Commissione parlamentare d'inchiesta sul terrorismo in Italia e sulle cause della mancata individuazione dei responsabili delle stragi, XIII legislatura (2001), *Elaborati presentati dai commissari*. Rome, Vol. I, Tome II, 313–410.

Mantica, A. and V. Fragalà. 2001d. 'Aspetti mai chiariti nella dinamica della strage di piazza della Loggia. Brescia 28 maggio 1974' in Commissione parlamentare d'inchiesta sul terrorismo in Italia e sulle cause della mancata individuazione dei responsabili delle stragi, XIII legislatura (2001), *Elaborati presentati dai commissari*. Rome, Vol. I, Tome II, 411–36.

May, V. 2004. 'Public and Private Narratives. Conference Report: Conference on Narrative, Ideology and Myth – Second Tampere Conference on Narrative' *Forum Qualitative Sozialforschung/Forum: Qualitative Social Research* [online journal], 5(1), January. Available at: http://www.qualitative-research.net/fqs-texte/1-04/1-04tagung-may-e.htm

Mayorga, P. 2003. *Il Condor nero. L'internazionale fascista e i rapporti segreti con il regime di Pinochet.* Milan.

Mazzantini, C. 1995. *I balilla andarono a Salò.* Venice.

Mendeloff, D. 2004. 'Truth-Seeking, Truth-Telling, and Postconflict Peacebuilding: Curb the Enthusiasm?' *International Studies Review* 6: 355–80.

Mieli, P. 2001. *Storia e politica. Risorgimento, fascismo e comunismo.* Rizzoli.

Mingione, E. 1993 'Italy: The Resurgence of Regionalism', *International Affairs* 69(2): 305–18.

Minow, M. 2000. 'The Hope for Healing: What Can Truth Commissions Do?', in R.I. Rotberg and D. Thompson (eds), *Truth v. Justice: The Morality of Truth Commissions.* Princeton, 235–60.

Moioli, V. 1990. *I nuovi razzismi.* Rome.

Monti, A. 2006. *Il 'golpe Borghese'. Un golpe virtuale all'italiana.* Bologna.

Neglie, P. 1994. 'Il Movimento sociale italiano fra terzaforzismo e atlantismo', *Storia contemporanea* 25(6): 1167–95.

Nuti, L. 2002. 'The United States, Italy, and the Opening to the Left, 1953–1963', *Journal of Cold War Studies* 4(3): 36–55 (Special Issue: *Italy and the Cold War*).

O'Leary, A. 2003. 'Commissions for the Truth? Narrative and the Legacies of Political Violence in Contemporary Italy'. Paper delivered at the SIS Conference, University College Cork, July 2003.

Paine, R. 2001. '"Am I My Brother's Keeper?" (Genesis IV:9): Violence and the Making of Society', *Qualitative Sociology* 24(2): 169–89.

Pansa, G. 2003. *Il sangue dei vinti. Quello che accadde in Italia dopo il 25 aprile.* Milan.

Pansa, G. 2005. *Sconosciuto 1945.* Milan.

Papo de Montona, L. 1999. *Storia e tragedia senza la parola fine.* Rome.

Parlato, G. 2006. *Fascisti senza Mussolini. Le origini del neofascismo in Italia, 1943–1948.* Bologna.

Pecchioli, U. 1995. *Tra misteri e verità. Storia di una democrazia incompiuta.* Milano.

Pelizzaro, G.P. 1997. *Gladio Rossa – Dossier sulla più potente banda armata esistita in Italia.* Rome.

Pezzino, P. 2001. *Storie di guerra civile. L'eccidio di Niccioleta.* Bologna.

Pisano, I. (2004). *Io, terrorista. Parlano i protagonisti.* Milan.

della Porta, D. and M. Rossi. 1984. *Cifre crudeli: bilancio dei terrorismi italiani.* Bologna.

della Porta, D. and S. Tarrow. 1986. 'Unwanted Children: Political Violence and the Cycle of Protest in Italy, 1966–1973', *European Journal of Political Research* 14: 607–32.

Rafalko, F.J. (ed.). 1998. 2. *A Counterintelligence Reader: World War II, Volume Two.* Washington, DC, released in 2004 and available at: http://permanent.access.gpo.gov/lps54742/counterintelligencereader/ci/docs/ and http://www.fas.org/irp/ops/ci/docs/index.html

Rao, N. 1999. *Neofascisti. La destra italiana da Salò a Fiuggi nel ricordo dei protagonisti.* Rome.

Rao, N. 2006. *La fiamma e la celtica. Sessant'anni di neofascismo da Salò ai centri sociali di destra.* Milan.

Raw, C. 1992. *The Money Changers: How the Vatican Bank Enabled Roberto Calvi to Steal 250 Million Dollars for the Heads of the P2 Masonic Lodge*. London.

Registry of the European Court of Human Rights. 2003. *Admissability Decision in the case of Sofri and Others v. Italy*, http://www.echr.coe.int/Eng/Press/2003/june/Decision-Sofri&Others.htm

Ronchey, A. 1982. *La democrazia bloccata i comunisti e il 'fattore K'*. Milan.

Rotberg, R.I. and D. Thompson. 2000. *Truth V. Justice. The Morality of Truth Commissions*. Princeton.

Rouhana, N. and D. Bar-Tal. 1998. 'Psychological Dynamics of Intractable Ethnonational Conflicts. The Israeli-Palestinian Case', *American Psychologist* 53(7): 761–70.

Ruggiero, M. 2006. *Nei secoli fedele allo stato. L'arma, i piduisti, i golpisti, i brigatisti, le coperture eccellenti, gli anni di piombo nel racconto del generale Nicolò Bozzo*. Genoa.

Rumiz, P. 1997. *La secessione leggera. Dove nasce la rabbia del profondo Nord*. Rome.

Rusconi, G.E. 1993. *Se cessiamo di essere una nazione*. Bologna.

Salerno, A. 2006. *Era polare. La pazza storia dell'Italia di Berlusconi*. Milan.

Salimbeni, F. 1998. *Le foibe : un problema storico*. Trieste.

Santino, U. 1997. *La democrazia bloccata. La strage di Portella della Ginestra e l'emarginazione delle sinistre*. Palermo.

Santomassimo, G. 2004. *Antifascismo e dintorni*. Rome.

Scaliati, G. 2005. *Trame nere. I movimenti di destra in Italia dal dopoguerra ad oggi*. Genoa.

Sechi, S. 'Una storia da tenere nascosta', *Avanti*, 12 December 2006.

Semprini, G. 2003. *La strage di Bologna e il terrorista sconosciuto. Il caso Ciavardini*. Milano.

Shenhav, S.R. 2006. 'Political Narratives and Political Reality', *International Political Science Review* 27(3): 245–62.

Smith, T.E. 1991 *The United States, Italy and Nato, 1947–52*. London.

Spazzali, R. 1990. *Foibe: un dibattito ancora aperto. Tesi politica e storiografia giuliana tra scontro e confronto*. Trieste.

Stellati, C. 2001. *Un'ideologia dell'Origine. Franco Freda e la controdecadenza*. Padua.

Streccioni, A. 2006. *A destra della Destra. Dentro l'MSI, dai Far a Terza Posizione*. Rome.

Tajfel, H. 1978. *Differentiation between Groups*. London.

Tarchi, M. 1995. *Esuli in patria: i fascisti nell'Italia repubblicana*. Parma.

Tarchi, M. 1997. *Dal Msi ad An*. Bologna.

Tassinari, U. M. 2005. *Guerrieri. 1975/1982 storie di una generazione in nero*. Naples.

Taylor, C. 1989. *Sources of the Self: The Making of Modern Identity*. Cambridge.

Telese, L. 2006. *Cuori Neri. Dal rogo di Primavalle alla morte di Ramelli 21 delitti dimenticati degli anni di piombo*. Milan.

Tompkins, P. 1995. *L'altra Resistenza. La liberazione raccontata da un protagonista dietro le linee*. Milan.

Tompkins, P. 2005. *L'altra Resistenza. Servizi segreti, partigiani e guerra di liberazione nel racconto di un protagonista*. Milan.

Travaglio, M. 2004. *Montanelli e il cavaliere. Storia di un grande e di un piccolo uomo*. Milan.

Travaglio, M. and P. Gomez. 2003. *Lo chiamavano impunità. La vera storia del caso SME e tutto quello che Berlusconi nasconde all'Italia e all'Europa*. Rome.

Trigilia, C. 1994. 'Le basi sociali della crisi politica', *Stato e Mercato* 42: 406–12.

Tullio-Altan, C. 1995. *Italia: una nazione senza religione civile. Le ragioni di una democrazia incompiuta*. Udine.

Turi, R. 2004. *Gladio Rossa. Una catena di complotti e delitti, dal dopoguerra al caso Moro*. Venice.

Valdevit, G. (ed.) 1997. *Foibe. Il peso del passato: Venezia Giulia 1943–1945*. Venice.

Various Authors. 1998. *L'Italia delle stragi*, 2 vols. Milan.

Various Authors. 2005. *Brescia: La memoria, la storia. Testimonianze, riflessioni, iniziative*. Brescia.

Veltri, E. and M. Travaglio. 2001. *L'odore dei soldi. Origini e misteri delle fortune di Silvio Berlusconi*. Rome.

Ventrone, A. (ed.). 2006. *L'ossessione del nemico. Memorie divise nella storia della Repubblica*. Rome.

Villa-Vicencio, C. and W. Verwoerd (eds). 2000. *Looking Back, Reaching Forward: Reflections on the Truth and Reconciliation Commission of South Africa*. Cape Town.

Vinciguerra, V. 1989. *Ergastolo per la libertà. Verso la verità sulla strategia della tensione*. Florence.

Vinciguerra, V. 1993. *La strategia del depistaggio*. Bologna.

Vinciguerra, V. 2000. *Camerati addio. Storia di un inganno, in cinquant'anni di egemonia statunitense in Italia*. Trapani.

Vivarelli, R. 2000. *La fine di una stagione. Memoria 1943–1945*. Bologna.

Wagner, P. 2002. 'Identity and Selfhood as a Problèmatique' in H. Friese, ed., *Identities. Time, Difference and Boundaries*, New York and Oxford, 32–55.

Weinberg, L. and W.L. Eubank. 1988. 'Neo-Fascist and Far Left Terrorists in Italy: Some Biographical Observations', *British Journal of Political Science* 18: 531–53.

Williams, P.L. 2003. *The Vatican Exposed: Money, Murder, and the Mafia*. Amherst, NY.

Wilson, R.A. 2003. 'Anthropological studies of national reconciliation processes', *Anthropological Theory* 3(3): 367–87.

## Judicial sources

For Piazza Fontana:

*Sentenza-ordinanza del Giudice Istruttore presso il Tribunale Civile e Penale di Milano, dr. Guido Salvini, nel procedimento penale nei confronti di Rognoni Giancarlo ed altri*, 18 March 1995, 3 February 1998, 2 March 1998, 18 March 1998, Milan. Entire text available at: http://www.uonna.it/indsalv.htm

Corte di Assise di Milano. 2001. *Sentenza*, 30 June.

Corte di Assise di Appello di Milano. 2004. *Sentenza*, 12 March.

Suprema Corte di Cassazione, Sezione Seconda Penale, *Sentenza n. 21998/2005*, 3 May 2005, Rome, available at: https://www.odg.mi.it/docview.asp?DID=1876

For the 1973 Attack against the Milan Questura:

*Sentenza-ordinanza del Giudice Istruttore presso il Tribunale Civile e Penale di Milano, dr. Antonio Lombardi, nel procedimento penale nei confronti di Maggi Carlo Maria ed altri*, 18 July 1998.

Corte di Assise di Milano. 2000. *Sentenza*, 11 March.

Corte di assise di Appello di Milano. 2002. *Sentenza*, 27 September.

Suprema Corte di Cassazione. 2003. *Sentenza*, 11 July.

Corte di Assise di Appello di Milano. 2004. *Sentenza*, 1 December.

Suprema Corte di Cassazione, Sezione Prima Penale. 2005. *Sentenza*, 13 October.

## Sources from the *Commissione stragi*

Commissione parlamentare d'inchiesta sul terrorismo in Italia e sulle cause della mancata individuazione dei responsabili delle stragi, XIII legislatura. 2001. *Elenco Audizioni, Aggiornamento al 17 gennaio 2001*, http://www.parlamento.it/parlam/bicam/terror/audizioni/aud.htm

Commissione parlamentare d'inchiesta sul terrorismo in Italia e sulle cause della mancata individuazione dei responsabili delle stragi, XIII legislatura, 2001. *Elaborati presentati dai commissari*. Rome.

Commissione parlamentare d'inchiesta sul terrorismo in Italia e sulle cause della mancata individuazione dei responsabili delle stragi, XIII legislatura. 1996. *Il terrorismo, le stragi e il contesto storico-politico (Proposta di Relazione Pellegrino)*, http://clarence.dada.net/contents/societal/memoria/stragi/index.htm

Commissione parlamentare d'inchiesta sul terrorismo in Italia e sulle cause della mancata individuazione dei responsabili delle stragi, XIII legislatura. 2000. *Settima relazione semestrale sullo stato dei lavori*, comunicata alle Presidenze il 12 ottobre 2000, available at: http://www.parlamento.it/parlam/bicam/terror/relazioni/home.htm#1

Commissione parlamentare d'inchiesta sul terrorismo in Italia e sulle cause della mancata individuazione dei responsabili delle stragi, XIII legislatura, 78th session, 22 March 2001, available at: http://www.parlamento.it/parlam/bicam/terror/stenografici/steno78.htm

## Interviews

Giano Accame, 7 October 2005, Rome.
Gabriele Adinolfi, 5 October 2005, Rome.
Adalberto Baldoni, 7 October 2005, Rome.
Paolo Bolognesi, 19 October 2005, Bologna.
Marcello De Angelis, 6 October 2005, Rome.
Stefano Delle Chiaie, 14 October 2005, Rome.
Giuseppe Dimitri, 11 October 2005, Rome.
Saverio Ferrari, 31 October 2005, Milan.
Giuseppe Valerio Fioravanti, 6 October 2005, Rome.
Aldo Giannuli, 24 October 2005, Milan.
Manlio Milani, 25 October 2005, Brescia.
Gian Paolo Pelizzaro, 5 October 2005, Rome.
Ferdinando Pincioni, 20 October 2005, Milan.
Sandro Provvisionato, 14 October 2005, Rome.
Guido Salvini, 2 November 2005, Milan.

# Websites

Almanacco dei Misteri d'Italia, http://www.almanaccodeimisteri.info/

Clarence Società-Banca dati della Memoria, http://clarence.supereva.com/contents/societa/
     memoria/

Associazione familiari delle vittime della strage alla stazione di Bologna del 2 agosto 1980,
     http://www.comune.bologna.it/iperbole/2agost80/present2.htm

Centro di documentazione storico politica su stragismo, terrorismo e violenza politica,
     http://www.cedost.it/

Misteri d'Italia, http://www.misteriditalia.com/

Osservatorio Democratico sulle nuove destre, http://www.osservatoriodemocratico.org/

http://www.repubblica.it/online/fatti/fontana/fontana/fontana.html

# Index